The Zinoviev Letter

The Zinoviev Letter

LEWIS CHESTER

STEPHEN FAY

HUGO YOUNG

J. B. LIPPINCOTT COMPANY
PHILADELPHIA & NEW YORK
1968

Contents

Illustrations
Following page 108

The Labour Cabinet, 1924 (*Bassano & Vandyk Studios*)

A *Pravda* cartoon

Arthur MacManus (*Thomson Newspapers*)

Christian Rakovsky (*Thomson Newspapers*)

Grigory Zinoviev (*Radio Times Hulton Picture Library*)

The forgers' room (*E. Reichart*)

Alexis Bellegarde and his *daughter* (*by permission of Mme Irina Bellegarde*)

No 117 Eisenacherstrasse (*E. Reichart*)

Donald im Thurn (*by permission of Mr John im Thurn*)

Im Thurn's Admiralty pass (*by permission of Mr Edmund Kindersley*)

The London Steamship and Trading Corporation office party 1923

Guy Kindersley (*by permission of Mr Edmund Kindersley*)

The cigarette case (*Thomson Newspapers, by permission of Mr Nicholas Kindersley*)

Red Scare poster (*Radio Times Hulton Picture Library*)

Stanley Baldwin and Lord Younger (*Thomson Newspapers*)

Sir Stanley Jackson and Sir Reginald Hall (*Radio Times Hulton Picture Library*)

Colonel Vernon Kell (*Thomson Newspapers*)

Captain Sidney Reilly (*Thomson Newspapers*)

Sir Eyre Crowe (*Thomson Newspapers*)

J. D. Gregory (*Thomson Newspapers*)

Red Letter Day (Daily Mail)

Letter from im Thurn to Kindersley, October 1924
(*by permission of Mr Edmund Kindersley*)

Low's cartoon on the eve of the debate (*by permission of the trustees of the Low Estate and the* Evening Standard)

Im Thurn acknowledges the Tory payment (*by permission of Mr Edmund Kindersley*)

Thomas Marlowe (*Thomson Newspapers*)

Major Joseph Ball (*by permission of Mr Alan Ball*)

Extract from *The Times* of Marlowe's letter to *The Observer* (*Thomson Newspapers*)

Mme Irina Bellegarde (*Sally Soames, Thomson Newspapers*)

Acknowledgements

First, we should like to acknowledge the assistance given to us by the people who helped us discover the two vital pieces of new evidence on the Zinoviev letter: Madame Irina Bellegarde, the widow of one of the forgers, and her son Michael; and Mr Edmund Kindersley, who gave us access to his father's papers. The common author's cliché which runs 'without whose help this book could never have been written' is, in their cases, unquestionably true.

We also received invaluable assistance from Dr Nicolay Andreyev, Lecturer in Slavonic Studies at Cambridge University, and his wife, who led us patiently through the complexities of émigré politics. Mr John Barnes, lecturer in Government at the London School of Economics, helped us with the intricacies of British politics in the 'twenties. Mr Jacek Niecko played an essential role by drawing our attention to previously unconsidered evidence from Polish sources. Lord and Lady Davidson gave us their own recollection of the affair.

Mr John im Thurn willingly provided information about his family's history. We should also like to thank Mr Percy Cohen, formerly of Conservative Central Office, Mr John Ross Campbell of the Communist Party of Great Britain, and the University of Birmingham Library, which allowed us access to the Austen Chamberlain papers. Miss Judith Todd was a resourceful research assistant.

The Sunday Times has been generous ever since publication of our original article, 'The Red Letter Forgery', on 18 December 1966. Mr C. D. Hamilton, editor-in-chief, kindly allowed us the free use of material which was the copyright of *The Sunday Times*. The enthusiasm of the editor, Mr Harold Evans, spurred us on. His chief assistant, Mr Ronald Hall, read our manuscript critically, and made useful suggestions. Miss Evelyn Irons in New York, Mr Robert Lindley in Buenos Aires, and Mr Ritchie

McEwen in Prague, all helped us with research. But most of all we should like to thank Mr Antony Terry, the Bonn correspondent of *The Sunday Times*, who was a co-author of our original story, and whom we would have liked, had distance not made it impossible, to be a co-author of this book.

With this book more than most, the customary disclaimer is imperative: responsibility for the facts, deductions and conclusions is ours alone.

The Zinoviev Letter

Executive Committee,   Very Secret
    Third Communist International.
                                            To the Central Committee,
                                            British Communist Party.
Presidium,
    September 15th, 1924.
    Moscow.

Dear Comrades,

The time is approaching for the Parliament of England to consider the Treaty concluded between the Governments of Great Britain and the S.S.S.R. for the purpose of ratification. The fierce campaign raised by the British bourgeoisie around the question shows that the majority of the same, together with reactionary circles, are against the Treaty for the purpose of breaking off an agreement consolidating the ties between the proletariats of the two countries leading to the restoration of normal relations between England and the S.S.S.R.

The proletariat of Great Britain, which pronounced its weighty word when danger threatened of a break-off of the past negotiations, and compelled the Government of MacDonald to conclude the Treaty, must show the greatest possible energy in the further struggle for ratification and against the endeavours of British capitalists to compel Parliament to annul it.

It is indispensable to stir up the masses of the British proletariat to bring into movement the army of unemployed proletarians whose position can be improved only after a loan has been granted to the S.S.S.R. for the restoration of her economics and when business collaboration between the British and Russian proletariats has been put in order. It is imperative that the group in the Labour Party sympathising with the Treaty should bring increased pressure to bear upon the Government and Parliamentary circles in favour of the ratification of the Treaty.

Keep close observation over the leaders of the Labour Party, because these may easily be found in the leading strings of the bourgeoisie. The foreign policy of the Labour Party as it is, already represents an inferior copy of the policy of the Curzon Government. Organise a campaign of disclosure of the foreign policy of MacDonald.

The I.K.K.I. (Executive Committee, Third [Communist] International) will willingly place at your disposal the wide material in its possession regarding the activities of British Imperialism in the Middle and Far East. In the meanwhile, however, strain every nerve in the struggle for the ratification of the Treaty, in favour of a continuation of negotiations regarding the regulation of relations between the S.S.S.R. and England. A settlement of relations between the two countries will assist in the revolutionising of the international and British proletariat not less than a successful rising in any of the working districts of England, as the establishment of close contact between the British and Russian proletariat, the exchange of delegations and workers, etc., will make it possible for us to extend and develop the propaganda of ideas of Leninism in England and the Colonies. Armed warfare must be preceded by a struggle against the inclinations to compromise which are embedded among the majority of British workmen, against the ideas of evolution and peaceful extermination of capitalism. Only then will it be possible to count upon complete success of an armed insurrection. In Ireland and the Colonies the case is different; there there is a national question, and this represents too great a factor for success for us to waste time on a prolonged preparation of the working class.

But even in England, as other countries where the workers are politically developed, events themselves may more rapidly revolutionise the working masses than propaganda. For instance, a strike movement, repressions by the Government etc.

From your last report it is evident that agitation-propaganda work in the army is weak, in the navy a very little better. Your explanation that the quality of the members attracted justifies the quantity is right in principle, nevertheless it would be desirable to have cells in all the units of the troops, particularly among those quartered in the large centres of the country, and also among factories working on munitions and at military store depots. We request that the most particular attention be paid to these latter.

In the event of danger of war, with the aid of the latter and in contact with the transport workers, it is possible to paralyse all the military preparations of the bourgeoisie, and make a start in turning an imperialist war into a class war. Now more than ever we should be on our guard. Attempts at intervention in China show that world imperialism is still full of vigour and is once more making endeavours to restore its shaken position and cause a new war, which as its final objective is to bring about the break-up of the Russian Proletariat and the suppression of the budding world revolution, and further would lead to the enslavement of the colonial peoples. 'Danger of War', 'The Bourgeoisie seek War', 'Capital fresh Markets' – these are the slogans which you must familiarise the masses with, with which you must go to work into the mass of the proletariat. These slogans will open to you the doors of comprehension of the masses, will help you to capture them and march under the banner of Communism.

The Military Section of the British Communist Party, so far as we are aware, further suffers from a lack of specialists, the future directors of the British Red Army.

It is time you thought of forming such a group, which, together with the leaders, might be, in the event of an outbreak of active strife, the brain of the military organisation of the party.

Go attentively through the lists of the military 'cells' detailing from them the more energetic and capable men, turn attention to the more talented military specialists who have for one reason or another left the Service and hold Socialist views. Attract them into the ranks of the Communist Party if they desire honestly to serve the proletariat and desire in the future to direct not the blind mechanical forces in the service of the bourgeoisie, but a national army.

Form a directing operative head of the Military Section.

Do not put this off to a future moment, which may be pregnant with events and catch you unprepared.

Desiring you all success, both in organisation and in your struggle.

With Communist Greetings,
President of the Presidium of the I.K.K.I.
ZINOVIEV

Member of the Presidium: McMANUS.
Secretary: KUUSINEN.

Prologue

This book tells the story of a successful conspiracy, or more precisely, a series of successful conspiracies. The Zinoviev letter, with its chilling exhortation to British Communists to gird themselves for the revolution, effectively destroyed the electoral chances of Britain's first Labour Government when it went to the polls in October 1924. It also eclipsed any prospect of the Anglo-Russian trade treaties being ratified by the British Parliament. Both consummations were devoutly wished by all the conspirators who had made the letter's publication possible. It was, most of all, a triumph for the tiny group of White Russian émigrés who had originally penned this particular example of Bolshevik extremism over the forged signature of Grigory Zinoviev, the Russian president of the Third International.

But their efforts alone could never have achieved success. To bring the exercise to fruition, the co-operation of other parties was needed – parties who had to be bluffed into believing that the letter was genuine before they could throw their weight behind the enterprise. These were the phase-two conspirators, men who, having once convinced themselves of the letter's authenticity, with only the most exiguous evidence, were prepared to employ the most elaborate and sometimes highly dubious devices to ensure its publication. Into this category fell an oddly-assorted bunch: the British intelligence service, Conservative Central Office, the Foreign Office and the *Daily Mail*. Each group of conspirators had its own methods, and at times they worked in almost complete ignorance of what the others were doing – so much so that even after the event none of those involved could be sure who deserved most credit for engineering this most unscrupulous, and potent, election 'gimmick' in British political history.

Coming, as it did, at the climax of a vituperative Conservative campaign against the Labour Government's trade and loan negotiations with Soviet Russia, publication of the Zinoviev letter was calculated to have the maximum effect. It seemed to confirm every middle-class prejudice about the implacable nature of the Bolshevik menace. The result was that, on 29 October 1924, a high percentage of the voters went to the polls thoroughly indoctrinated with the idea that only the Conservatives could save the country from Moscow.

Just what effect the 'Red scare' technique had on the actual election result is, and will always remain, a matter for conjecture. Psephology was not even in its infancy in those days. Certainly, it frightened people to the polls. The turn-out for the October 1924 election (the third in three years) was a prodigious 80 per cent; this compared with 74 per cent at the previous election. But to say, as many Labour stalwarts did at the time, that the Zinoviev letter was entirely responsible for the Government's defeat, is to claim more than the sketchy evidence warrants. The Labour vote in fact grew by more than a million, though the party as a whole lost fifty seats. The most significant consequence of the election was the political annihilation of the Liberal Party.

They lost over a hundred seats, to end up with a meagre forty-two members in the Commons – a slump from which they never recovered. The Conservatives reaped the harvest, building up an unassailable overall majority of over two hundred seats. At the time, some of the franker Conservatives suggested that the Zinoviev letter might have been responsible for one-third of their 155 gains. It is certainly credible, if unprovable after this interval of time, that the ability of the Conservatives to form a majority government was attributable to the Red Bogey campaign – of which the Zinoviev letter constituted the most dramatic part. The Liberals, for all their vigorous Red-scare-mongering in the later stages of the election, had a record of being soft on the Soviet Union. The Tories had been hard liners all along. Theirs was the more unequivocal anti-Socialist ticket.

But the reverberations of the Zinoviev letter conspiracy did not end with the 1924 election. Labour, having jumped from the status of working-class pressure group to Government office in one bound, now had to work out a new philosophy of Opposition – as the potential alternative government. Their failure to tackle this problem effectively can be attributed in large measure to the Zinoviev letter experience. The conviction that they had been tricked out of office blinded the Party to the need for reconstruction and, perhaps more important, to the evidence that Ramsay MacDonald's leadership was already dangerously out of touch with the aspirations of the Party's rank and file. When the realization finally came in 1931, it broke the Party's back.

More important still, however, was the letter's effect on the general development of Anglo-Soviet relations. Its publication marked a definite turning point in Soviet Russia's view of the West, and in the West's view of Soviet Russia. Up to the autumn of 1924 Britain had led the gradual process of diplomatic rapprochement with the Soviet Union, giving a lead that found many imitators on the continent. Indeed, it is difficult to imagine that the United States could have remained aloof from this trend.

After the publication of the Zinoviev letter, with its inevitable strengthening of the die-hard wing in the Conservative Party, the whole process went into reverse. Under Baldwin, the British Government led the diplomatic retreat from Moscow. Soviet Russia became more isolated, and, of necessity, more isolationist. American recognition of the Soviet regime came grudgingly and late, in November 1933, while in Europe the Soviet Union was almost brutally frozen out of arrangements for collective security.

The Zinoviev letter hardened attitudes, and hardened them at a time when the Soviet Union was becoming more amenable to diplomatic contact with the capitalist world. The apologists of world revolution were being superseded by infinitely more pliant subscribers to the Stalinist philosophy of 'Building Socialism in One Country'. Thus, after successfully weathering all the early contradictions in Soviet diplomacy, Britain gave up when the going was about to become much easier. And it gave up largely because the two middle-class parties suddenly perceived that their short-term electoral advantage was best served by a violent anti-Bolshevik campaign.

The Zinoviev letter episode seems to us to be significant for two other reasons: it represents one of the classic instances of Whitehall's ability to purvey fiction as fact, and purvey it long after there is massive evidence of fraudulence. It also represents an equally classic instance of dereliction of journalistic responsibility. The journalistic situation has, to an extent, been repaired. It is, for instance, difficult to imagine another Zinoviev-type letter getting past the clinical scrutiny of the Kremlinologists. The treatment of the Zinoviev letter in the British press in 1924 was abysmal: each newspaper's policy was determined by the prejudices of its proprietor. They were, in the most unfortunate sense, organs of opinion, and provided an instructive example of the absurdity of the argument that the health of the press depends on its ability to reflect a broad spectrum of views. The health of the press, now as then, seems to us to depend on a simpler, but more demanding, function – its ability to find out and present the facts.

The Foreign Office, which originally authenticated the Zinoviev letter, has, of course, no such function. Still, it is tiresome to find the Foreign Office of today sitting pat on the departmental errors of nearly half a century ago. No assistance was given to us by the Foreign Office staff in our research for this book. Their official attitude is still that the Zinoviev letter was the work of Zinoviev, though the department prefers not to have to answer the question direct. After our original article in *The Sunday Times* in December 1966, a few questions on the subject were put to Mr George Brown, the Foreign Secretary, by Labour Party backbenchers in the House of Commons. Mr Brown did not give any direct answer to the question of the letter's authenticity, though he did manage a throw-away reference to 'fanciful stories in the newspapers'.

The structure of the book needs explanation. The narrative line is not straightforward. It seemed to us essential to put the Zinoviev letter in as wide a historical context as possible. The first four chapters, therefore, are an attempt to give this perspective. They also serve another purpose. They constitute an account of the overt story of the Zinoviev letter as it has hitherto been believed. The actual story of how the letter was forged, authenticated and circulated starts in chapter five and, with minor departures, the narrative is consecutive thereafter.

It is a complex story. It is based on an accumulation of newly-discovered documents, gathered from various sources; but the evidence is by no means complete. The involvement of the intelligence services means that some areas of the story are totally undocumented. Equally, the role of politicians was of the kind which is carefully removed from their papers and memoirs.

At times we are obliged to speculate. But we have always made it clear when this is the case, and we have always founded our speculation on the facts and documents which are available. This is the way in which any unauthorized history involving the intelligence services must be written; and on the whole it tends to be a more fruitful exercise than the rehearsal of romantic escapades doctored to satisfy the present controllers of MI5 and MI6. There are no footnotes, but references for each chapter are listed at the back of the volume. The important references, however, are detailed at the appropriate point in the text itself.

1

How the Bombshell Burst

Connoisseurs of press 'leak' techniques had some advance warning. On the morning of 22 October 1924, the *Morning Post* ran a cryptic little paragraph containing the information 'There called at the Conservative Central Office yesterday a man who had been sentenced to death by Zinoviev'. The version in the *Daily Mail* was somewhat fuller but scarcely more illuminating. 'Among the callers,' it ran, 'at Conservative Central Offices, Bridge Street, Westminster, yesterday, was a man who had escaped from Russia after being sentenced to death by Zinoviev, the Bolshevik leader.' Later that morning, however, the London correspondent of the *Manchester Evening Chronicle* brought a little provincial bluntness to bear on the substance of the 'leak'. His story, published in the afternoon editions of the *Evening Chronicle*, was speculative but had, at least, the common journalistic decency to put its main point in the introduction.

'There is a report here,' he wrote, 'to which much credence is attached that before next polling day comes a bombshell will burst and it is connected with Zinoviev.'

The identity of the mysterious caller at Central Office was of no great relevance. What, essentially, was being rehearsed was a subtle, but to most journalists familiar, form of blackmail by newspaper. Central Office was delicately putting it about that it was in a position to make a Zinoviev 'revelation' as part of an elaborate campaign to force a Government department into making an uncomfortable disclosure. In simple terms, Central Office was hinting that if the department did not own up, then the Conservatives could, and would, tell all themselves, which

1

would be even more uncomfortable for the department concerned. The department would then look as if it had concealed a matter of vital public interest. Thus, the abstruse little paragraphs in the *Daily Mail* and *Morning Post*, two of the most uninhibited supporters of the Conservative cause, were not designed for the edification of the general reader. They were inserted for the attention of a highly select readership at the top of the British Foreign Office.

The ploy was apparently successful. On 25 October, just four days before polling in the general election, the 'bombshell' burst. The Foreign Office, with almost exaggerated frankness for so reticent a department, had decided to keep the public informed. The decision had been exceptionally sudden. For while assiduous readers of the *Manchester Evening Chronicle* may have been half braced for the shock, the Labour Government evidently was not. Before publication, the majority of the Labour Cabinet knew no more about the Zinoviev letter than the humblest commoner. They, like almost everybody else, first read about its contents in the national newspapers.

The *Daily Mail*'s presentation was undoubtedly the most powerful. In descending order, its seven decks of headline type read:

CIVIL WAR PLOT BY SOCIALISTS' MASTERS
Moscow Order To Our Reds
Great Plot Disclosed Yesterday
Paralyse the Army and Navy
And Mr MacDonald Would Lend Russia Our Money
Document Issued By Foreign Office
After 'Daily Mail' Had Spread The News

In any competition for examples of slanted, tendentious head-line-writing it would be difficult to emulate the *Daily Mail*'s achievement on that day. In this instance an acute case of the sub-editor's congenital disease – over-inflamed imagination – appears to have been potently allied with a violent political animus towards the Labour Government. Even so, the bare facts of the story were bloodcurdling enough.

The *Mail*'s version, and that carried by all the other newspapers, was based on the contents of two dramatic documents just released by the Foreign Office: a copy of an inflammatory

2

letter allegedly from the Third International, the Moscow-based directorate on Communist tactics throughout the world, to the British Communist Party, and an official protest Note from the British FO to the Soviet chargé d'affaires in London. There was nothing in the Note to suggest that the Foreign Office had any reservations about the authenticity of their explosive find.

Copies of the letter, it appeared, had come to light as a result of the initiative of the British secret services. It was marked 'Very Secret', bore the masthead of the Executive Committee of the Presidium of the Third Communist International, and was graced with the signature 'Zinoviev' (Grigory Zinoviev had been president of the Third International since its inception in 1919). Its 1,200-word contents seemed to confirm the implacable nature of the 'red menace'. 'It is indispensable,' the letter stated, 'to stir up the masses of the British proletariat.'

It mentioned the burning political issue of the time – the Anglo-Soviet trade and loan treaty negotiations – and urged that 'the proletariat of Great Britain . . . must show the greatest possible energy in the further struggle for ratification' of the treaties as a means of furthering 'the revolutionising of the international and British proletariat'. Closer contacts between British and Russian workers were commended 'to extend and develop the propaganda of ideas of Leninism in England and the Colonies'. Most alarming of all, however, was the tailpiece on Communist tactics in the Services. 'It would be desirable,' the letter said, 'to have cells in all the units of the troops.' And followed this up with: 'The Military Section of the British Communist Party . . . suffers from a lack of specialists, the future directors of the British Red Army.'

If the truth – a commodity seemingly of no great interest to much of the press at the time – had been known, however, nobody would have had much cause for alarm. The British Communist Party suffered from more crippling deficiencies than a lack of military specialists. Perhaps the most important of these was a straightforward failure to attract adherents to the cause; unlike the Communist parties in France and Germany, it never succeeded in building up a mass following. In October 1924 the total British card-carrying membership was a meagre 3,500 – and that was subject to rapid turnover.

3

The British Communist Party's method of penetration into the armed services was unconventional but not specially fruitful. Essentially, it consisted of enclosing Communist broadsheets in small brown envelopes which also contained a tip for the big race of the day. The envelopes were placed in hedgerows around Salisbury barracks by a local CP loyalist in hopes that betting men among the passing soldiery would open them and realize the poisonous nature of their allegiance to the Crown.

The impotence of the British CP, however, was irrelevant to the issue, at least as far as the Tory press and most Conservative politicians were concerned. The Zinoviev letter established to their apparent satisfaction that in seeking rapprochement with Russia, Ramsay MacDonald's Labour Administration was prepared to underwrite the subversion of the British Empire.

In the last four days of the election campaign the Labour Party was vigorously battered with the implications of Zinoviev's alleged treachery. Winston Churchill, finding his natural emotional home on the die-hard wing of the Tory Party (a homecoming made possible by a secret deal early in 1924 between Churchill, Baldwin, and Austen Chamberlain to accept Churchill back into the fold as long as his behaviour remained on the right side of the outrageous), performed with massive orotundity. Stanley Baldwin, the Conservative leader, with what seemed like rare prescience at the time, had already made an election campaign reference to Zinoviev, five days before the famous letter was published. 'It makes my blood boil,' he told a meeting at Southend-on-Sea on 20 October, 'to read of the way in which M. Zinoviev is speaking of the Prime Minister of Great Britain today.' And Conservative Central Office had already fashioned a 'Red Bogey' poster showing Ramsay MacDonald turning his back on three downcast Britishers to greet two grim-faced Cossacks. The legend ran: 'So this is Socialism VOTE UNIONIST'. It all dovetailed neatly with a Zinoviev letter climax to the campaign.

In isolation the Zinoviev missive might have been dismissed as the triviality it undoubtedly was. Documents of this nature, both forged and genuine, were constantly being 'found' by the intelligence agencies of the Western powers. There were in the early 'twenties, in the words of one of MacDonald's biographers, 'Enough "Red Letters" fluttering around Whitehall to paper the walls of the Foreign Office'. Even supposing the Zinoviev letter had been genuine, its contents merely instructed the British CP to do what it was constitutionally obliged to do anyway, if only it could muster the support. Planning for the bloody revolution, after all, was, or ought to have been, its vocation. But the letter's publication at a time when all the latent middle-class hysteria about Bolshevism had been made explicit by a vicious election campaign invested it with a totally spurious significance.

The elaborate, behind-the-scenes machinations which led to the use of the Zinoviev letter in the campaign, in a way which took the official 'finders', the Labour Government, by surprise but found the Conservative opposition in a state of total readiness to exploit its potential, are dealt with at length in the middle chapters of this book. Meanwhile, it is worth recalling the overt events of the 1924 election campaign. From this record it is possible to isolate two major factors which helped to give the Zinoviev letter its explosive impact: the supreme irrationality of political debate at the time, and the mental exhaustion of the Labour Prime Minister, Ramsay MacDonald. The first gave the letter a contemporary relevance. The second meant that the Labour Party missed every tactical opportunity to stifle or offset the consequences of the letter's publication.

Even before the election was announced, the more perceptive members of the Labour Cabinet were anticipating an unpleasant political roughhouse. Speaking in Birmingham, on the first week-end in October 1924, John Wheatley, the Minister of Health, declared melodramatically, 'Britain is entering a political class war.' If, he continued sarcastically, the Labour Government were to reverse its policy towards the Soviet Union, by dropping the proposed loan to Russia and spending instead £50 million on crushing the Bolshevik regime, there would not be any talk of a general election.

Talk there certainly was. Its intensity had been growing during the previous week, and the Labour Government was not strong enough to resist it. It was the most insecure minority Government of the century. MacDonald controlled less than one-third of the House of Commons. In the election late the previous year Labour had won 191 seats, the Conservatives 258, and the Liberals 159. Thus, the first Labour Government relied wholly on the support of the Liberals; and by the beginning of October, the Liberals' good will was rapidly disappearing.

Throughout the summer, they had been ambivalent towards MacDonald's trade and loan negotiations with the Soviet Government. Like virtually all other representatives of the middle class, they had serious reservations, although these had never been formally stated. But, on 1 October, Asquith announced that the Liberals would move a motion in the House of Commons to reject the trade treaty.

Simultaneously, the Conservatives stated that they were about to introduce a motion censuring the Government for its handling of the prosecution of a leading British Communist, John Ross Campbell.

The *Daily Herald*'s political correspondent, who had greater access to the Prime Minister than any of his journalistic colleagues, reported confidently on 2 October that MacDonald would advise an election if the Government was defeated on the Conservative motion. The prospects of victory in the Commons did not seem good. 'Prepare for a General Election' the same edition of the *Herald* was headlined.

In a country where unemployment was hovering around the million mark, neither the Anglo-Russian treaties nor the 'Campbell Case' could objectively be considered the central issues of the day. They were, however, the ones that dominated the last weeks of Labour in office. And it was to be the 'Campbell Case', an almost total irrelevance, that ultimately brought the Government down. The case does, at least, offer in microcosm an insight into the tactical ineptitude of the Labour Party and the unscrupulousness of Conservative electioneering tactics.

John Campbell, acting editor of the *Workers' Weekly*, the official organ of the British CP, was charged on 5 August under the Incitement to Mutiny Act of 1795. He had published an allegedly seditious article addressed to the armed forces of the Empire. It was basically a 'Don't Shoot' appeal – pretty routine Communist stuff. The exhortation to the British armed forces was phrased: 'Let it be known that, neither in the class war nor in a military war, will you turn your guns on your fellow workers.'

News of the prosecution had met with much amazement in

6

the Labour Party. It was pointed out during a turbulent session in the Commons on 6 August that the article in question was merely an appeal to troops not to allow themselves to be used for strike-breaking purposes. The Attorney-General, Sir Patrick Hastings, who had ordered Campbell's indictment, was taken aback by the unfavourable reaction to his efforts of his party colleagues. A recent convert to Labour, Sir Patrick had evidently entered on the prosecution with little appreciation of its political ramifications. Still less did he realize that he was doing the Communists a favour. Nation-wide publicity and a spot of political martyrdom were like manna to a party that had singularly failed to make any impact by more conventional methods. Campbell, a chirpy Clydesider, emerged as admirable left-wing hero material. Not only did he escape the 'conchie' label: it was revealed that he had been disabled in the war and decorated for exceptional gallantry.

Advised that a conviction was doubtful on the legal merits of the case, the Attorney-General withdrew the indictment. This provoked an immediate outburst in the newspapers, which presented the issue as one of political interference with the course of justice. The Labour Government was lambasted with accusations of bowing to the wild men of the Left.

The charge was not an entirely false one. The Left were certainly lobbying fiercely. George Lansbury, the most articulate Left-wing backbencher, for one, was very active as the unofficial mediator between the Cabinet and the Communists. And he was confident enough some days before the official announcement to tell Campbell that there was 'nothing to worry about'. The withdrawal of the charge was, however, logical. If the case had proceeded, and Campbell had been acquitted, the only outcome would have been a lot of free and advantageous publicity for the CP – something which all parties would normally prefer to avoid.

But the Conservatives, naturally, were determined to make the most of the matter. When Parliament reconvened on 30 September, the tone of the questions addressed to Hastings and MacDonald indicated that the Government would not escape lightly. The Prime Minister agreed to set aside 8 October for a full debate on the Case. On that day the Government was duly defeated by 364 votes to 198.

7

For the Tories it was a tactical victory as well as a strategic one: they withdrew their motion, having persuaded the Liberals to incur the odium of demanding an inquiry into the Campbell case. If blame was to be distributed for the Government's downfall, and for yet another trek to the polls (the third in three years), a large proportion of it was indeed going to be borne by the Liberals.

As soon as the result of the debate was announced, MacDonald adjourned the House, and said he would see the King the following day. From the steps of Number 10, Downing Street he told the crowd: 'Tonight they have had a hard task to defeat us, but they have not heard the last of us yet.' The election campaign had begun.

Next day, after seeing the King, the Prime Minister announced the date of the election: 29 October. The campaign was to be one of the briefest on record, 20 days, and one of the most intense. Always the patrician, MacDonald took it all very coolly. He sounded more like a Tory when he impressed on his supporters: 'We will fight the clean fight.' The following morning, he even took delivery of a new Jacobean drawing-room suite for No. 10.

He spent that day, Friday the 10th, mapping out his itinerary for 'the clean fight'. It was to be perhaps the most arduous election tour ever undertaken by a British party leader, taking him at the rate of 20 speeches a day and more from one extremity of the country to another. He did not know that on that very day, the Zinoviev letter, which was to guarantee the election a place among the most uninhibited of the century, reached the Foreign Office.

The week-end was spent quietly. On the Sunday, MacDonald celebrated his fifty-eighth birthday. The only news the *Herald* could find to get excited about was a cable sent by Lord Rothermere to his staff on the *Daily Mail*: 'Be careful,' he told them, 'Ramsay might win'. It was the first shot by the *Herald* across the bows of the *Mail* in a dog fight which was to continue throughout the campaign. To Labour members with a fondness for the conspiracy theory of political activity, Rothermere's telegram must have seemed to justify Sidney Webb's gloomy premonition: 'This will be a dirty election.'

MacDonald left London on Monday, 14 October. A week-end's reflection had evidently persuaded him to take Webb's warning to heart, though he still retained his pose of dignified detachment from any baser elements in the campaign: 'They will hit you below the belt all the time,' he told the enthusiasts who went to Euston to see him off, 'but don't you do the same.' The message seemed to go down well. 'The people pressed around him, and women with babies in their arms rushed forward to shake him by the hand,' the *Herald* reported rhapsodically.

On the way north the train made whistle stops at Rugby, Crewe, Carlisle, and Motherwell. In Glasgow, MacDonald made the first of a series of major set speeches in which the Russian Treaty and the Campbell case were the ever-present theme. Thus, he made it clear from the start that he was not afraid to grasp the Bolshevik nettle; indeed, he seemed determined to make not the slightest effort to escape from the issue which the anxious middle-class viewed with the greatest alarm. It was as if he had decided to confirm rather than forget Wheatley's ominous diagnosis.

Certainly he was confident enough in Glasgow. Referring to the firmly-held belief of Stanley Baldwin, the Conservative leader, that Labour would hang themselves if given enough rope, he replied: 'They discovered that the rope they gave us was going around their own necks, and not round ours.'

The following day must have been the most arduous of the campaign. Setting out from Glasgow at nine in the morning, MacDonald spoke in Bishopbriggs, Kirkintilloch, Kilsyth, Stirling, Alloa, Bannockburn, Larbert, Falkirk, and Linlithgow before *lunch*. And then he addressed a large rally in Edinburgh. By the middle of the afternoon, as the motorcade went south through the fog to Portobello, Musselburgh, Dalkeith, and Earlston the Prime Minister was visibly tiring. At Jedburgh, where he was scheduled to make his 21st speech of the day, his voice failed. But he recovered quickly enough to make another big speech in Newcastle that night. Again, it was the Russian issue which dominated all others, and again MacDonald seemed confident. "If you want to frighten all the old ladies of both sexes,' he told an enthusiastic crowd of 4,000 who had begun to queue for the meeting six hours before it started, 'all you have to do is put on a red sheet and cry "Bolshie", and hire your

9

leader-writers to write out of the fullness of your ignorance about Bolshevism.' The jocularity went down well with the overwhelmingly working-class audience.

Meanwhile the Zinoviev letter, so ordinary in appearance but so explosive in its potential, was slowly making its way through the Foreign Office's cumbersome machine. Early on the 15th its existence was formally registered, and it was sent off to the Northern Department.

The pace of the campaign was already making a serious mark on the Prime Minister. The *Daily Herald*'s special correspondent wondered how he could stand it day after day. The truth was really that he could not. But equally, no other Labour leader could stop in hundreds of towns and villages on a journey through England and meet such support. On the Wednesday he addressed 6,000 people in Leeds, 2,000 in Dewsbury, 6,000 in Batley, 10,000 in Cleckheaton, and 20,000 in Huddersfield before driving into Manchester for his third successive evening rally, at Belle Vue. There his theme was still the Treaty, and his reception was again rapturous.

That night, since he was Foreign Secretary as well as Prime Minister, the Foreign Office boxes reached him. They included, for his routine consideration, the Zinoviev letter.

The following morning, 16 October, as he drove towards Birmingham, the letter was on its way back to London. On it, MacDonald had written a minute to the Office stating that great care was to be taken to establish its authenticity; but while the investigations were proceeding a Note of protest to the Russian chargé d'affaires, Christian Rakovsky, was to be drafted, so that no time would be lost if its authenticity was established. It was a reasonable response, although the letter had hit him at a moment when his competence to deal with it was impaired by fatigue.

By the time MacDonald reached Wolverhampton that afternoon, the *Herald* reporter was getting very worried: 'He was visibly tired, but he made a short fighting speech.' Yet another long evening speech in Birmingham that night, written and delivered, as always, without the expert assistance of a team of secretaries and speech writers, added to the exhaustion. Next day, he continued his journey south, through Worcester and Malvern, and then into Wales and his own constituency, where

10

the reception was rowdily enthusiastic. After five days' campaigning, his themes remained the same: they were still the Treaty and the Campbell case. On the morning of Friday 17th, MacDonald's minute reached the Foreign Office.

The week-end was spent in Wales, virtually without incident. There was no reply from the Foreign Office to his minute. Indeed, the only thing to disturb the sudden calm was an article in the *Daily Mail*, claiming that MacDonald had received a silent welcome from his constituency. H. W. Nevinson, in the *Herald*, was outraged: 'Except in a few parasitic and mouldering old towns and villages, he was received everywhere with the utmost enthusiasm,' he wrote.

For the next week, another stump round the country was scheduled. Travelling east, MacDonald arrived at Leicester, where his tiredness was again a cause for comment. The following day, he spoke to 4,000 people in the Hippodrome in Sheffield in the morning and, belying his haggard appearance, told the faithful what they had come to hear: 'This campaign is to me like a whiff of victory.' That afternoon he drove to Gloucester, and eventually to Bristol for another major speech, arranged with complete disregard for his stamina, largely because Winston Churchill had spoken there the same day. He then turned north once more, to visit his son's constituency in Nottinghamshire.

While their Minister was travelling back to the North, the Foreign Office unaccountably sent the draft of the requested Note of protest to MacDonald's constituency in Aberavon. He was not to see it for two more days, or reply for three. By that time, what chance he had to be the controller rather than the victim of what happened to the letter had vanished.

For reasons which are far from clear, he did not see the draft immediately even when he returned to Aberavon. There was a delay before he replied. But by Wednesday the 22nd the Zinoviev letter was already circulating to the Admiralty, the War Office, Scotland Yard and the Home Office. It was no longer the Foreign Office's exclusive property.

Ironically, this was the day on which MacDonald seems to have tried to switch the direction of the Labour campaign. He dropped the Bolshevik issue and turned his attention to the fact that taxes had been cut during the eight months of Labour

11

Government. In London, the *Herald*, likewise, was now be-labouring the *Daily Mail* for its allegedly inaccurate use of employment figures, Rothermere's diligent operatives having used them to conclude that unemployment had risen during Labour's term.

It was the 23rd, Thursday, before MacDonald saw the F.O.'s draft. He studied it between bouts of canvassing and attacks on food profiteers. His alterations to the draft were sent back to London the next morning. They arrived there at roughly the same time as Thomas Marlowe, the editor of the *Daily Mail* and the man who was later to be widely acclaimed for his energy and courage in publishing the Letter, secretly received his first copy of it.

That night, at a meeting in Tai Bach in Glamorganshire, Mac-Donald was telling his supporters: 'Let us show the other side better manners than they show us.' He had no idea that the Foreign Office had already released the text of the protest Note to Rakovsky, as well as the letter itself, that afternoon. Nor did he know that 'the other side' had displayed the quality of their manners more clearly than ever, by conniving at – indeed, in-ducing – this publication.

Every newspaper, except the faithful *Herald*, headlined the news of the letter on its main news page. In the context of an election in which the major issues were Britain's relations with Russia and the Government's relations with the Communist Party, it was obviously sensational news. The Conservatives grabbed the opportunity with relish, and also with an alacrity which some Labour leaders found distinctly suspicious. On the same Saturday, Lord Birkenhead, Lord Curzon, Winston Churchill and four other senior Tories attacked in a well-briefed chorus. The Labour Party was confused. MacDonald was silent.

On Sunday, the newspapers continued to hammer away at MacDonald, and MacDonald still remained silent. On Monday, the *Herald* declared the letter to be a forgery, but it was a lonely voice. Of its rivals only the *Manchester Guardian* and the *Sunday Express* had even minor reservations about the authen-ticity of the letter.

That night, at the end of another twenty-speech day, Mac-Donald finally broke his silence. Speaking in Cardiff, he implied that it was civil servants in the Foreign Office who were to blame. They had acted precipitately. He had not been convinced of the letter's authenticity, and had asked them to protest only after they had satisfied *him* that the letter was genuine. On the audience, the speech had a reassuring effect; but the newspapers interpreted it as a cowardly attack on his civil servants ('who cannot,' as the refrain goes, 'answer back.').

Over the week-end, the Foreign Office had sent two officials from the Northern Department down to Wales, to explain to the Foreign Secretary why they had behaved as they had the previous Friday. But MacDonald, it seems, was too exhausted to absorb what they told him. In any case, the explanations were too late. By Monday, the election was only thirty-six hours away, and there was probably nothing MacDonald could have done, even if he had had all his wits about him.

On the eve of polling-day, he made one faltering attempt to retrieve the situation. It was a pathetic, and totally ineffective, diversion. He had received reliable information, he said, that four days before the Foreign Office got news of the Zinoviev letter it was being discussed in a London club. Already he had selected the argument to which he was to stick with fair consistency whenever the subject of the letter was raised in later years: that the real issue was not its authenticity, but the way its exploitation was organized in some dark outpost of the Conservative party.

Only the *Herald* was left to whistle up Labour's spirits. Its eve-of-poll headline put a brave face on a hopeless situation: 'The Red Plot will become Labour's Red Letter Day.' The optimism was misplaced. As the first results trickled in on the evening of the 29th, it was obvious that Labour had lost office. The measure of their defeat became known next morning. They had lost 40 seats, the Tories had gained 161. The biggest losers were the Liberals, who, having slid from a representation of 159 seats to one of 40, were, for political purposes, exterminated. They never recovered, whereas Labour did.

The tragedy of Ramsay MacDonald was that he did not know half the story. It was bad enough that his twenty-day absence on the stump prevented him from keeping in adequate touch with the activities of his own officials at the Foreign Office. Had he been at his desk in Whitehall, the handling of the letter would no doubt have been very different. But had he been there, of course, the letter would never have taken a place among the classic documents of British party politics: to raise an essentially unexceptional missive to this eminence, an election on the Red issue was required.

What was far worse for MacDonald was the story his officials could never have told him, because they did not know it. They knew much less about the origin of the letter than they thought they did. They had only the vaguest comprehension of the letter's other life: its impact simultaneously elsewhere in London, its currency among Conservative Party leaders, its divisive effect on the intelligence services, the use to which it was put by a dedicated, anti-Socialist secret agent. The officials remained largely ignorant of these factors, even though they were the very influences which compelled the Foreign Office to publish the letter.

One thing, however, was clear at the time: publication of the Zinoviev letter constituted the biggest election campaign 'windfall' for the Conservative Party in this or any other century. After nine months of cautious administration Britain's first Labour Government went to the country liberally smeared with the gravest of all electoral liabilities, 'being soft on the Reds'. The irony of the situation was that the mud should stick after a governing exercise of almost paralysing respectability.

2

The Revolution that Never Was

The crude element of misrepresentation in the final phases of
the 1924 election campaign – suggesting that the MacDonald
Government was at best the dupe of Bolshevik aims and at
worst the abettor – fell naturally into a well-grooved tradition.
Ever since the end of the First World War persistent attempts
had been made to paint the Labour Party as the apostle of Red
Revolution. Confronted by the ominous phenomenon of a
successful workers' take-over in Russia, the Conservative Party,
like every other right-wing party in Europe, hardened in its attitude towards any manifestation of working-class political organization. Fear bolstered the expedient political hypocrisy of
making a competitor for power appear more horrendous than
the facts warranted. To be anti-Bolshevik abroad was to be
anti-Labour at home. And Tory publicists soon achieved facility
in visiting the sins of the Communists upon the dignified heads
of the Labour leadership. Thus, the exploitation of the Zinoviev
letter was no more than a classically successful example of a
well-established method of political infighting.

Before Labour assumed power there may have been some
justification for such a technique. Viewed from Tunbridge
Wells, or Bournemouth, or more disingenuously from Conservative Central Office, the Labour Party's avowed interest in
Socialism looked very like the Marxist brand (Clause 4, which
was reduced to a semantic dispute in 1960, had been written
into the Labour Party's new constitution in 1918; and in those
days there seemed to be a serious intention to draw into common ownership 'the means of production, distribution and exchange'). The Labour Party contained a convinced minority

15

who shared the Communist belief that capitalism was about to get its come-uppance; and, like the Communists, they blamed capitalism for 'imperialist wars'.

The Bolshevik revolution of 1917 had not, however, been greeted with undiluted approval by the Labour Party; the bloody methods used to establish it were not to every Socialist's taste. Nevertheless it had made an instant impact on the party. The vision of working men in charge of Europe's most spacious land mass had a bracing effect on Labour's self-respect. A modern parallel, perhaps, is the interaction of influence between the achievement of majority rule in African countries, and the civil rights movement in the United States. For this reason, the Labour Left had shown none of the resentment of the Coalition leaders at the Russian revolutionaries' early peace with the Germans. Essentially, there existed between the Soviet Union and the British working-class party an affinity, which could be summed up in a phrase which now sounds impossibly romantic: the brotherhood of the common man. This, above all, was what distinguished Socialists from other politicians. It was the source of the illusion, as fantastic as it was fatal, that they would bring Bolshevism to Britain.

But the potency of the illusion has to be reckoned with in any analysis of the political situation that preceded publication of the Zinoviev letter. It was an illusion that suited the Conservative Party, both in the context of domestic politics and in the wider ambit of Empire, where the party saw itself as the custodian of British interests in the global struggle against an implacable Bolshevik enemy. And it was an illusion, given the right-wing bias of the press, that the Conservatives were well able to propagate.

When it came to ends justifying means, the British party of Empire had nothing to learn from the Bolsheviks. In contrast, the Labour Party, while it talked of class war, felt that political hostilities should be limited to the ballot box and, in extremis, strike action. Indeed, its leadership had demonstrated its distaste for Bolshevik methods long before it was called on to form a Government. Rejecting the Moscow-based Third International, MacDonald and Arthur Henderson did everything in their power to build up the prestige of the rival Second International, making it a vehicle for spreading the ideology of democratic socialism – a concept which struck Lenin as absurd. For this, MacDonald was vilified with much greater frequency and relish by the Moscow leadership than, for example, Winston Churchill ever was. One, in their eyes, was a traitor to his class; the other simply could not help himself.

Lenin, who died of a brain haemorrhage just as Labour took office, had previously classified MacDonald in predictably uncompromising terms. The Labour leader was, he said: 'a bourgeois pacifist and middle-class reformer, cherishing the illusion of a non-class state . . . [one who] recognized the class struggle only as a figure of speech, just as do all deceivers, sophists and pedants of the bourgeoisie.' As the British Communist Party – formed from a rag-bag of Marxist fringe groups in July 1920 – was obliged to share the views of its Russian tutors, MacDonald always treated it with circumspection. With the backing of successive Labour Party conferences, he consistently rejected the demands of the CP for formal affiliation to the movement. One factor, however, gave tenuous justification for the Tory charge that the Labour Party was subject to Communist infiltration. Individual Communists were free to join the party and, if they could secure adoption, become Parliamentary Labour candidates. In the first 1923 election, two were returned to Parliament. Shapurji Saklatvala, a wealthy Parsee, was elected as official Labour candidate for Battersea North, and Walton Newbold, a former Quaker, was returned for Motherwell without Labour opposition. Neither made much impact; and both lost their seats in the election later in the same year. Thus during the period of MacDonald's administration, there were no Communists, avowed or otherwise, in the House of Commons.

Nonetheless, the election which ushered Labour to power for the first time produced some bizarre examples of Conservatives falling victim to their own propaganda. On receiving news that Labour was to take office, one old-established Sussex family packed all its plate and valuables and headed for the coast 'before the Bolsheviks closed the channel ports'. But this kind of hysterical response to the workers in office infected many more august pundits.

It was, for instance, the avowed view of Winston Churchill, the defeated Liberal candidate for West Leicester, that 'the

17

enthronement in office of a Socialist Government will be a serious national misfortune such as has usually befallen great States only on the morrow of defeat in war'. The *English Review* amplified this doleful thought: 'We stand at the moment,' it wrote, 'when the sun of England seems menaced with final eclipse. For the first time in her history the party of revolution approach their hands to the helm of the State, not only, as in the seventeenth century, for the purpose of over-throwing the Crown, or of altering the Constitution, but with the design of destroying the very basis of civilized life.'

Estimating how far such dire prognostications were justified is of crucial importance to the task of framing a context for the exploitation of the Zinoviev letter. If they contained a grain of truth, then the Zinoviev affair could be regarded an unconventional but, given the issues at stake, a wholly proper method of dragging the country away from an anarchic abyss. If they were absurd misrepresentations of the Labour Party's aims, then only one construction can be put on the use made of the letter – it was a crude political gimmick to serve party political ends. For the rest of this and the subsequent chapter, we propose to examine Labour's record in office during 1924 to establish which hypothesis most aptly fits the facts.

Initially, the danger of the 'final eclipse', to which the *English Review* referred, was stayed for some weeks after the December 1923 election. The Conservatives, still the largest single party in the Commons, with 258 seats, waited for the formal, but inevitable, defeat in the House. Baldwin's espousal of the Protection issue had killed any chance of another arrangement with the Liberals, yet fear of Labour administration kept the idea alive. Among other notions aired at the time, inspired by that dreadful prospect, were a Conservative administration, headed by a less divisive character than Baldwin, like Balfour or Austen Chamberlain; and, oddest of all, a non-parliamentary Government of 'national trustees'.

But when the Conservatives were defeated on 21 January, George V cut through all the verbiage by doing what he was constitutionally obliged to do: he sent for Ramsay MacDonald, as the leader of the second largest party in the House, and asked him to form a Government. He did so with the complete approval of the level-headed elements in both the other parties.

18

Asquith was attracted by the idea of his Liberals being the party who 'really control the situation'. Neville Chamberlain was struck by the perceptive thought that a minority Labour Government 'would be too weak to do much harm but not too weak to get discredited'.

MacDonald himself was well prepared for the summons. The party's high command – MacDonald, Sidney Webb, J. H. Thomas, Henderson and Snowden – had already discussed their attitude at a meeting in Webb's house. They decided that the left-wing proposal to introduce bold Socialist measures in the King's Speech and get rapidly but heroically defeated on them in the House, would be a worthless gesture, with disagreeable electoral consequences. A Labour Government, it was decided, should proceed cautiously. By its example it should show that responsible government was not necessarily the prerogative of 'a governing class'. Snowden later recalled urging on his colleagues the view that 'we must show the country that we were not under the domination of the wild men'. Even at this early stage in the history of British democratic socialism, the democratic had got the better of the socialism.

It was, then, in a mood of somewhat pusillanimous high purpose that MacDonald went to see George V. The confrontation proved amiable enough. MacDonald expressed his earnest desire to serve King and Country, confessed a few worries about the inexperience of his party and hoped the King would understand his problems vis-à-vis the extremists in it. The King, for his part, confessed an aversion for the Labour Party's fondness for singing the Red Flag. MacDonald solicitously explained that some of the party had got into the way of singing it, but, by degrees, he hoped to break down the habit.

On this unctuous note, the standard-bearer of the working-class struggle for political power took up the seals of office. King George V recorded in his diary that night: 'Today twenty-three years ago dear Grandmamma died. I wonder what she would have thought of a Labour Government.' It might have been more fruitful to speculate on the posthumous thoughts of Keir Hardie.

MacDonald, a conciliator of great talent, had many ideas about what to do with his new authority, but bursting asunder the capitalist integument was not one of them. The Cabinet he selected proclaimed the conservatism of his ambitions. George Lansbury, the charismatic leader of the Left, was passed over (it was not until 1945 that Labour leaders learned the elementary parliamentary lesson of muzzling their zealots with office). There was only one truly radical figure in the entire administration – John Wheatley, the Clydesider, who took over the Ministry of Health, and who was later to declare, after nine months in office, that politics now consisted of class warfare.

MacDonald himself took the Foreign Secretaryship and, predictably, was soon working himself into the ground. The other plums went to J. R. Clynes (Deputy Leader), Sidney Webb (Board of Trade), Arthur Henderson (Home Office), Snowden (Chancellor of the Exchequer), and J. H. Thomas (Colonial Office). To prove the Government's freedom from class bias, and to get an invaluable bolstering of experience, the Cabinet included a Tory, Lord Chelmsford (Admiralty) and a former Liberal minister, Lord Haldane, as Lord Chancellor. Haldane's political views were never fully clarified. Immediately after the 1923 election, for example, he had written to Baldwin urging him to carry on 'the King's Government'. Baldwin wrote back and 'begged' Haldane 'to join the Labour Government and help them out'. It is perhaps significant that, of all the people MacDonald chose to consult, Haldane appeared to have the most influence.

A revolution of a kind had been achieved. No fewer than eleven of twenty Cabinet members were, after all, of working-class origin. But their impact on the archaic ceremonial of office was negligible. The three new appointments to the Royal Household did, it is true, baulk at wearing knee-breeches; but they accepted the proposition of Levee dress (trousers, coat, cock-hat and sword). Lord Stamfordham, the King's Private Secretary, was able to inform them that such articles of attire could be obtained from Moss Bros., 'a well known and dependable firm', for a cut-rate of £30 and up.

Clynes later summed up the euphoric self-satisfaction of the workers in power with the words: 'As we stood waiting for His Majesty, amid the gold and crimson of the Palace, I could not help marvelling at the strange turn of Fortune's wheel, which had brought MacDonald the starveling clerk, Thomas the engine-driver, Henderson the foundry labourer and Clynes the mill-hand, to this pinnacle beside the man whose forbears had been kings for so many generations. We were making history.' But the history which Labour was to make had as much to do with the absorptive powers of the Establishment as the rise of the working-class.

In home affairs the new Government inherited a potentially crippling problem – an unemployment figure of well over a million. It was a problem to which they, like the other parties, could offer no solution. There was a vague feeling in the movement that the imposition of Socialism would somehow make all economic problems wither away. But Socialist solutions were out, partly because of the delicate Parliamentary situation but mainly because the leadership no longer believed its own propaganda. By turning his back on the 'class war', MacDonald deliberately abandoned the emotional drive that could lead to radical change in the economic organization of the country. Keynes by this time already arrived at the idea that unemployment could be alleviated by means of higher expenditure on public works. But the Labour Party, if anything, were more conventional in their approach to capitalist economics than the capitalists themselves.

On the economic front, balanced budgets, low public expenditure and hoping for the best were the orders of the day. The thinking behind Snowden's Budget, the first ever by a Labour Chancellor, was indistinguishable from that of his Tory predecessors.

Anticipating a surplus of £38 million, Snowden cut a variety of duties, abolished some of the protective advantages enjoyed by the motor-car industry, and removed the special tax on Corporation profits. The Chancellor's proud boast in the Budget speech was of measures 'vindictive against no class and no interest'. It did not, however, measurably benefit the class that returned his party to power. Haldane wrote to one of his upper-class friends: 'I told you that Snowden would prove to be an orthodox financier. There is nothing socialistic about his budget.'

There was not much that could be considered socialistic in other activities on the home front. Strikes among the dockers and London tramwaymen prompted a threat to use the Emergency Powers Act (i.e. bring in the troops), despite the Labour

Party's vigorous denunciation of this legislation when it had been introduced by Lloyd George. MacDonald was mortally offended that workers should strike while Labour was in office.

There were the occasional reforms. Significantly, the only one of lasting benefit was initiated by Wheatley, the Cabinet's lone radical. His Housing Act gave statutory recognition to the fact that housing was a long-term problem. He increased the subsidy, insisted that subsidized houses must be built for rent and returned the main responsibility to local authorities. By promising that the scheme would operate for fifteen years (in fact, it ceased to operate after eight) he secured a major expansion of the building industry. But other reforms were more piecemeal: mild improvements in the provision of unemployment benefits and old-age pensions; an increase in agricultural wages; a liberal approach to education policy, extending the system of grants and maintenance allowances.

In defence and colonial policy nothing was done that could perturb the most reactionary Tory grandee. Indeed, J. H. Thomas, Colonial Secretary and unofficial Cabinet jester, was to make an imperial virtue of his inaction. 'The Government,' he proclaimed at the British Empire Exhibition, 'intended above all else to hand to their successors one thing when they gave up the seals of office, and that was the general recognition of the fact that they were proud and jealous of, and were prepared to maintain, the Empire.' Such sentiments as these may have been inflated in order to demonstrate the 'soundness' of the British working-man in office; but they were also uttered with conviction. Jimmy Thomas, never one of nature's Machiavellis, really meant it.

The lassitude of the Labour Government in home and colonial affairs was, however, offset by frenetic activity on the diplomatic front. Here, more than anywhere else, was the area in which Ramsay MacDonald chose to make his mark. He intended to press on with the business of resolving international difficulties by 'the strenuous action of good-will'.

At the London Conference in July 1924, he earned the right to boast of 'the first really negotiated agreement since the war'. Tension between France and Germany was eased largely as a result of his intervention. The French agreed to a plan for ending their occupation of the Ruhr, while MacDonald, having

22

agreed to the Dawes plan, which brought reparation payments within the capacity of the Germans, persuaded the French to accept it as well. This was a triumph which involved abandoning much of what the Labour Party had stood for in the preceding five years (i.e. no reparations, and a revision of the Treaty of Versailles). But its contribution to an improved atmosphere in European politics was undeniable.

Other atmospheric improvements were initiated at the League of Nations in Geneva where the British delegates, and Henderson in particular, played an important part in drafting the Protocol for the Pacific Settlement of International Disputes. MacDonald himself became the first British Foreign Secretary (and only British Prime Minister) to go to the League Assembly, thus emphasizing the high priority given by his Government to the organization of collective security. Ultimately, discussion on the Protocol – providing elaborate procedures for arbitrating international disputes, and support for victims of unprovoked aggression – fizzled out. The Labour Government fell before it was ratified. The Conservatives dropped the policy altogether.

Still, it was a statesmanlike failure. Moreover, it did great things for the movement's self-esteem. Whatever opponents might say, the party of working-class protest had demonstrated that it could perform very adequately on the international stage. MacDonald, it seems, was as surprised by this as anyone, and gave it due weight in his opening election speech in October 1924, when he remarked on 'this extraordinary phenomenon of a Labour Government that has met kings and rulers of the earth, that has conducted itself with distinction and with dignity; this Labour Government that has met ambassadors, that has faced the rulers of Europe on terms of equality; this Labour Government that has sent its representatives forth and its representatives have been held as statesmen. . . .' Even if this sounded much like the forelock toucher surprised by the squire's handshake, it went down remarkably well.

By then, however, the essential record was clear. No party with a left-wing label could honourably have done more to eradicate the fears and suspicions of its opponents. At home, not entirely because only five members of the Cabinet had any previous ministerial experience, scarcely anything had been done to interfere with the well-grooved procedures of the Civil

Service machine. Overseas, old party dogmas had been patriotically sacrificed in the unrelenting search for peace. The evidence in October 1924 was that the middle-classes had nothing to fear. Winston Churchill and his fellow prophets of doom had been proved entirely false.

The only wonder is that an administration so anodyne could ever have fallen victim to accusations of consorting with the Bolsheviks, or to an election campaign based on a Red Scare. It would certainly be a mistake to look for any logical reason. But if there is an explanation to be found, it lies in the only feature of its policy which seemed to distinguish the Labour Government from its predecessors: its policy of diplomatic rapprochement between London and Moscow.

3

Why the Red Scare Took Hold

The tinder for a 'Red Scare' election had been assembled long before the Zinoviev letter supplied the vital spark. It was, ironically, the cautious MacDonald who specified the issue which, subsequently distorted out of recognition, was to drag him down. On becoming Prime Minister, he had promptly declared his intention of ending 'the pompous folly of standing aloof from the Russian Government'. The sentiment was very much in line with the Labour leader's general approach to foreign affairs – friction between nation states was, in his view, an aberration that could be cured by understanding and 'the strenuous action of goodwill'. Despite the phraseology, the statement was not as radical as it sounded. Relations between the capitalist nations and the Soviet Union after the war had been anything but pacific. Improvements, however, had been made. And the British Government, with occasional relapses, had played a leading role in facilitating this advance.

Thus, MacDonald's policy towards Russia was, in many ways, a logical development of what had gone before. It was Lloyd George, the master realist, who had perceived soon after the war that British involvement on the side of the 'White' Russians against the 'Reds' was a sterile, and potentially expensive, policy. From 1920 onwards, he had exerted his authority as Prime Minister in the Coalition towards the task of drawing the Soviet Union into the community of nations. He argued, reasonably, that continued baiting of the new Russian bear would serve only to aggravate its belligerence.

The Russians, realists themselves, responded to this initiative, and in March 1921 Lloyd George concluded an Anglo-Soviet trade agreement, which was to become the model for a range of Soviet agreements with other European countries. A *Punch* cartoon depicted Lloyd George, who a few years earlier had 'refused to shake hands with murderers', in the act of directing his hairy and primitive-looking Bolshevik visitors to the tradesmen's entrance of Number 10 Downing Street. Under the 1921 agreement, Britain undertook not to attach or take possession of any gold, funds, securities or commodities exported from Russia. The Soviet Government, for its part, recognized 'in principle' its liability to pay compensation to private firms who had supplied goods to Russia and not been paid. There was also an undertaking to refrain from 'hostile propaganda' against the British Empire. In essence, the treaty gave reassurance to British businessmen wanting to develop trade with Russia who were constrained by the fact that no formal diplomatic relations had been established.

A year later Lloyd George went for even bolder solutions. As part of the international conference at Genoa, he attempted to settle a whole range of outstanding problems relating to the Soviet Union – war debts, settlement of claims for expropriated owners, *de jure* recognition, and the terms for foreign capital investment. The conference was a failure. On the capitalist side its mood had been damaged by the elaborate attempts of British and American oil interests to double-cross each other over prospective Soviet oil concessions. William Borah, Republican Senator for Idaho, and leader of the political lobby for recognition of Russia by the United States, commented sarcastically that the issue at Genoa 'was what amount of the natural resources and raw materials of Russia each one of the allied powers could get ahold of'. Even so the very fact that Soviet delegates had been prepared to attend such a conference, and discuss their liability for claims against their Tsarist predecessors, was a mark of progress.

These advances, however, were accompanied by a large measure of dissension on the British side. The 1921 agreement represented a victory for the Prime Minister and the Board of Trade. But the departments in most constant contact with the Soviet Union were the Foreign Office, the War Office and the India Office, none of which really approved of the new arrangement. Indeed, the Foreign Office under Lord Curzon, even in

26

those days the caricature of an old-fashioned imperialist, seems to have taken some trouble to disrupt the agreement. Kamenev, who became a member of the ruling triumvirate in Russia after Lenin's death in 1924, has left on record an interesting appraisal of the comparative world views of Lloyd George and Curzon. Lloyd George, he thought, 'realized that he was living in the twentieth century, though he had not always the courage to make the necessary deductions and act on them'; Curzon, on the other hand, 'is determined that, if this is not the nineteenth century, he will behave as if it were'.

In view of its subsequent part in releasing the Zinoviev letter, the Foreign Office's attitude under Curzon is particularly interesting. Less than six months after the 1921 agreement, the episode of the Curzon Note emphasized the reckless suspicion with which it regarded any Soviet dealings.

On 7 September, Curzon dispatched a violent protest to the Soviet Government, complaining of activities which were contrary to its undertaking to refrain from propaganda 'against the institutions of the British Empire'. While his overall charge, that anti-British activities in Asia still continued, was broadly true, the Note seems to have been based on very dubious information.

It purported to quote reports made to the 'Central Committee' of the Communist International by Stalin, 'the president of the eastern division of the Third International', by Eliava, and by one Nuerteva, described as 'director of propaganda under the Third International'. The Soviet reply indignantly noted that none of these three people had ever exercised any functions under the Third International. The British counter-reply, in November, made the extraordinary retort that 'it was never said of any of these persons that they belonged to the Third International, though that is not a point of substance'.

In addition, the first British Note had quoted a speech of Lenin on 8 June. When it was pointed out that Lenin had not made a speech on that day, Curzon, nothing daunted, shifted the alleged speech to 5 July. The official record of Lenin's speech on that day, however, contains no passage resembling that quoted in the British Note. If it achieved nothing else, this incident at least illustrated how intemperately the Foreign

Office was capable of acting in response to Soviet documents which displayed even a patina of authenticity.

In May 1923 Curzon, with somewhat more justification, launched another savage protest to the Soviet authorities. His 'Ultimatum', a long memorandum of twenty-six paragraphs, listed all the aggravations Curzon had suffered since the trade agreement had been signed: it included claims arising out of the deaths of two British agents, complaints about the detention of British fishing vessels and a splenetic indictment of the activities of the Third International and Soviet diplomats in the Far East. Once again, however, the British Government weakened its case by quoting highly suspect secret reports and wrongly alleging that Sokolnikov, the People's Commissar for Finance, was a member of the Third International committee charged with financing foreign communist parties. The Russians, however, since at this stage they had more to lose than the British from a rupture of the trade agreement, were conciliatory in their reply.

For the British the upheaval over Curzon's Ultimatum had been an emotional release, but it brought the inevitable shame-faced reaction: perhaps Curzon had gone too far after all. The general political atmosphere, always excepting the die-hard wing of the Tory Party, was almost penitent: some kind of amends to the Soviet Union ought to be made. Diplomatically, something was done to avert the possibility of a similar flare-up in the future. The Foreign Office and the Soviet Government agreed a 'friendly procedure' for trying to sort out their diplomatic differences in private before striking public attitudes with the dispatch of a formal Note. This 'friendly procedure' was well observed for more than a year. Its first abrogation came with the publication of the Zinoviev letter.

Thus, when the Labour Government took office, the course of Anglo–Soviet relations, after numerous vicissitudes, was moving into a calmer phase. The country was already conditioned to accept the party's 1923 election manifesto pledge to undertake 'the resumption of free economic and diplomatic relations with Russia'. Diplomatic recognition, which the Labour Government bestowed on 2 February 1924, nine days after taking office, was, nonetheless, a bold step. It released Moscow, for the time being at least, from the omnipresent fear

28

of foreign attack. It was also the signal for a series of recognitions by other European countries. It had, however, one grudging element: the first official diplomatic representative of the Soviet Government was to be a chargé d'affaires and not a fully fledged ambassador. In this, the Labour Party was once again acting in deference to the King's wishes. George V had raised personal objections to receiving an ambassador from a Power which he regarded as responsible for the assassination of Tsar Nicholas II, his cousin, and the imperial family.

At home, MacDonald's first diplomatic initiative received a passably good press. The *Morning Post* regarded recognition as a 'leap in the dark' and Curzon termed it 'a grave mistake', but in this attitude they stood virtually alone. J. L. Garvin, the famous Conservative editor of the *Observer*, was delighted. He had consistently supported a rapprochement with Russia. The Liberals, with Lloyd George prominent, unanimously supported the measure. 'Europe stands on the threshold of a new era,' the *Manchester Guardian* affirmed on 10 February.

The *Daily Herald*, naturally, was overjoyed. For the Labour Left, recognition had an emotional significance which was not shared by its pragmatic opponents.

Whereas Lloyd George thought it a realistic way to treat a potentially dangerous enemy, many in the Labour Party regarded it as a felicitous gesture towards an awkward but sympathetic friend. This difference in attitude was to become crucial when Anglo–Soviet policy obscured all other issues. Lloyd George's view on Russia was a tactical expedient, capable of being reversed if a new political strategy seemed necessary.

Even for the Labour Party, however, the policy of Russian appeasement was based on hard-headed business assumptions. As we have seen, MacDonald was anything but starry-eyed about the Soviet Union and its British apologists. He wanted friendship with the Russians, but he also wanted to get something out of it.

Insofar as the Government had any remedy for unemployment, it lay in the allegedly vast opportunities presented by the Russian market. MacDonald was not alone in cherishing this false optimism. Mussolini, too, showed by his intensive wooing of Moscow that he believed this would end his country's economic malaise. Likewise, American business interests were jealous of any development in Anglo–Soviet rapport.

MacDonald regarded recognition as merely the preliminary to wide-ranging negotiations which would settle all differences between the two countries. Of these, the most persistent was compensation for British owners of Russian property sequestered after the revolution. The expropriated owners were a vociferous and varied crowd. Some were small, like the woman who wanted to call on the Soviet representative in London, Christian Rakovsky, and collect rent for the three years he had lived in her house in Kharkov while he was Prime Minister of the Ukraine. Others, like the Lena Goldfields Company, which claimed £56 million compensation, had lost a great deal. The bosses of the larger victims were a political embarrassment to MacDonald because of their ready support, both financial and inspirational, for any anti-Bolshevik opening that was available. Their Association of British Creditors of Russia was itself a principal source of agitation. The most famous of their number, Sir Henri Deterding, the oil king, fought his own battle by sponsoring oil blockades in 1922 and 1923. The fact that he himself purchased petroleum from the official Soviet Naphtha Syndicate did not prevent him obstructing the sale of 'stolen' oil from Russia with unrelenting vehemence. He was suspected of financing the Menshevik insurrection in Soviet Georgia in the autumn of 1924; and later of involvement in a scheme to finance anti-Bolshevik measures from Germany with counterfeit Soviet currency. This versatile operator, who subsequently, in the 1930s, took up residence in Nazi Germany because the British were 'soft on the Communists', was bound to exert all his influence against any Anglo–Soviet economic settlement. In the spring of 1924, when MacDonald embarked on his attempt to rationalize relations with Russia, Deterding's influence on conventional City opinion was considerable.

The conference on the Anglo–Soviet Treaties opened in London on 14 April 1924. From the outset it became clear that, if the discussions were to succeed, the delegates would have to weather a lot of hostility from uninvolved financial opinion; and that the settlement of private claims would be the thorniest issue. The day the conference opened a memorandum was submitted to the British Government and Press by a group of orthodox City bankers. The Bankers' Memorandum demanded, among other things, that the Bolsheviks recognize Russia's public and private debts; that an equitable restitution of private property to foreigners be made; and that British businessmen be able to deal freely with private enterprise institutions in Russia. It was an intransigent document. Under Lenin's New Economic Policy, instituted in 1921, the Soviet Union may have departed somewhat from Marxist economic orthodoxy. But the British bankers were asking not for further small deviations, but for a virtual denial of the revolution.

It soon became evident that the Russians would consider settling pre-revolutionary debts only if they were advanced a large loan. 'The central question is the loan,' said Christian Rakovsky, the leader of the negotiating team, in an interview with *Izvestia* on 30 July. Moreover, the unfriendliness of the City made it inevitable that the loan would have to be guaranteed by the British Government.

The negotiations dragged on, against a mounting barrage of press criticism, only to break down suddenly, and seemingly irrevocably, on 5 August. It was an occasion for rejoicing in the Conservative newspapers. The collapse of Labour's Russian policy would, it was thought, be bound to lead to the downfall of the Government.

The sticking-point was failure to agree over the precise terms of compensation for the former owners. Despite the seeming stalemate, MacDonald resolved to postpone the adjournment of Parliament to allow time for one final effort to heal the breach. It is probable that this alone would have been enough to assure the resumption of the talks. As it was, they reopened with unexpected speed thanks to intensive activity on the Labour left. George Lansbury, James Maxton and E. D. Morel, some of the Conservatives' most conspicuous *bêtes noires*, were the chief conciliators. After consultations with Arthur Ponsonby, MacDonald's junior at the Foreign Office, they reported to Rakovsky that the British were willing to start again the very next day, 6 August.

By the 10th the settlement was won. There was to be a straightforward commercial treaty settling the Russian debts to be followed by a further treaty settling the Russian debts to the British owners, in exchange for a guaranteed loan. The loan was to be contingent upon a satisfactory settlement of the debts. Its sum was never publicly specified, because in the end it never came to be made. But the sum discussed in Cabinet was £30 million.

It was a businesslike, if complex, arrangement. Concretely, the treaty settled the problem of the existing Tsarist treaties; it provided for a fisheries settlement favourable to the British industry; it pledged both sides to refrain from propaganda and interference in internal affairs; and it was supplemented by a detailed commercial agreement. Whether or not Russia received the loan, these beneficial settlements stood.

Furthermore, the Soviets were now on record with an acknowledgement of responsibility for the claims of bondholders and expropriated private owners. A machinery was prescribed for the settlement of these claims; and if the machinery failed and the claims remained unsettled, the Bolsheviks got no loan. Overall, the treaty was not a final settlement, but it pointed the way to one in the future.

But by this time the Press was on the boil. 'British interests are betrayed', was the *Morning Post*'s shrill comment when the treaty was signed. The *Daily Telegraph* commented on the 'uselessness of the treaty'. For an agreement as guarded as this one the chorus of complaint was disproportionate and certainly did not justify the emotional right-wing rallying slogan, 'No Money for Murderers'. A glorious heritage, it was implied, had been besmirched by concluding a treaty with, in Winston Churchill's phrase, 'the blood-dyed tyrants of Moscow'. The *Evening News* summed up the opposition argument in its crudest terms. 'What Mr. MacDonald, Mr. Ponsonby and their fellow dreamers about Russia are doing is to pledge the British taxpayer to lend money to the conspirators who want that money to hasten the collapse of the British Empire. In other words, the British taxpayer is to finance his own ruin.' The fact that the Soviet loan was contingent on promises of debt settlement and good behaviour was completely overlooked.

The paranoia that had gone out of Anglo–Russian relations after the Curzon Ultimatum had returned with a vengeance. It had returned, however, not so much because Bolshevism seemed more malignant (in fact, as we shall see later, Soviet foreign policy was moving into a less intransigent phase), but because the Conservatives had perceived an issue that could, given the right kind of build up, drive Labour from office. Unfortunately, for the Labour Party, the same thought had struck some of the key members in the Liberal ranks. And it was the Liberals, a party which had earlier been in favour of a loan to Russia, who ultimately delivered the unkindest cut.

The man responsible for the changed Liberal stance was none other than Lloyd George, the one-time apologist of Anglo–Soviet rapprochement. In fact, it was not Lloyd George's position that had changed so much as the political realities of the day. By now he was obsessed with the domestic political scene and his own chances of making a comeback. Unlike Asquith, the official Party leader, he recognized that the Liberals could have no future if the Labour Party made a good showing in office. He was anxious for action, and a quick annihilation of Labour before people got too used to the idea of Labour government. The treaty with Russia gave him his chance. It was shocking, he disingenuously maintained, to lend money to the Bolsheviks; and even more culpable when the loan was 'a fake' and 'a thoroughly grotesque agreement'. During the summer recess, Lloyd George, with the reluctant acquiescence of Asquith, swung the majority of the Liberals behind this policy of opposition. And MacDonald's chances of getting the Anglo-Soviet treaties ratified when the House reassembled began to look slim.

In the event, of course, the election was called before the Anglo-Soviet treaties could be put before the House. But it was the course of its negotiation that created the climate for the campaign, enabling the Conservative Party to paint Mac-Donald as the dupe and abettor of Bolshevism's subversive aims. In fact, of course, MacDonald's Labour Party for the most part had been extremely cautious in all its dealings with Communists both abroad and at home. It was to demonstrate this at the party conference in London on the eve of the 1924 election. Delegates voted overwhelmingly in favour of a resolution that no member of the Communist Party should be eligible for endorsement as a Labour candidate for Parliament or for a local Council. Another resolution, from Sutton Labour Party, making all Communists ineligible for membership of the Labour Party, was carried by 1,804,000 to 1,540,000. The policy imposed on the British CP by the Third International, of 'exposing' the Labour Government, had alienated many who had earlier sympathized with Communist affiliation. With the passing of the Sutton resolution, the way was open to edge Communists out of the Labour Party completely. The Labour Party no longer needed telling that the British CP was not just a 'hotted-up' version of the pre-war Marxist groups.

But these resolutions had no effect on the Conservatives' election tactics. Their electoral stance was already fixed on the Red issue, even though during the preceding months the terms of the debate on this subject had rarely been elevated above the level of a slanging match. In this too, the election followed the pattern. It would probably have done so even without the sinister intervention of the Zinoviev letter. As it was, this served as the epitome of something which MacDonald, in his exasperation, had expressed a few days before he fell. At the time his outburst was criticized as one more example of his unfitness for high office. In retrospect he does not seem to have been so inexact when he inquired of his opponents: 'Why, instead of having a great battle on a political principle, do they go sniffing about like mangy dogs on a garbage heap?'

4

Zinoviev: Injured Innocence in Moscow

The strange phenomenon of smoke without fire is more common in politics than other areas of human activity. But it was not the only explanation for the success of the 'Red Scare' election campaign. While the Labour Party had good reason to feel aggrieved at the unscrupulous tactics of their political opponents, the Soviet Government had less cause for righteous indignation. The Zinoviev letter was accepted as completely authentic by many responsible people, for one simple reason – Russian foreign policy had conditioned them to expect this kind of subversive activity. MacDonald's curious behaviour in the crisis may well have been caused by this conditioning. Zinoviev had not written the letter; but even MacDonald, the Socialist Prime Minister, believed it possible.

Since a widespread acceptance of the Zinoviev letter's authenticity was an essential element in its successful exploitation, it is necessary to look at the two main factors that gave it credibility – paradoxes in Soviet foreign policy and the character of Zinoviev. In discussing them, it will be essential at some stages to vault ahead of the narrative in subsequent chapters. The plotting involved in the Zinoviev letter forgery never crosses into Russia itself; but, as the letter's publication gravely affected the Soviet Union's relations with the capitalist world, it is convenient to deal with its Soviet impact in this chapter.

Essentially, throughout 1924, there were two Russian foreign policies – one orthodox, designed to work the Soviet Government's passage into the fraternity of nation states, and one revolutionary, designed to undermine capitalism wherever it flourished. Zinoviev, as the president of the Third International (Comintern), personified the revolutionary policy. He directed the tactics of Communist parties throughout the capitalist world. He was the official trouble-maker; a task he discharged with a zeal that sometimes had embarrassing consequences for the orthodox wing of Soviet diplomacy.

All the contradictions in Soviet foreign policy were neatly exemplified in relations with the MacDonald Government. At the time when the Anglo-Soviet Treaty negotiations were delicately poised in the summer of 1924, Zinoviev was pronouncing: 'The chief task of the Communist International is now transferred to England in all fields.' And at the fifth Congress of the International in July 1924, the British CP figured first on the list of parties honoured for special mention in the general resolution on tactics. British Communists were urged 'to struggle against the so-called Labour Government of MacDonald by clearly exposing to the masses its bourgeois and anti-worker character'. A separate resolution on the British Labour Government described it as 'the faithful servant of his majesty the king of the empire of capitalists'. Such unflattering references to the British Government were scarcely calculated to improve the treaty talks. Nor was the macabre imagery of Zinoviev's injunction to British Communists to form a united front with the Labour Party. Support should be given to the MacDonald Government, he said, 'as a rope supports a hanging man'.

Significantly, the British Communist delegates failed to rise to Zinoviev's ominous analogy between the position of MacDonald in 1924 and Kerensky in 1917. They, at least, were fully aware that Britain was some way from the red revolution. But in the euphoric mood of a Comintern Congress, they received no thanks for their caution. 'The English comrades,' sneered one European delegate, 'are members of the Labour Party on weekdays, and Communists in a mild sort of way on Sundays for recreation.'

The Soviet Government was, of course, aware of the problems created by a militant Communist International. And in June 1924 *Pravda* ran a revealing 'friendly caricature' depicting Zinoviev spouting furiously from a raised dais, while behind him crouched Chicherin, the Commissar for Foreign Affairs, crumpled with embarrassment. The Soviet Government's explanation of this equivocal Russian outlook was blandly disingenuous – they pretended it did not exist. By 1924 all overt connection between the official foreign affairs bureau, the Narkomindel (run by Chicherin), and the International had been severed. And from this date on it became a commonplace of Soviet diplomatic utterances that the International was absolutely independent of the Soviet Government.

Chicherin once told a bewildered German diplomat that no more conclusions could be drawn from the presence of the headquarters of the Third International in Moscow than could be deduced from the fact that the headquarters of the Second International was situated in the Brussels of Leopold II. This, of course, was nonsense. However scrupulous the division between the personnel of the Narkomindel and the International, both served essentially the same master – the all-powerful Politburo of the Soviet Communist Party.

Bolshevik foreign policy had not always been so capricious. In the early days it was simply revolutionary. 'There is no more erroneous or harmful idea,' Lenin wrote, before the Bolshevik coup in Russia, 'than the separation of foreign from internal policy.' The message was clear: revolution at home should always be matched by revolutionary insouciance abroad. Throughout the civil war period this attitude had a certain validity: even the most zealous Russian Communists found it hard to conceive a consolidated revolution without some kind of spontaneous proletarian combustion in other European countries. But when hostilities ended in 1921, the Bolsheviks were left in possession of a ravaged and substantially reduced Russian homeland, and nothing else.

Revolution had not swept Europe. The bold advance of the Red Army on Warsaw had been thrown back, and Lenin was forced to cut his losses by the humiliating Treaty of Riga (18 March 1921). About ten million Ukrainians and White Russians passed under Polish rule. Such, it seemed, were the consequences of placing world revolution before the interests of Soviet Russia. Everywhere else the revolutionary mood had lost impetus. In Britain and the new Czechoslovakia, probably

37

the two healthiest states in Europe, the success of Bolshevik propaganda had reached a modest peak in the middle of 1920 and then rapidly declined. America was virtually unscathed. Italy, France and Germany, it is true, had developed mass Communist parties of a kind, but to Bolshevik eyes they all seemed singularly lacking in revolutionary spirit. Renewed hope of a German revolution briefly flickered after the occupation of the Ruhr in 1923, only to be extinguished by the farcical ease with which the German Communist rising was suppressed in October of the same year.

Meanwhile Russia was in a state of devastation. Only the ironical fact that the Marxist vision, framed for an advanced industrial community, had been realized in an overwhelmingly agricultural country, gave it the opportunity of survival. Yet even in agriculture, the attempt to impose a Marxist solution almost brought disaster.

Nothing could be done about the sequestration of land by the peasants – the Black Partition. And the Bolshevik Government had been obliged to recognize that the land now belonged to the village communities. It did, however, lay claim to all the produce; a proportion was assigned as wages to the peasant, the rest was to be surrendered to the State without payment. The peasants' response was anything but communistic. They refused, in most cases, to produce any more than they consumed. Punitive columns had to be sent into the countryside to seize grain for the towns. In many cases they seized the peasants' own supplies, and sometimes even confiscated the seed grain which was kept in reserve for the next crop. Drought and an almost complete transport breakdown compounded an already nightmarish situation. A malaria epidemic broke out.

The end result was the supreme humiliation for a revolutionary government – capitalist charity. Foreigners had to be admitted to organize relief for the starving. The American Relief Administration, led by Herbert Hoover, did especially able work, apart from conducting some fruitless commercial espionage on the side.

But relief work could only be a stop-gap; political action on a massive scale had to be taken. Lenin, with immense political courage, decided to put his revolution into reverse. On

15 March 1921 he introduced his New Economic Policy. Far from being new, NEP was, in fact, a reversion to many of the techniques of the old free enterprise system. The peasants were now allowed to sell their products, after paying a heavy tax in kind. Private trade was licensed and factories were handed over to trusts or even individuals. For some idealists the trauma was too much. When the trams started to charge fare money again several Muscovites committed suicide. On the foreign affairs front there were even graver betrayals of revolutionary aspiration: envoys and missions went out in ever increasing numbers, cap in hand for capitalist loans and trading agreements. Lenin, not for the first time, was pragmatically amending his own doctrine. NEP was Lenin's last achievement. After a stroke in the spring of 1922 he retired, though he kept a remote control on affairs until his death on 21 January 1924.

With NEP the new ambivalent diplomacy was born: on the one hand Moscow had to maintain its role as the headquarters for the world revolutionary movement, on the other it had to negotiate treaties and agreements to ensure the survival of the only successful Communist revolution so far. Since both policies had, to a large extent, to be conducted in the open, the Soviets rapidly achieved a well-merited reputation for duplicity and double-dealing in their relations with other powers. Not that the capitalist powers were above reproach – torn as they were by a desire to undermine the socialist regime and a resolution to be first in the queue when the more lucrative trading and industrial concessions were being handed out.

Britain was the first to take advantage of this development with the commercial treaty of March 1921 and an exchange of trade missions. The lead of Britain was followed in 1922 by Germany and Norway, and by most other European countries by 1924. In that year Britain once more led the field in its recognition of the Soviet Government, much to the chagrin of the new fascist dictator, Mussolini. Italy and France followed soon after. Harding's and Coolidge's Republican Administrations in America remained aloof from these developments, despite the activity of the lively pro-Soviet lobby led by Senator Borah. The American attitude was a curious one. It seems to have been based on the erroneous impressions gleaned by the American Relief Administration on its mission in 1921. In

December 1921, Hoover, the head of the ARA, wrote a letter to Charles Hughes, the head of the State Department, rebutting a suggestion that encouragement should be given to German firms to ship American goods to Russia. It is worth quoting because the viewpoint expressed informed American policy towards the Soviet Union for over a decade, and because of its classic misreading of Bolshevik psychology. Hoover argued that 'the relief measures will build a situation which, combined with the other factors, will enable the Americans to undertake the leadership in the reconstruction of Russia when the proper moment arrives'. For this reason he urged that 'the hope of our commerce lies in the establishment of American firms abroad, distributing American goods under American direction, in the building of direct American financing and above all, in the installation of American technology in Russian industries'. Such relations could, however, Hoover concluded, only be established after 'fundamental changes' in Russia. Hoover maintained this strange view when he became President of the United States. The Soviet system of managing the economy struck him as 'utter foolishness'; and he resolutely resisted pressure to recognize the Soviet Government, even after the Great Slump had revealed a few bugs in the system he was running. It was left to the Roosevelt administration to recognize the Soviet régime in November 1933.

Back in 1924, however, the Russians were not obsessed by the problem of American recognition. Enough progress had been made in Europe to offset any transatlantic disappointments. In those days Britain was still marginally ahead of the United States as the diplomatic pace-setter. The successful completion of the Anglo–Russian Treaty talks in August 1924, was described in an official Soviet communiqué as 'laying the foundations of a new relation between the USSR and the greatest world-capitalist power'. The treaty with Britain, Kamenev said, was 'indubitably a turning-point in the whole world situation of our union'.

This, of course, was two months before the publication of the Zinoviev letter and the electoral triumph of a Conservative Party with a powerful, die-hard right wing. And the turning point when it came was towards a new low in Soviet relations with the capitalist world. There is no better circumstantial evidence for the fraudulence of the Zinoviev letter than this central fact: it ruined the most important initiative of orthodox Soviet policy – the Anglo-Russian Treaties were never put before the Commons for ratification by the new Conservative Government.

Zinoviev himself lost no time in disclaiming all responsibility for the notorious letter. On 27 October, just two days before polling in the British election, he attempted to clarify his position to the foreign press in Moscow. He had never written the letter, never sanctioned the issue of a letter of this kind, and never given instructions for such a letter to be prepared. Furthermore, on the alleged date of its signature, 15 September, he personally had been taking a well-earned breather from the affairs of international Communism – on holiday in Kislovodsk. In his view, the letter was 'from the first to the last word, a forgery'.

Such testimony from, in British eyes, a wholly suspect source had no effect whatsoever. Would a subverter of Zinoviev's ability ever admit his subversion? The denial was worthless. Zinoviev, however, made one more exasperated effort at establishing his innocence. There are no bounds to the righteous indignation of a professional subverter who feels he has been 'framed' for a job he did not do. It strikes at something much deeper than morality; it tampers with the rules of the game.

Something of this flavour came through in the 'Declaration of Zinoviev on the Alleged "Red Plot" ' published in the December 1924 issue of *The Communist Review,* a journal catering for Marxist intellectuals in Britain. 'It would seem,' Zinoviev wrote scornfully, 'as if the Executive Committee of the Comintern take pleasure in writing letters which are very convenient to statesmen of the type of Hughes [Charles Hughes, the American Secretary of State for Foreign Affairs] and Curzon. And in a strange manner these alleged letters – like eggs at Easter – fall into the hands of the retrospective bourgeois ministers, precisely when they need them in this or that campaign against their own working-class, or against the Soviet Government.'

Charles Evans Hughes came high on the ranking list of Zinoviev's most unpopular Western statesmen. In December 1923, Hughes had responded to a Soviet diplomatic overture in the most hostile fashion, and the day after doing so had released the text of a letter allegedly from Zinoviev to the Workers' Party of America (at that time the legal cover of the American Communists). The letter had concluded with the hope that 'the party will step by step conquer (embrace) the proletarian forces of America, and in the not distant future raise the red flag over the White House.' A declaration by the Workers' Party that the letter was a forgery, which it very likely was, did not shake the official attitude.

Zinoviev's 'Declaration' on the British letter was equally vain. The Tories, who had been swept back to office on the crest of the 'Red Scare' campaign, lost no time in staking their reputation on the letter's authenticity. On 21 November, Austen Chamberlain, the new Foreign Secretary, claimed, in a stuffy missive to the Soviet chargé d'affaires in London, that the information at his Government's disposal 'leaves no doubt whatsoever in their mind of the authenticity of M. Zinoviev's letter'. The nature of this clinching evidence was never revealed for reasons, the House of Commons was told, 'of safety to individual life'. As far as the Conservative Cabinet was concerned there was nothing more to be said.

Izvestia headlined its story on the British Foreign Secretary's line: 'Chamberlain outdoes Curzon', the supreme Bolshevik insult. Moscow's indignation, however, meant nothing to Labour's political opponents in Britain. From their point of view Zinoviev and his Bolshevik comrades were merely indulging in a noisily elaborate cover-up.

In fact, the Moscow leadership all appear to have shared Zinoviev's genuine incredulity that any foreign department could have been persuaded to put its imprimatur on what looked to them like the crudest of forgeries. Had any of Zinoviev's comrades suspected the letter of being genuine, there is scarcely any doubt that the blunder of 'being found out', and effectively annihilating the carefully negotiated Anglo-Russian treaties, would have been used against the fiery Comintern boss. Yet in a period of bitter internecine struggle within the Soviet Communist Party, there is absolutely no evidence of this ever happening.

In October 1924, Grigory Evseevich Zinoviev was at the height of his political career. One of the veterans of the revolution with an impeccable background of incarceration, exile and Bolshevik propaganda activity, he was, at the age of forty-one, still a serious contender for supreme power. Inside Russia, he had just achieved the uncertain immortality of having a town named after him (his birthplace, Elisavetgrad in the Ukraine was restyled Zinovievsk). Outside Russia, his position as president of the Third International had made Zinoviev the most famous of the Russian leaders after Lenin and Leon Trotsky.

But Lenin was dead and Trotsky was already on the way out: embarked on the long course that would lead to expulsion, exile, and ultimately the fatal blow of an assassin's ice-pick in a Mexican hotel room sixteen years later. And Zinoviev, one of the triumvirate who took virtual control of Communist Party affairs after Lenin's death in February 1924, was among the principal witch-hunters.

The other two triumvirs were Kamenev, Trotsky's brother-in-law, and a stocky Georgian bureaucrat called Joseph Stalin. In the ruthless leadership struggle that was getting under way, Zinoviev seemed commendably well placed. He had travelled through Germany in the famous sealed train en route for the Revolution in April 1917, as Lenin's closest adviser and lieutenant. When Lenin died, therefore, Zinoviev found it comparatively easy to build himself up as the first high priest of the Leninist creed. The master himself had left a somewhat jaundiced appraisal of Zinoviev's main rival: Stalin, Lenin had said, was too 'uncomradely' and might spoil everything by his roughness.

After the revolution Zinoviev had assumed almost dictatorial power in Petrograd (later Leningrad), where he distinguished himself by the brutality of his methods in crushing the bourgeoisie. His Leningrad power base – a potent one in the days when Leningrad, as the most advanced industrial city in Russia, considered itself the true standard-bearer of the proletarian masses – remained intact throughout 1924.

The Zinoviev success story had not, however, been accomplished without arousing some powerful enmities in the party. And Lenin's death, while it enhanced his acolyte's prestige, inevitably increased his vulnerability. Zinoviev had become the front-runner for power at a time when men of quite another cast were moving into positions of authority. These were men who had little experience of the outside world; dedicated Communists, but still more dedicated Russians, anxious to repair a country devastated by years of conflict. They were essentially pragmatists; and Joseph Stalin personified their mood. To some of them, inevitably, the more charismatic apologists of world revolution began to seem more trouble than they were worth. Like Trotsky, Zinoviev, a vain, brittle-tempered man, fell into this category.

Although Stalin's enunciation of the doctrine of 'Socialism in One Country' was not fully developed until well into 1925, there were signs of a reaction against Zinoviev's pyrotechnic displays as president of the International, even before the Zinoviev letter episode. Ironically, just at the time when the Soviet Union was moving most strongly towards a genuine accommodation with the capitalist world, Britain, which had assisted the process in its early stages, opted out. After the ruckus over the Zinoviev letter Anglo–Soviet relations went from bad to abysmal. The events of the General Strike in May 1926 accelerated the process. Moscow, seeing the Marxist prophecy on the brink of fulfilment, alienated even moderate English opinion by its exhortations to the strikers. It was all an illusion. When, by the Bolshevik analysis, the killing had to start, the strikers dutifully caved in. Old revolutionary hands in Moscow must have read with incredulity of the football match between strikers and the police, in which the strikers won by two goals to one and the chief constable's wife kicked off.

The reaction on the Soviet side, inevitably, was further disenchantment with the efforts of the International to promote revolution (Marx had anticipated that England would be the first to succumb). In Britain the die-hards were strengthened in their resolve to teach the Bolsheviks a lesson. On 17 May 1927, Britain severed diplomatic relations with the Soviet Union.

The ever-receding prospect of world revolution had inevitably affected the status of the Communist International. The duplicity of Soviet foreign policy became self-defeating. It got in the way of 'building Socialism in One Country'; and it provided the easiest of targets for the lively anti-Soviet forgery industry. When it was realized that a tricky diplomatic initiative by the Soviet Union might be ruined by the 'revelation' of a subversive action by the International, the number of such 'revelations' escalated impressively. The Zinoviev letter was by far the most notorious exercise of this kind, but there were many others. In April 1927, the Soviet Government sponsored an English edition of *Anti-Soviet Forgeries* – probably in a desperate attempt to influence British public opinion before the impending diplomatic rupture. The book adduced evidence of twenty major forgeries, ranging from a secret treaty between the International and the Croat Republican Peasants Party to a letter delicately smearing the pro-Soviet American Senator Borah. The Zinoviev letter was given pride of place, although no light was thrown on its origins.

As the International's star dwindled, so did Zinoviev's. Throughout 1925 his influence in the inner councils of the Soviet Communist Party was gradually eroded. Initially, the tensions between Stalin and Zinoviev in the triumvirate had been concealed by their joint desire to keep Trotsky out of the succession. By April 1925, however, with Trotsky temporarily banished to the Caucasus for his 'political health' (he had already 'resigned' the key post of Commissar for War) the scene was set for a direct confrontation between Zinoviev and Stalin.

It was an unequal contest. Stalin, already a manipulator of genius, had, as Secretary of the Communist Party, control of all the levers of patronage. He held the confidential files; members had to come to him for advice on party tactics. In December 1925 there was a blazing row at the party Congress, in which Zinoviev and his Leningrad following were crushingly defeated. Stalin rubbed his triumph in by detaining Zinoviev in Moscow while the Leningrad organization was systematically dismantled.

The following year brought further humiliation for Zinoviev. It did, however, polarize the dispute in an intelligible way. Trotsky, bouncing back for more punishment, formed a coalition with Kamenev and Zinoviev against Stalin. This was a natural alliance: all three were International Jews, and as such naturally claimed priority for the message of world revolution. They were also in favour of a more strongly industrial emphasis in the management of the economy. Stalin's doctrine of 'Socialism in One Country' downgraded the importance of the

45

International and dictated a peasant-orientated policy at home until the revolution was consolidated. Needless to say, Stalin's policy, in a country with over eighty per cent of its population living outside the towns, had more grass-roots appeal.

Forsaking his normal reserve, Stalin confidently branded the opposition alliance as 'a gang of European adventurers' – a telling blow, after the failure of the General Strike in Britain. By the end of the year Trotsky had been removed from the Politburo and Zinoviev deprived of his presidency of the International. A few months later both were expelled from the party.

Their reactions to expulsion neatly demonstrated the differences in their characters. Trotsky, unrepentant to the end, had to be bundled out of the country into exile where he fought for his concept of 'permanent revolution' until his death. Zinoviev apologized, kept his head down, and was quietly readmitted into the party in 1929. (Stalin, however, was never reconciled to him: on 25 August 1936 Zinoviev was convicted of high treason and shot.) With the European adventurers out of the way, Stalin tidied up the embarrassing problems presented by the Comintern by not allowing it to meet for six years. When it reappeared again, in September 1935, it was as a docile agent of Soviet policy. Its headquarters were moved away from the centre of Moscow.

For Zinoviev on the way out in 1927, there was, however, one minor consolation. The Soviet authorities finally uncovered, to their satisfaction, the origins of the Zinoviev letter. In the summer of 1927, Druzhelovsky, a forger of some eminence (*Anti-Soviet Forgeries* had devoted a chapter to the output of his forgery 'arsenal'), who had entered Russia illegally, stood for trial in Moscow. He confessed to having helped forge the Zinoviev letter with a group of White Russian emigrés in Berlin.

Some months later the issue of the Zinoviev letter was briefly revived in the House of Commons. The Conservative Government once more pledged its confidence in the letter's authenticity. On 22 March 1928, three days after the debate, the Soviet Government made one last effort to put the record straight. M. Chicherin issued the following statement to the press:

During the trial by a Soviet court of Druzhelovsky, a manufacturer of forgeries, his evidence, as recorded by shorthand minutes, shows that he possessed information of how the so-called Zinoviev letter was fabricated in Berlin. His evidence shows a bright light upon this affair. Druzhelovsky worked in Berlin on the instructions of Paciorkowski, a Polish captain, who, according to Druzhelovsky, was connected with other Intelligence Services. Druzhelovsky, in his evidence, communicated detailed and concrete evidence of the so-called Zinoviev letter by the Russian refugees Zhemchuzhnikov, Bellegarde, and Gumansky, who worked under Paciorkowski and the British Intelligence. Zhemchuzhnikov told Druzhelovsky that the 'Zinoviev letter' which was fabricated in Berlin, was simultaneously by several ways transmitted to London. The most precise and detailed evidence of Druzhelovsky categorically refutes the existence of the so-called 'Zinoviev letter'.

Chicherin concluded piteously: 'If this affair were investigated other proofs could be presented, but the British Cabinet persists in declining an inquiry.'

In Britain only the *Manchester Guardian* ran Chicherin's statement at any length. The newspapers were bored by the controversy. As far as the Conservative Party was concerned, of course, the protestations of the Soviet Government were still not worth listening to. Theirs was a potent fiction – the Zinoviev letter had been written by Zinoviev, the British secret service had acted with honour and resource, and the men who had been responsible for informing the public of the letter's contents had done a service to the nation. Against the monolithic simplicity of this account, the Soviet version, full of strange-sounding names and reeking with central European intrigue, just did not have a chance. The Parliamentary controversy over the Zinoviev letter was at an end.

5

How the Zinoviev Letter was Forged

A veteran diplomatic correspondent of great eminence was once asked by a tyro journalist the secret of his amazing in-sight into affairs. The formula revealed by the diplomatic correspondent was both ingenious and simple. He would spend the morning reading the foreign affairs columns in all the daily newspapers; having done that he would go to one of the finest restaurants in town for a substantial lunch, and then, over a few brandies, ponder 'what, at this juncture, could be the most despicable, underhand action taken by one power against another.' He would then go home and write down his post-prandial reflections in the form of a speculative news story. The technique, said the correspondent, had led to the achievement of 'an unbroken succession of scoops'.

Cynicism on this scale is, of course, a rare art form, and one not easily mastered by most people or, for that matter, by many journalists. Without it, however, no member of the British public in 1928 could have believed the story of the origins of the Zinoviev letter put about by the Soviet Government. Anyway the Chicherin statement came too late to have even the slightest influence on the House of Commons debate on the subject, and to this day, the Foreign Office has rested on the position that the Zinoviev letter was written by Zinoviev. Its ability to do so must in large measure be attributed to a widespread quality that is the reverse of cynicism, but probably no more desirable – namely naïveté. One of the more curious characteristics of Anglo-Saxon electorates is that when formal pronouncements are made by their foreign affairs departments, they tend to take them at face value. As most continental countries do not appear

48

to share this delusion, the condition would appear to have something to do with the fact that most Anglo-Saxon communities are insulated from the consequences of their diplomatic actions by large stretches of water.

As it happens, the Soviet Government's vain insistence back in March 1928 that the Zinoviev letter had been forged in Berlin was based on the truth. But even if the British would not listen, the diplomatic community on the continent at the time must have found it eminently credible. For one thing, the locale was absolutely right. Berlin was the capital of European intrigue. Diplomatically, anything could happen there, and quite frequently did.

Berlin was where the capitalist East met the Bolshevik West. It had, before 1924, that extreme rarity – a Soviet embassy, complete with ambassador. Governments which officially were not on speaking terms with the Bolsheviks could communicate on the Berlin diplomatic network (in much the same way as the Americans speak to the Red Chinese now through the neutral medium of Warsaw). In Berlin the Poles and French could hatch their mutually beneficial schemes to keep Germany down and Russia isolated. In Berlin, too, all the contradictions in the policy of the Soviet Union towards the capitalist world were made manifest.

Berlin was also, of course, the centre for technical and industrial contacts between Russia and the Germans. Officially, the Soviet Government, though not the Third International, had the most cordial relations with the Weimar Republic. Only one month after the October rising the Soviet Embassy in Berlin held a brilliant reception attended by a large company of concession-hungry German officials, bankers and industrialists. The occasion was the anniversary of the Bolshevik revolution in Russia. But Berlin was also the publishing headquarters of *Ost Information,* an uninhibited anti-Bolshevik journal given to the revelation of 'Secrets of the Kremlin' for private circulation. Curzon's splenetic, and largely erroneous, diplomatic Note of 1921 seems to have borrowed generously from the lucubrations of this little publication. Berlin, above all, had in the early 1920s the most intelligent and resourceful White Russian community of any European capital.

In 1917 Lenin had expelled not only foreigners but many of

49

his internal political enemies. Many did not even wait to be asked to go.

The diaspora, as they called it, the scatterings of pre-Bolshevik Russia, spread to all parts of the globe. Many of the churchmen found a home from home in the newly-created Yugoslavia, which was Orthodox. Scholars and students were warmly welcomed with a generous provision by the new Czechoslovakia. Some made it to England and America. A larger number settled in Paris, where Diaghilev's ballet had already earned plaudits for Russian culture before the First World War. In all something like 1,000,000 Russian émigrés decided, or were persuaded, that Lenin could include them out of his Socialist utopia. Abroad, united in the grievance of having been burgled by the same gang, they were naturally clannish. But the most fully developed expression of a self-contained White Russian émigré community came in Berlin. Nothing quite like it, with the possible exception of the expatriate Jacobite society in Paris in the early eighteenth century, had ever been created before.

In the early 1920s, Berlin became, in many ways, more representative of Russian opinion than Russia itself. It was a natural resort for émigré politicians – offering proximity to their mother country and a first-class listening-post on contemporary Bolshevik affairs. Culturally, the community, which settled mainly round the Charlottenburg district in west Berlin, strove to make itself as near a replica of pre-revolutionary Russia as possible. Berlin housed for a time the 'Moscow Arts Theatre Beyond the Frontier'. There were numerous émigré publishing houses. Vladimir Nabokov, the most famous novelist produced by the diaspora, earned early distinction by compiling the first Russian crossword puzzles for an émigré newspaper. At one stage the city produced three daily papers in Russian – ranging from the monarchist to the Menshevik persuasion.

Political enmities conceived in Imperial Russia transferred, without much diminution of tension, to the German capital. In March 1922, for example, Nabokov's father, an able liberal politician in Imperial Russia, was shot by a monarchist at a public meeting in Berlin. It was all a ghastly mistake: the assassin, Taboritsky, later a Nazi and Gestapo collaborator, had come to shoot Nabokov senior's friend, a leading liberal politician and former Foreign Secretary, but Nabokov had tried to defend him.

One thing, however, united all émigré political creeds – a passionate anti-Bolshevism. And at this timé the joke figure of the émigré general, keeping his Imperial uniform in a closet and taking it out for a monthly dusting against his return to Russia, was not so very funny. The hot war between the 'Whites' and the 'Reds' had ended only three years earlier; and the difficulties that Lenin had experienced in introducing the New Economic Policy gave immense heart to Russian opponents of the régime. In 1924, unrealistically as it turned out, émigrés still entertained genuine hopes of a triumphant return to Russia. And, like the Bolsheviks, they did not just sit and wait for the tide of history to turn in their favour.

It was Berlin, inevitably, that spawned the most intransigent counter-revolutionary organizations. Some, like 'The Brotherhood of Russian Justice', did not draw the line at political murder as a method of reprisal. Others, like the Brotherhood of St George (a name based on the Order of St George, the Tsar's highest military honour), were more sophisticated in their tactics. Their single-minded aim was to keep the Soviet Union diplomatically isolated. The equation for them was simple: diplomatic contact led to trade, which led to capitalist investment which eventually would strengthen the Soviet régime and diminish the chances of ever bringing it down. Any stratagem which could jeopardize this process was, far from being traitorous, the most patriotic of gestures. Of all the curiosities to which the Bolshevik revolution gave birth, few were more bizarre than these idealistic counter-revolutionary groups.

The twilight world of spying and political forgery suddenly became inhabited by a host of aristocratic amateurs. Some were pathetic failures in this role, others, however, brought a new verve and daring to what, in reality, is normally one of the drabbest departments of diplomatic activity. Two of them, Alexis Bellegarde, aged twenty-six, and Alexander Gumansky, aged twenty-seven, both members of the Brotherhood of St George, composed the Zinoviev letter.

The widow of Alexis Bellegarde, Mme Irina Bellegarde, is still alive and lives in London. It is largely upon her evidence that the true story of the Zinoviev forgery is based. She

51

witnessed the forgery as it was performed, and she is the sole survivor of those who did. This chapter derives in the main from her recollections. This whole book, in fact, originated with her decision to reveal a secret she had kept for forty-two years. But she is not the only source for it. In order to show why we have not had to treat her evidence with the same chronic scepticism that one would exercise towards, for example, a claimant to the inheritance of the Tsars, it is worth describing how we came across her story.

In December 1966, the Zinoviev letter returned briefly to the newspaper headlines, after it had been disclosed that the Zinoviev file in the Foreign Office records was incomplete. This disclosure was made, remarkably, in a new official edition of documents in British foreign policy. One of the auxiliary papers to the letter itself was reported missing. During the consequent discussion, *The Sunday Times* was put in touch with Mme Bellegarde, who wanted to tell her part of the story for the first time.

With all due scepticism we interviewed her. As it turned out, her fluency, her unfaltering consistency and her transparent integrity were impressive enough. But they were not all. The facts which she gave suddenly made other facts, already in the public record but never given credence, fall into place. The names she gave of those who were involved coincided to a great extent with those given forty years ago in the Soviet version of the story. The details she gave about her husband's later life as a secret agent were verified from official sources in London. In fact, every verifiable aspect of what she said proved, when checked, to be true. All that had prevented her from publicizing the story before was a fear for the safety of those involved – itself an illustration of her seriousness of purpose.

There can be no credible doubt that what she has said is a true account of what she can remember of such a distant event. That there are minor differences between what she remembers and what the Soviet Union said at the time is merely a further confirmation that hers is a genuine recollection rather than a modern concoction. It must be said that her version does not tally in every respect with that advanced by Chicherin to the foreign press on 22 March 1928. With the exception of Paciorkowski, the Polish captain mentioned in the Chicherin statement, Mme Bellegarde knew all the people – Druzhelovsky, Gumansky, Zhemchuznikov and, of course, Bellegarde – said to be involved in the enterprise. But she does not always assign them the same roles as did the Soviet authorities. For example, Zhemchuzhnikov, who was Mme Bellegarde's brother, did not, according to her version of events, have any part in the affair; he was probably dragged into Druzhelovsky's 'confessions' because of his close family relationship with the Bellegardes. The other discrepancies between the Druzhelovsky and Bellegarde versions are better dealt with after the sequence of the forgery has been explained.

The Bellegardes, as the name suggests, were originally French aristocrats with the usual unconventional history of such families. The great-grandfather of the Zinoviev letter plotter, Count Charles Cassier de Bellegarde, was a general in the French Army before the Revolution. When revolutionary France became uncomfortable, the Count moved briefly to Germany; once there, however, he decided to write to Catherine the Great with a view to taking his family to settle in Russia. Catherine replied with imperial generosity: Count Bellegarde and his son, a former colonel in the French army, would be more than welcome. They could come 'with their rank and medals'.

The Count died on the journey to St Petersburg, where he was ultimately buried with full military honours, but the son survived to found a new aristocratic line in Russia. He rose in the Imperial service to the post of commandant of the fortress of Viborg in Finland. His own son, in turn, rose even higher, and for a period held the position of Governor of Estonia – an office he seems to have discharged along progressive lines. He went out of his way to ensure a fair trial for a troublesome Estonian nationalist called Pyats, who faced arrest and instant execution. Later in the 1930s, Pyats, then president of Estonia, was able to offer the Bellegarde family refuge when its activities became offensive to the Nazi regime.

In 1912 Bellegarde became a Senator, but when the Bolshevik revolution started, Senator Bellegarde and his son, an officer in the Russian army, decamped rapidly, first to Riga, and then, in 1918, to Berlin. They both abominated Bolshevism and were soon immersed in the miasmic world of émigré counter-revolutionary politics. Soviet sources suggest they became extremely influential. *Anti-Soviet Forgeries* relates that when the Brotherhood of St George became suspect and was dissolved in the mid-1920s, it re-emerged as the clandestine Svyatogor League. The President of the Council of this League was, according to the same source, Bellegarde senior; the Propaganda Department was headed by his son, Alexis.

It was Alexis Bellegarde who took part in the Zinoviev letter escapade. On the dates of events leading up to the forgery in 1924, Mme Bellegarde cannot be precise, but her grasp of their sequence is both authoritative and convincing. They begin in the late summer of that year, when Gumansky burst excitedly into Bellegarde's third-floor apartment in 117, Eisenacherstrasse, in the Charlottenburg district. Gumansky, another former officer in the Russian Imperial Army, was an intimate family friend of the Bellegardes. He was also a plotter of considerable talent. The reason for his excitement on this occasion was a proposition he had just heard that could devastate the Anglo-Soviet treaty negotiations then being conducted by the MacDonald government. He then outlined the concept of the Zinoviev letter.

Gumansky hinted darkly that the request for such a letter had come from 'a person in authority in London'. Whether this was true or not, Mme Bellegarde assumed from the outset that the letter would be used by some member of the English Establishment for his own purposes. As these purposes were bound to be anti-Bolshevik, they naturally chimed in with the sympathies of the Bellegarde circle.

Mme Bellegarde was in her early twenties at the time, pregnant with her first child, but an interested observer of all that followed. The decision to go ahead and draft the letter was taken with very little deliberation. Who, if anyone, was the link between the Berlin émigré cell and the shadowy sponsor of the letter in London, is not clear. It could possibly have been a slightly older acquaintance Vladimir Orlov, whom Mme Bellegarde recalled as a man who 'constantly travelled around Europe, and appeared to have important connections in London'. Orlov certainly understood the business. In July 1929 he was found guilty of forging documents and fraud, by a Berlin court. He and an accomplice had tried to sell forged documents to an American journalist; the documents were designed to prove that the American Senator William Borah received bribes for advocating recognition of Soviet Russia by the United States. In 1924 Orlov was a close friend of Gumansky but regarded 'with the deepest suspicion' by Bellegarde.

The actual drafting of the letter was done entirely by Gumansky and Bellegarde. Their initial problem, however, was the acquisition of some authoritative-looking notepaper with Third International emblazoned across the top. They decided to sound out another Russian contact of theirs, Druzhelovsky (the 'manufacturer of forgeries' in Chicherin's statement), who used to frequent the restaurant opposite the Bellegardes' apartment. The restaurant, Stolnikov's Dining Room, was run by a close friend, and was a cheap and popular meeting place for émigré plotters.

In this convivial setting, Druzhelovsky agreed to try and steal some genuine Third International notepaper from the Soviet Embassy in Berlin. Mme Bellegarde disagrees with the Soviet authorities' estimate of Druzhelovsky as a master forger. She took him for a clerk at the Soviet Embassy – 'a little man badly in need of some ready money'. She considered his part in the enterprise a meagre one; and that poorly carried out. For, after weeks of nail-biting anxiety waiting for the notepaper, Druzhelovsky arrived with just one sheet. Bellegarde found this very frustrating. 'It meant,' said Mme Bellegarde, 'they had only one chance; the first attempt had to be right.'

The early drafts were done on rough paper and took another two weeks or so. The two young anti-Bolsheviks spent much of this time consulting revolutionary primers and Marxist texts to get just the right flavour of polemic. The published speeches of Zinoviev himself were an immense help.

The evening of the actual forgery was a memorable occasion. The final draft, transferred to the precious notepaper, lay on her front room table awaiting the Zinoviev signature. There were four people present: M. and Mme Bellegarde, Gumansky and a Latvian friend called Edward Friede who had served with the anti-Bolshevik, Baltic 'Patriot Volunteers'. Friede was the odd man out: he was not a professional plotter and much the least intelligent of the group. He had, however, one special accomplishment – his favourite party piece, after a few vodkas, was forging other people's signatures. He duly copied out Zinoviev's signature from a facsimile on a Communist International circular.

Mme Bellegarde recalls an atmosphere of intense exuberance. Everyone was buoyed up with excitement: it was a schoolboy prank as much as an ultra-serious blow against the Soviet regime. The average age of the occupants of the room was twenty-six. None of them probably realized the full consequences of their action; Gumansky alone may have done. It was Gumansky, the motivating force throughout, who took the Zinoviev letter away from the apartment and sent it through the channels that led to London and the crescendo of the 'Red Scare' election campaign.

When the explosion came, Mme Bellegarde recalls being 'absolutely amazed': neither she, nor, it seems, her husband, realized that the letter would be used as a party political weapon in the British election campaign. It had, of course, been conceived and composed before MacDonald announced that he would go to the country. Even so it was an occasion for rejoicing in the tiny émigré cell that had made it all possible. And a slap-up celebration was organized at Berlin's most fashionable Russian restaurant, Moniko's, in the Motz Strasse. Druzhelovsky was not invited. The party comprised the Bellegardes, Gumansky and his wife, and Friede. There was a cabaret of gipsy dancing. Gumansky settled the bill. 'It was,' recalled Mme Bellegarde, 'all tremendous fun.'

At this point it is necessary to examine the discrepancies between the story as told by Mme Bellegarde and the story advanced by the Soviet authorities on the basis of Druzhelovsky's 'confessions' in 1927. The first and most obvious point is that Druzhelovsky made no mention of Edward Friede as the man who actually forged Zinoviev's signature. This particular variation, however, does not affect the general structure of the story: indeed, it tends to corroborate Mme Bellegarde's version. The Bellegardes clearly did not care for Druzhelovsky, and after he had performed his allotted task he was frozen out of the drafting stages. He never had any contact with Friede, who was a late-comer to the plot.

More serious is the difference between Mme Bellegarde's and the Soviet authorities' estimate of Druzhelovsky himself.

Mme Bellegarde, who thought Druzhelovsky a lowly clerk in the Soviet Embassy, tends to be of the opinion that his role was deliberately inflated by his captors, simply because he was the only one ever brought to justice. (Bellegarde and Gumansky were sentenced to death *in absentia*.)

On the balance of evidence this seems unlikely. For one thing the Soviet capacity for re-writing history was not nearly so highly developed at this stage as it was to become in the later Stalinist phase. More important, however, is the internal evidence in *Anti-Soviet Forgeries*, which was published in England in April 1927. This volume devotes separate chapters to the Zinoviev letter and Druzhelovsky's forgery 'arsenal' in Berlin – but no suggestion of a link between them is made. In another section, as we have seen, the same book mentions the 'white guardist' activities of Senator Bellegarde and his son. In this section there is mention of a precise link between Druzhelovsky and Gumansky, but nothing associating Gumansky or the Bellegardes with the Zinoviev letter forgery. The book does, however, provide a potted biography of Druzhelovsky:

> A native of Mogilev province in Russia, the son of an official in the police service. During the great war, he was an officer in the Russian air service. Subsequently he worked with the Polish General staff . . . he went to Riga at the time of the conclusion of the Russo–Polish Peace Treaty in 1920, and there did valuable service for the Poles. Having returned to Warsaw, he was convicted of treasonable practices in the year of 1922 or 1923, and was deported to Danzig. Thence he went to Berlin.

The conclusion seems inescapable: in April 1927 the Soviet authorities simply did not know that Druzhelovsky, Gumansky and the Bellegardes had been associated in the Zinoviev letter forgery enterprise, though they were aware of many of the émigrés' other activities. Had they known, it is hardly conceivable that they would not have made a determined effort to have the case immediately reopened in Britain, before diplomatic relations were severed in May 1927.

The fact that no such attempt was made seems to indicate that Druzhelovsky's 'confessions' did not take their most interesting turn until just before, or during, his trial in the late summer of 1927. And, of course, until the Zinoviev letter revelation came out, there was no real necessity, from a Soviet propaganda point of view, to inflate his reputation artificially. How was it, then, that Mme Bellegarde, a highly perceptive woman, understood that he was merely a clerk at the Soviet Embassy? Clearly, if the *Anti-Soviet Forgeries* biography is anything like accurate, Druzhelovsky would be among the last people ever to gain admittance to the Bolsheviks' most important diplomatic establishment in Europe.

One explanation seems possible. Druzhelovsky was essentially Gumansky's contact. Of the three plotters who gathered in the Eisenacherstrasse apartment, Gumansky was the most professional by far. It would be in his nature, and in the nature of the business, not to reveal more than absolutely necessary about other characters in the enterprise. Druzhelovsky, the son of a police officer, and clearly the social inferior of the Bellegardes, must have been very easy to pass off as 'a little man' at the Embassy.

One other factor suggests, almost conclusively, that Druzhelovsky was much more influential in the Zinoviev forgery enterprise than Mme Bellegarde ever realized: his mention in the confession of the Polish captain Paciorkowski.

Mme Bellegarde knew nothing of his involvement, nor anything of the mechanism by which the letter came to circulate in London after leaving her apartment. But all the evidence points to the conclusion that when Gumansky left with the letter in his pocket, the whole enterprise moved from one half-world of intrigue to enter yet another. This world was, if anything, even more furtive than that of the forgers. Theirs contained an element of amateur recklessness which was not the best guarantee against the truth ever coming out. The next stage of the letter's path to London was controlled by people rather more experienced in covering their tracks: the European intelligence services. The key to this world seems to have been supplied by Captain Paciorkowski.

In 1924 Paciorkowski was the press attaché at the Polish Embassy in Berlin. There seems, however, to be little doubt that his main function was of a more clandestine nature. Three years after the Zinoviev letter was published, Paciorkowski was a lieutenant-colonel in the Deuxième Bureau of the Warsaw General Staff. Apart from Druzhelovsky's 'confession', there is one other hearsay reference to his involvement in the forgery of the Zinoviev letter. This was made, in January 1928, at the trial in Leipzig of a talented forger called Johann Schreck. Schreck was convicted of forging documents and offering them for sale to the Polish Secret Service as coming from the German War Office. Most of the forgeries, in the main, were designed to prevent Germany's admission into the League of Nations: and the main customer for them, the prosecution alleged, was a man with the code name 'Dr Berger', who was, in fact, Paciorkowski. One of the witnesses at the trial, Karl Mertens, said that he had met an English publisher in Geneva a year previously who told him that he believed Paciorkowski was responsible for the forgery of the Zinoviev letter.

The evidence at this trial is less reliable – it was suggested that the Zinoviev letter might have been forged at Schreck's Berlin address – but it offers another pointer to the nature of Paciorkowski's activities in Berlin. There is no reason to think that Paciorkowski was acting in anything but the interests of his own Government.

The Polish Government at this stage was, if anything, more eager to cripple the Soviet regime than White Russian émigrés themselves. The émigrés had lost everything, whereas the Poles still had a lot to lose: by the Treaty of Riga, which ended the Russo–Polish war in 1921, they had taken over large tracts of what had formerly been Russian territory. After the peace, the Polish Government naturally strove to keep the Russian regime as weak and isolated as possible; a corollary of this was the denigration of the Soviet Union's closest friend – Weimar Germany.

The prospects of success of the Zinoviev letter enterprise must have been greatly enhanced by the involvement of Polish intelligence.

At that time a large proportion of the Russian section of the British intelligence was staffed by British subjects formerly resident in Russia, whose desire to believe anything discreditable to the Bolsheviks often outstripped their critical faculty. Even so it is highly doubtful whether even the rabidly anti-Bolshevik British secret service agencies could have accepted the Zinoviev forgery direct from émigré hands. Polish intelligence would be in a much better position to supply a credible 'route' for the letter's progress from Moscow.

The Poles, too, may well have been responsible for the central irony in the whole story of the Zinoviev forgery: the document so laboriously prepared in Berlin was never used in the tortuous manœuvres that led to the exposure of its contents in London. After the Zinoviev letter had exploded in the press it became apparent that none of the British intelligence services had seen the original. They had all worked on copies. Why the original was never passed on and flourished as authentic is not clear. But it is possible to speculate the reason – it probably was not anything like good enough.

Since we are now assuming that Druzhelovsky was never in a position to steal Comintern notepaper from the Berlin Embassy, there remain two alternative possibilities. Either someone stole the paper for him or the Third International masthead was a product of his somewhat erratic forgery factory. The copies, it is worth mentioning here briefly, though a textual analysis of the letter is the subject of another chapter, all had a mistake in the full title of the Third International.

We can well imagine Paciorkowski deciding that an ineptly forged original would not do. He may also have decided that the contents could be improved or topped up. Changes, certainly, were made in transforming the original into copies. Mme Bellegarde is sure that the only forged signature on the letter that left her flat was Zinoviev's. Yet the copies that turned up in Britain were purported to be based on an original that included Kuusinen, the Secretary of the Comintern, and MacManus, the British representative on the Comintern Presidium, among the signatories.

It must, however, be confessed that we can at this stage do no more than speculate on Paciorkowski's precise role. Nonetheless, there is now extremely good evidence that the Polish Government at the very highest level was extremely proud of the part played by their intelligence services in the forgery of the Zinoviev letter. The evidence comes from the diary of Maciej Rataj, who was the Speaker of the Polish House of Deputies between 1923 and 1928. The diary, published in Warsaw in 1965 by Ludowa Spoldzielnia Wydawnicza, is entitled *Maciej Rataj Pamietniki* and covers the years 1918–27. The entry for 9 November 1924, just fifteen days after the Zinoviev letter was published in London, records an interview

Rataj had with the Polish Prime Minister, Wladyslaw Sikorski. It warrants quotation in full:

> Sikorski's visit at 6 p.m. He reported on his visit to Paris. Very pleased and proud with the result. 'They can turn me out of office now because I have done my work.' In his activities conducted behind the scenes in France he was using right-wing statesmen who regarded Poland as a trump card against Herriot's pro-German tendencies. He visited Millerand, Poincaré, and Maginot. Sikorski maintains that he was the author of the 'Zinoviev Letter' addressed to the English Communists. This letter brought about the downfall of MacDonald's Labour Government during the General Election.
>
> The instructions contained in the alleged letter actually came from the 3rd International in Moscow and our General Staff was in possession of them. They were used in the form of a 'letter'. Details appropriate to British conditions and Zinoviev's signature were added. Gregory of the British Foreign Office, a Conservative and candidate for the office of Minister Plenipotentiary in Warsaw was helpful in exploiting the forgery.
>
> If Sikorski is telling the truth, his success is remarkable and he can be proud that he decided the results of the English elections.

There can be few more charmingly illustrative examples of the old adage that while it may be the working-classes who preach class war, the upper-classes simply practise it. The reference to Gregory is fascinating. J. D. Gregory, head of the Northern Department at the Foreign Office, was the man who actually signed the Note of protest to the Russian chargé d'affaires that was released at the same time as the Zinoviev letter. A release, as we have seen, that MacDonald later maintained was made without his authority. But Gregory's role belongs to another chapter. Meanwhile, what did Sikorski mean when he said that he was 'the author of the "Zinoviev Letter"'? And that the instructions 'actually came from the 3rd International'? Both statements seem to muddy the outlines of the story so far.

In fact there is no essential conflict. Sikorski, it seems, was taking, as head of state, credit for work done by one of his departments. And the 'instructions' from the Third International were much vaguer than the diary entry implied. Later on in the volume of the Rataj diary for the year 1924, there are more entries on the same subject. These, according to the editors, constitute rough notes which were normally the basis for the contents of the actual diary, which was sometimes written up after a considerable delay. If this is the case, then the following text was written before the entry for 9 November 1924 was composed:

A few days before the elections, during the election campaign, the Foreign Office acquired confidential instructions designed for the English Communists and signed by Zinoviev, Chairman of the Third International. The instructions recommend that there should be a strong propaganda campaign and social revolution in England and her Dominions.

Sikorski informed me that the instructions were a forgery and were the work of our Deuxième Bureau.

Foreign Office officials persuaded MacDonald to despatch a note to the Soviet Government because these instructions violated international practice and the specific pledges given by the Soviet Government. MacDonald yielded to the suggestions put forward by his Conservative civil servants. He acted on the day preceding the elections [sic] and this was fatal to the Labour Party! The great Conservative victory was due to the work of the Polish Deuxième Bureau.

The Soviet Union protested their innocence and demanded investigations. Nobody believed them. Although these particular instructions were indeed a forgery, there was nevertheless strong Bolshevik propaganda of this kind in existence.

The forgery in this entry does not appear to be based on specific 'instructions' at all. It tallies very much better with Mme Bellegarde's recollection that it was cobbled together from a variety of Communist propaganda texts and dressed-up to suit the British market. We can now speculate on a more coherent structure for the whole Berlin enterprise. Gumansky, or more probably Paciorkowski, had the original idea. If it was Paciorkowski, he would almost certainly have farmed the forgery work out to Druzhelovsky and Gumansky. The original forgery, however, was never designed to dish the Labour Party in the election -- it was simply hoped that its 'revelations' would ruin the Anglo–Russian treaty negotiations. Gumansky may have used the line about 'a person in authority in London' to draw Bellegarde into the enterprise. Bellegarde was a brilliant linguist and exceptionally fluent in English. He was also, apart from being anti-Bolshevik, a passionate Anglophile. He would undoubtedly have felt he was doing Britain a favour by promoting a scare that would force her to disengage from any arrangement with Soviet Russia.

Soon after the forgery is completed, Paciorkowski perceives that there is likely to be a general election in England. Lobby stories to this effect appeared in British newspapers before the end of September. He realizes that the letter could be much more devastating than he originally thought: he therefore adds a few refinements to Zinoviev's 'instructions', keeps the original, and endeavours to circulate copies. The project is a huge success. And Sikorski, with the aplomb of a pleasurably surprised departmental chief, basks in the glory.

The Zinoviev letter story now moves to London, leaving the world of the Bellegardes and Gumanskys. Meanwhile, it is worth recording what happened to them all. Druzhelovsky was shot for his crimes against the Soviet Union. Gumansky appears to have devoted his life to intrigue, sometimes on behalf of the French, sometimes for the Poles, but always against Soviet Russia. 'Politics,' says Mme Bellegarde, 'were his living and his life.' She has no doubt that he was extremely well paid for his part in the Zinoviev affair. Indeed, he appears to have prospered throughout his life. In Prague, where he settled in the late 'thirties, he possessed the ultimate status symbol: a telephone. His neighbours dubbed him 'the provocateur'. His end, however, was disquietingly abrupt. In the summer of 1938, Gumansky, by this time out of favour with the Nazi regime, boarded a train that was to take him from Prague to Rome. He never arrived in Italy: his widow always assumed that he was abducted by the Gestapo as the train passed through Austria, and killed.

Alexis Bellegarde appears to have served the White Russian cause without financial motive. After the Zinoviev affair he worked in the American consulate in Berlin for nine years. Then in 1934 his father was involved in a skirmish with the Nazi authorities (they objected to the measures he had taken to safeguard the funds of an expatriate Russian Jewish organization), so the entire Bellegarde family decided to move to Estonia. Later, during the Second World War, Bellegarde returned to Germany and did important work for British intelligence as a member of the Abwehr, the German counter-espionage agency.

He finally escaped to Sweden by bluffing a Gestapo frontier man that they had met at a party given by Reichsmarschal Göring – a possibility so flattering that the Gestapo man omitted to check the Bellegardes' forged papers. After such triumphs, Bellegarde arrived in England with his wife and three children on 10 March 1945, broken in health and virtually penniless. He died of tuberculosis in Hampstead on 17 September 1945.

Edward Friede lived longest. He settled down to the trade of bookbinding in Berlin, and does not appear to have taken part in any other émigré escapades. During the war he worked for the Germans as an interpreter in Russian. He had a heart attack and died in 1955. His widow, who is still alive, recalls that he used to promise her that when there was a change of regime in Russia, he and his friends would return home to important jobs.

6

London: The Tories Enter the Conspiracy

By late September the Labour Government was riding inexorably for a fall. In fighting so hard for their Russian policy, MacDonald and his colleagues had erected a formidable obstacle to their own survival. The Liberals, urged on by Lloyd George, were on the verge of finally opposing the Treaties and the loan. This meant, inevitably, the abandonment of their earlier determination not to allow the Government to fall. The Campbell Case was in its final stage of Government bungling. The Red Scare, a self-propagating nightmare, was approaching the heights of hysteria. The 'treasonable' loan and the 'seditious' newspaper editor were both symptoms of it and a focus for it. MacDonald, it was clear, would soon be forced to go to the country; it required only that the Liberals should unite for the kill. Although they had no predetermined plan, the Berlin forgers had acted at a moment which could not have been more opportune. They wanted, as their primary object, to embarrass and discredit the Bolshevik regime. But had they planned also to ensure the ruin of Ramsay MacDonald, they timed their effort to perfection.

The first Whitehall department to learn that the letter had arrived was the Foreign Office. This was on 10 October, two days after the Government had been overwhelmingly defeated on a Liberal confidence motion over the Campbell issue. Having decided to dissolve the House of Commons if it was defeated, the Labour Cabinet now faced an election in which the Bolshevik threat was certain to be the dominant political issue.

Slow though they were to grasp the fact, the Foreign Office received, on the eve of the election campaign, the most inflammatory piece of tinder ever supplied to fuel a Red Scare.

When MacDonald took over the Government in January 1924, he had also taken over the Foreign Office. Like the rest of Whitehall – not to mention London society – the Office anticipated the arrival of the Socialists, after their limited victory in the 1923 election, with mixed feelings. Their doubts were fixed on more important matters than the ability of the new men to handle a knife and fork. Unlike several London hostesses, they did not expect barbarians; but they did view with foreboding the potential disruption of their measured conduct of foreign policy. For one thing, they were afraid that Labour would try to abolish the intelligence service; it did, after all, conflict utterly with the fervour for peaceful internationalism. For another, they suspected that the Socialists were not 'sound': that they had no feeling for the diplomatic power of the British Empire. But much the most unsound proposal of all was the prospect of dealings with the crowd of gangsters which passed for a Bolshevik Government. In this, of course, their worst fears were justified: after only momentary vacillation, the Labour Government granted unconditional recognition to the Soviet regime.

The permanent Secretary, who had the job of initiating MacDonald into the mysteries of diplomacy, was Sir Eyre Crowe. In the pantheon of devoted servants revered in the Foreign Office, Crowe takes a very high place. Dedicated, cool, precise and incorruptible, Crowe represented an ideal of the orthodox British diplomat. With a German mother and a German wife went a Germanic attention to detail. He was hard on himself, but unfailingly kind to his subordinates. His life was one of clockwork regularity, interrupted only by Curzon's tenure of the Foreign Office, which no official survived without regretting the incontinent demands on his time at the least expected hours. He lunched every day with his number two, Lord Tyrell, at the Travellers' Club, except on Thursday when he lunched with the Portuguese Ambassador at the Carlton. Every night at nine o'clock he took the 19 bus home to Chelsea. If he was anti-Bolshevik, it was out of a highly developed respect for order and tradition rather than ideological fervour.

The text of the Zinoviev letter reached Crowe's department

on 10 October, during the five-day lull before the election campaign began in earnest. It was not, as we have seen, the original forged document, merely a copy. This itself was a vital element in the controversy which has surrounded the affair ever since. The original was never seen by anyone in authority. Neither the Foreign Office, nor any of the committees which later tried to establish the truth, ever discovered anyone else who had actually seen the original. It was mistakenly assumed at the time to be in the hands of the ostensible addressee, the British Communist Party: an accusation easily believed but never objectively substantiated – indeed, proof appears never to have been even attempted.

Next day, Saturday, 11 October, routine inquiries began in the Foreign Office to decide whether the letter should be treated any differently from the many similar revolutionary pronouncements allegedly originating with the Bolsheviks. Sunday intervened, and it was only on the Tuesday, the 14th, that the document was registered as having been officially 'received' by the Foreign Office registry. One of the first officials to see it was William Strang, then a second secretary in the Northern Department. Strang (now Lord Strang), who was later to rise to the Permanent Secretary's chair, has recorded that he did not at first consider the letter anything out of the ordinary. He had seen many similar instructions, and the Government had made plenty of protests against them. He was about to send the document up to the head of the Department with a short minute, when he was contacted by the office of the Permanent Secretary himself. Neville Bland, Crowe's private secretary, told him in urgent terms that Crowe had already seen a copy and attached unusual importance to it. More than that, Crowe thought it merited not merely a protest but publication. Bland's message was that the Northern Department should consider this before making its submission. For some reason unknown to Strang, the seemingly commonplace paper was being treated as something for decision by the Foreign Secretary himself.

Naturally Strang scrapped his plan to write a routine minute. Instead he prepared a new and longer minute, in which he spelled out arguments for and against publication. He did not, however, deal with the vexed question of authenticity. All available evidence suggests that this had been removed from the

67

debate this early: before the document had completed its normal progress through the Northern Department. Certainly it is known that Crowe became convinced that the letter was genuine at an early stage. He had seen – probably sent direct to his private office by MI1C, the intelligence department controlling espionage overseas – another copy for himself, and presumably had been convinced by the nature of his source that no further inquiry was necessary. Strang's actions certainly imply this. If any doubt about the letter's authenticity had been conveyed to him, it is fair to assume that he would have given his own opinion in his minute; but his own retrospective account makes it clear that his minute was confined simply to the question of publication.

Lord Strang does not recall whether his conclusion was for publication or against it. In any event, the letter then filtered up through official channels to the head of his department, J. D. Gregory. Don Gregory was, with Crowe, the principal Foreign Office official involved in the Zinoviev affair. But they were strikingly different personalities. Where Crowe was meticulous and single-minded, Gregory was a brilliant, impulsive man, who did not believe for a moment that the diplomatic life precluded the social round of London drawing-rooms. Indeed, Gregory seemed to make diplomacy a rationalization for a vigorous social life, and delighted in his acquaintance with fringe figures in the émigré European aristocracy. Nor was he as skilful as Crowe in sublimating his private beliefs in his public work. He was, in fact, a diplomat with strong personal views on the proper course of British foreign policy. Chief among these was a fervent anti-Bolshevism.

Ever since Labour came to power he had opposed their policy of rapprochement with Moscow. Only in August he had worked energetically to impede what he viewed as the over-generous terms of the trade treaty, garrulously leaking details of the negotiations which reflected badly on the Russians to, of all people, the Diplomatic Correspondent of the *Daily Herald*, in, of all places, the crowded bar of the RAC club. He had always had a deep interest in the affairs of Eastern Europe, especially the anti-Bolshevik strain. Supremacy over the Northern Department, and hence an insistent voice in British diplomacy in northern Europe, was a fulfilment of his natural interests. Some of his closest friends were Poles and Tsarist Russians. In May, for example, he had welcomed a representation from White Russian exiles and told them that he would gladly see them 'unofficially' at any time – even though, strictly, they did not warrant diplomatic status.

These and other personality traits of Gregory's led, later, to his becoming a natural focus of suspicion among Labour M.P.s who were determined to prove that MacDonald had been sabotaged by his officials over publication of the letter. However, on 14 October, when the letter reached him, Gregory minuted as follows: 'I very much doubt the wisdom of publication. The authenticity of the document would at once be denied.'

This, of course, was not Crowe's view. Strang, and presumably Gregory, knew that he had already tended to favour publication. He now confirmed this, and minuted to MacDonald accordingly.

MacDonald, however, was not in London. He had already begun his election campaign, leaving only Arthur Ponsonby, a junior Minister, at the Foreign Office. He had left London on the 13th, Monday, and spoken in Glasgow that night. On the 14th he had started south, on his motor tour of the country.

Wherever MacDonald went, Foreign Office red boxes remorselessly followed. At the end of a hard day's speaking, he was faced in his hotel room with a thick pile of Government files requiring attention and decision. It was impossible to escape them, and MacDonald, at the cost of many hours' sleep, did not try to. On the night of 15 October, around midnight, he arrived in his hotel room in Manchester after a major campaign speech at Belle Vue. Among the files, he came across the Zinoviev letter, with the minutes of Crowe and Gregory attached. It was quite undistinguished from the other mass of business. Indeed, MacDonald was later to claim with remarkable naïveté that it was only ten days later, when the letter was published, that he realized it had any political significance whatever.

The same degree of political innocence did not, however, afflict quite everyone in London. MacDonald may have viewed the letter as just another minor contribution to the stack of papers which pursued him round the country. He certainly would not have done so had he even an inkling of the network which was at that very moment being established between the Conservative Central Office, several Whitehall departments, and one of the principals of an obscure White Russian trading company in the City.

When the Foreign Office received its copy of the letter on 10 October and rapidly concluded that it would have to be published, the recipients did not know that news of its arrival in Britain had reached other quarters at least forty-eight hours earlier. But this was, in fact, the case. Already the first moves had been made in a plot which was to culminate in the Foreign Office, whatever its collective better judgement, authenticating and publishing the letter four days before the election.

London life in the 'twenties might have been made for conspiracy. The Great War had left an imprint on the society as well as on the economy. New strands had been woven into the fabric of the city. Two of them, in particular, formed a connecting thread between the many elements which developed an interest in the Zinoviev letter.

The first was MI5. MI5 had been founded by a single officer in 1909, largely as an experiment in counter-espionage. It was an experiment which quickly proved its worth and, when war broke out, rapidly expanded in size. By 1918, MI5 had 850 employees. It had attracted a patchwork assortment of every type of man into the war effort, and once a man has been in intelligence he can never entirely escape from it. When the war ended, many, naturally, drifted back to the universities, to business, to the City. But, equally naturally, they did not all lose touch with their old agency, still less with their old friends. The job of any intelligence agency is to keep eyes and ears in every quarter which might prove remotely fruitful. MI5 did not lose this opportunity to maintain its contacts. The result was that in the 1920s London contained a quite disproportionate number of people with a taste for intelligence and some experience in its arcane ways. They knew one another, they knew the system, and some of them knew the Director of MI5, Col. Vernon George Waldegrave Kell. Kell, a veteran of the Boxer campaign, was the founder of the agency. In 1924 it was discreetly announced that he had retired from the War Office. In fact, this was simply another playful bluff. Kell was still running MI5 when the

Second World War began; and he was certainly to prove a significant figure in October 1924.

The other potentially conspiratorial element which the European upheaval gave to London society was the émigré community – in particular the White Russian émigrés. After Berlin and Paris, London was the most favoured stopping-place for refugees from Bolshevism. There was the usual quota of disinherited aristocrats but also a number of energetic traders. All were bitterly opposed to the Bolshevik regime, and to any move which endowed it with the cloak of diplomatic legitimacy. Many believed that they would return, and they were not averse to any undercover politicking which might hasten that day. The MacDonald Government, being among the first Western powers to grant recognition, was anathema. Anything which might damage it would enjoy their full approval, especially if it damaged the Bolsheviks at the same time.

As it happened, there was at least one man in London who united both these elements in himself. Conrad Donald im Thurn was both a former MI5 agent and a director of one of the émigré commercial concerns, the London Steamship & Trading Corporation. Im Thurn was one of those agents who had not lost touch. And he was an Englishman among the Russians who shared their hatred of Bolshevism, and, by extension, Socialism.

The curious Old German name was deceptive. The im Thurns were, like many assimilated European families, more English than the English. The original family seat was at Schafhausen, near Lake Constance, but Donald's father had set up the family banking business in London at the turn of the century. Donald himself had been sent to Radley. The family was already mildly distinguished. By 1924 it had produced a Governor of Fiji (Sir Everard im Thurn), and a successful sailor who was later to get a Mediterranean command (Admiral John im Thurn). At school Donald was noted for the sterling British quality of being able to throw a cricket ball 'harder, straighter and farther than many men who play first-class cricket.' He was a swarthy, stocky fellow, who made up for his lack of intellectual distinction by what the school magazine later called 'considerable vigour and animal spirits'.

Im Thurn, like so many people, got into MI5 by accident.

Before the war he worked in an estate agency in Hampshire. Bad health prevented him signing on for active military service. In August 1914 he was leading a quiet family life in Bishops Waltham. His wife and children were at the seaside, in Boscombe. One Sunday, according to a possibly romanticized account of his entry into the secret service later given by his wife, as he was driving back from Boscombe, he saw a motor-cyclist by the side of the road who had been floored by one of the anti-motorist devices still common at the time, a wire stretched across from tree-trunk to tree-trunk. The motor-cyclist turned out to be a military despatch rider. Im Thurn left him to an ambulance, and himself carried the despatches to their destination, the G-o-C Southern Command. That officer, impressed by his enterprise, noted his name, and in due course im Thurn was asked to carry out a dangerous mission carrying despatches to Belgium. From this, a move to MI5 was, in the amateurish way that intelligence recruited people 50 years ago, a natural step. (Their amateurishness was symbolized by their use of Girl Guides as headquarters messengers in London during the war – although it could be argued that there was some method in their madness: the patriotism of Girl Guides is, after all, unquestionable.)

Im Thurn enjoyed his time in MI5. He was a conventionally brave, middle-class Englishman, and obviously a patriotic one. The adventurous life, in the country's cause, appealed to him, and there can be little doubt that when the war ended and he returned to private life, he missed the sense of belonging to an obscure but important group of patriot gentlemen. He turned to business in London, and soon became involved with a variety of companies run by Russian émigrés. Their main business was ships – principally the ships of the Russian Volunteer Fleet, freelance cargo vessels, some of which had been held in England after the 1917 Revolution on the grounds that they belonged to an unrecognized and potentially hostile power.

In October 1924 the elements of Donald im Thurn's past career, coupled with a piece of pure chance, contrived to involve him in an intelligence coup of greater magnitude than anything he ever handled for MI5. He got wind of the Zinoviev letter. What is more, he got wind of it forty-eight hours before the Permanent Secretary at the Foreign Office.

On 8 October, while the House of Commons was echoing to the last gasp of the MacDonald Government in the debate on the Campbell Case, Donald im Thurn kept an appointment with a friend. His friend wanted to tell him of alarming news he had received from Moscow. This was to the effect that Grigory Zinoviev, President of the Third International, had recently boasted of a great propaganda war he was about to launch in Britain in order to galvanize the woefully apathetic conduct of the Communist cause. In particular, Zinoviev had already sent instructions for action, which were to be put into practice as soon as the trade treaty was signed. To im Thurn, the zealous patriot, this was horrifying information. To im Thurn, the former MI5 man, it was an instant call to action: he himself had to do something about it. He asked his friend to find out whether the instructions had been received in London, and if so by whom. There they left it. That night the Government fell, and an election became certain.

The information about Donald im Thurn's 8 October rendezvous is disclosed in a newly-discovered diary which he kept for most of that hectic October. (The diary is reprinted in full in Appendix A). This is the document which holds the key to the unofficial story of the Zinoviev letter: the story which Crowe and his colleagues and successors never told, for the simple reason that they were almost certainly entirely unaware of it. The original of the diary has not survived. What has appeared is a copy of it, typed by Donald im Thurn or his secretary, and discovered in circumstances which put its own authenticity beyond doubt (among the papers of his only confidant, Major Guy Kindersley, M.P.). It portrays the daily machinations of a man driven by anti-Socialist zeal and guided by several years' experience in MI5. The question it does not resolve – the identity of im Thurn's shadowy informant, whom he refers to throughout as 'X' – is for the moment less important than the vivid detail of conspiracy which it does convey. What mattered, in October 1924, was that the Foreign Office did not have the letter to itself. All that need be deduced about X at this stage is that, whether or not he knew the letter was a fake, he was nearer to the conspiratorial centre of anti-Bolshevism than im Thurn was.

For the next three days, after 8 October, im Thurn was in a

quandary. He could not be sure of his information. He did not know exactly what Zinoviev's instructions amounted to, nor even that they had been received by anyone in London. X contacted him each day, and evinced a sense of rising optimism. On 9 October, a Thursday, he rang at six in the evening to say that there was nothing doing so far. 'Wonder what I ought to do,' wrote im Thurn. 'Do nothing, only hearsay so far.' The next day, X was more hopeful, and on the Saturday he was confident enough to be asking for time to 'dot the i's a bit more'. Im Thurn began the week-end with the instruction that he should be available to get the hard news on Monday.

That Monday, 13 October, X produced enough information to convince im Thurn that it was time for him to act. X told im Thurn, apparently in considerably greater detail than he had been able to give on the 8th, what the instructions, in the form of a letter, actually were. X also claimed to know something of what had happened to the letter since it arrived. It had reached London around 25 September. More than that, it had been seen, X thought, by at least one Member of Parliament, Jimmy Maxton, the Clydeside leader of the Left wing of the Labour Party. Evidently, Maxton had visited his friend, Christian Rakovsky, the Russian chargé d'affaires, who had immediately seen the political significance of the letter's appearing at this particular juncture in British politics. Rakovsky was said to have cursed Zinoviev, in front of Maxton, for sending it so foolishly at this moment. He cautioned Maxton against saying anything at all about its existence. It was apparently X's view that Rakovsky himself had a copy and was keeping it under diplomatic immunity from search by the authorities. However, X also reported that MacDonald himself, and Arthur Henderson, the Home Secretary, had heard of the letter's existence already: presumably, Rakovsky's alleged precautions were a little too late.

This 13 October entry is the most puzzling in the whole diary, because it consists not of im Thurn's own activities and observations, but of information supplied by X: information, moreover, of which X appears to be far from certain. It is not clear who was his source. And at face value, the implication it strongly conveys is highly improbable.

It implies that certainly Rakovsky, and probably Maxton,

74

had no doubt about the letter's authenticity. But most other evidence about Christian Rakovsky suggests that he was too fly a conspiratorial hand to be so rapidly convinced. He was a revolutionary from the early days. He had been with Lenin during his wartime exile in Switzerland, and accompanied him on the sealed train to the Finland Station which was the real augury of the Russian Revolution. After five years as President of the Ukraine he was transferred to London in 1923, to succeed Krassin as the Soviet trade representative. By training, he was a linguist and a cosmopolitan. His long years in Western Europe before the revolution had been put to good use. He had learned the niceties of Western society and diplomatic lore. By temperament, however, he was an exhibitionist and a mischief-maker. His arrival in London had been delayed by an anti-British speech he had made just before leaving: 'I go to Britain to stir up trouble,' he was reported to have said. When he eventually arrived, he took a fascinated pleasure in disrupting the social canons of London, while at the same time establishing himself as 'a new lion for London society', 'infinitely better educated than most Russian leaders', as the *Daily Graphic* admiringly reported. He gave a party to celebrate the re-opening as a Bolshevik enclave of the old Tsarist embassy at Chesham House. All London was there, and plenty others besides. Tweed-coated youths, sporting red carnations, mingled with the élite of the embassy crowd in their white ties. A toast was proposed to the success of the Red Army. Everyone wanted to taste the vodka. One guest summed up the intimations of the millennium which the party seemed to embody: 'Great, it's great! What else can you think when you get a countess and an engine-driver here together' – a paean not entirely devalued by the fact that the countess in question was the notorious dabbler in revolution, the Countess of Warwick.

Rakovsky was certainly amused by any trouble he could create. And doubtless the natural instinct of anyone wishing to invest the letter with the flavour of authenticity would be to ensure that a copy was sent to the Soviet representative in London. Rakovsky would, after all, surely be kept informed of Moscow's communications with its disciples in this country. On the other hand this very factor makes it highly unlikely that the Russian envoy – even if he did see it before publication – mistook the forgery for the real thing. He was familiar with the idiom of Zinoviev's pronouncements. To anyone who took the time to examine it, and who was aware of the ubiquity of forged diplomatic documents at the time, the Zinoviev letter must have seemed a thoroughly dubious piece of work.

It seems, therefore, unwise to treat X's report of the meeting between Maxton and Rakovsky as anything more than fortifying gossip. It may have been retailed to im Thurn by X in order to underpin his conviction that there really was something afoot: that Maxton, that dangerous fellow-traveller, and Rakovsky, that trained revolutionary, were plotting to conceal the letter. Alternatively, X himself, who had only heard of the letter's existence and apparently never possessed it or enabled im Thurn to possess it, may have been told this corroborative story: in other words, the deception may have been one stage further back. In either case, there could not ostensibly have been two more suggestive names for implication than Rakovsky and Maxton. In fact, as we know now, the least likely element is Maxton. If Maxton really had known of the letter's existence, forged or otherwise, it is inconceivable that he would have restrained himself from warning the Labour party leaders. Yet there is no evidence whatever that he did so. When MacDonald saw the letter among his papers in Manchester, it was his first knowledge of it. Moreover, his actions later were clearly based on total ignorance of the fact that anyone besides the Foreign Office knew of its existence. This would not have been the case if, as X told im Thurn, Maxton had actually been told about the letter by Rakovsky.

Im Thurn, however, had neither the time nor the inclination to weigh the evidence. Why should he? At the time it all seemed very clear-cut. What he had heard was enough to encourage him to set about discovering just who, if anyone, in the Government service knew that these dreadful instructions – with their incitement to mutiny and their evidence of Moscow's real intentions behind the amicable noises of treaty-making – had reached London. Next day, 14 October, he set out to resurrect his MI5 contacts.

In fact, the ease with which im Thurn gained an entry, and the familiarity with which he speaks of various agents of the intelligence services in later diary entries, suggest that the element of resurrection was fairly small. His facility of manœuvre would strongly support the theory that he had remained in close touch with the service after he had left it for the City. Insofar as it is possible to distinguish between full-time and occasional MI5 agents, it seems likely that Donald im Thurn remained, after the war, closer to the former than the latter.

His first contact, on 14 October, was with a man he calls 'A'. Like 'A', many of the people mentioned in the diary are represented only by an initial. But the code is not difficult to break down. This task has been simplified to some extent by the evidence of im Thurn's wife, who, years later, supplied a glossary on some of the names mentioned for another inquisitive historian. She identifies 'A' as unquestionably a man called Alexander, an MI5 acquaintance. In any case, at a later point in the diary im Thurn has omitted to disguise the name and spelt it out in full.

'Saw A.,' im Thurn writes, with the diarist's hasty disregard for syntax, 'who did not commit either way but drew deductions but thought he had original or photographic copy.' At his first stop, it appears, im Thurn was given enough clues to make him suppose that the intelligence service was not entirely in the dark. But Alexander remained very discreet. He did not make it explicit whether he definitely knew about the letter or not. When im Thurn told him as much as he knew, and asked for help, Alexander was sympathetic, but said that there was nothing he could do.

That day, im Thurn had another meeting with X. He received another piece of what now appears to be garbled, second-hand information. X told him that on 25 September, MacDonald had seen Arthur MacManus, the British Communist leader who was the putative addressee of the letter, and asked him whether he had heard from Zinoviev recently. MacManus, X said, had refused to answer.

Whether it was X or im Thurn who was the dupe, this seems a little too good to be true. X had previously reported that the date of the letter's arrival was about the 25th. He had also implied that MacDonald knew about it. Now he is suggesting that on that same day MacDonald immediately went to MacManus to check up. Even im Thurn exhibits by this time a trace of decent scepticism. He firmly prefixes his diary notation with 'he [X] asserts' – a usage which makes clear that he was unwilling to adopt the information as his own. It was a reasonable doubt, even though it did not in the least induce him to delay his plan of action. MacDonald, as we know, had no inkling of the letter in September. Moreover, he could scarcely have been to see MacManus then, because MacManus was in Moscow at the time. (Im Thurn, in fact, was not alone in overlooking this important detail. It was left to Maxton, years later, to point out that if Zinoviev had wished to send a blueprint for insurrection to the apathetic British CP, he would not have needed to risk sending a letter for anyone to read. He could simply have slipped it into MacManus's hip pocket for transmission during the next of his regular visits to London.)

As a final suggestive pointer in his message that day, X claimed that MacDonald, at this meeting with MacManus, had pointed out that, if indeed he had heard from Zinoviev, it would be unwise, even fatal, to let the news leak out at that moment. This is the first indication in the diary of any definite thought, on the part of im Thurn, that the Government might be working to conceal the letter. Of course, it would doubtless have occurred to anyone who knew what he did. And it is probably that from the beginning he realized the political gravity of the affair. But it is from this point that he seems to have started operating on that undivided assumption. Up to then, there was a distinct suggestion that he still wanted to discover whether the letter really existed. Now the object was simpler: to force the Government to expose what it knew.

On 15 October, im Thurn telephoned an old friend, Major Guy Kindersley, the Conservative MP for Hitchin. Kindersley was one of those reliable, plodding, utterly loyal Tory members who have always constituted the backbone, rather than the brains, of the party. Politically, he had two preoccupations. One was his constituency, which he lived in and nursed with diligent fondness. The other was the menace of the international Communist conspiracy. His Parliamentary career, from the time he first won Hitchin in 1923, is studded with questions and speeches which reveal an obsession with this topic. He and im Thurn spent many hours discussing it. Indeed, since im Thurn was himself fired by an equal fear of its purposes, Communism was probably the foundation of the friendship between the two men. Now this friendship was about to be put to an unexpectedly useful purpose.

Major Kindersley played a central, if unpublicized, role throughout the Zinoviev episode. He was the first man of influence to come to im Thurn's assistance. And, many years later, just before his death in 1956, he became the only one of the participants to write a limited, though authoritative account of what really happened. He, too, based his account on im Thurn's diary, albeit a bowdlerized version, and on the glossary supplied to him by Mrs im Thurn. He was the only other man known to have seen the diary, and it was among his papers that it was discovered. He was restrained, as will be seen later, from publishing his version of the story. But for modern historians it forms a valuable, and partly original, source.

From the Kindersley account, it is known that im Thurn's 15 October telephone call was not, in fact, his first. He had told his political friend on 10 October that something was up. Now, on 15 October, Kindersley came hot foot to im Thurn's office. Kindersley's reaction to the news was that Conservative Party headquarters should be informed. The man he decided to contact was, logically, Lord Younger.

Younger was not the chairman of the party, merely its Treasurer. He had, however, served as chairman earlier, and had proved one of its shrewdest, not to say sharpest, bosses. He had been a most effective exploiter of the honours racket, whereby party funds were replenished with impunity by the sale of peerages. He had virtually run the Conservative machine since 1916. In 1922, he had masterminded the breakup of the Coalition and Bonar Law's subsequent triumph at the polls. It was at this time that Birkenhead, in a singularly glib and ill-judged barb, ridiculed him as 'the cabin boy trying to run the ship'. In 1924 he was still the dominant figure at Central Office, although Sir Stanley Jackson, who was a more distinguished cricketer – he played for England as F. S. Jackson – than he was a politician, was the nominal chairman. For anyone with a proposition to make, Younger was the most likely person to consider it with a far-seeing and worldly eye.

At eleven o'clock on 15 October, Kindersley introduced the devious Scottish brewing magnate to the insignificant little man from the City. It was one of the more fruitful rendezvous in the history of British political intrigue. Blandly, im Thurn records: 'Told him news.' Younger never published his own reaction. It may safely be judged to have been one of delight. If the result of the election was not already certain, the means now existed, if only one or two ends could be tied up, to make it so. The Tory campaign, which had been based from the beginning on smearing the Socialists with the Bolshevik brush, was perfectly positioned to splash on another, and this time indelible, daub.

But im Thurn did not offer his news as an entirely unrepayable gift. He wanted what he called a 'guarantee against loss'. In other words, the deal would cost the Tories something from their well-endowed coffers. Someone, after all, had put himself in some danger by disclosing news of the letter.

It took Younger only the space of a lunch-time to arrange the guarantee. At 3.30, im Thurn had another meeting with him. This time, Jackson, as chairman, was present to give his formal agreement to it. Provisionally, they decided that the strategy should be directed to eventual publication of the news in *The Times*, at a date which would give it optimum political impact. Meanwhile, im Thurn was to continue his researches into the whereabouts of the letter in Whitehall.

The size of the guarantee is not mentioned in the diary. It was written at some point after the Tories had given their agreement in principle. In it, im Thurn speaks of the need to collect a total of £10,000. This was not for himself, he claimed, but for X. That, at least, is what he seems to have told the Conservatives, and there is no evidence which firmly suggests otherwise. The letter says that £2,500 of this has been guaranteed by another party, 'a relation of mine'. There is nowhere any single piece of evidence establishing just who this relation was. Speculation on the point is inseparable from consideration of the identity of X, and of the courier who carried the letter from the forgers in Berlin. The Tory obligation, however, is quite clear: to provide £7,500.

The same day he clinched the deal with Younger, im Thurn returned to visit Alexander, his MI5 acquaintance. He saw him at six o'clock, and the meeting prompted him to reverse his deduction of the previous day. He now decided that Alexander was not, after all, concealing his possession of a photocopy of the original letter. In fact, Alexander apparently had no idea who did have one. He could not discover where the letter was. It is clear from the diary that Alexander was now talking more freely about the matter. He confirmed, by his expressions of ignorance, that the existence of the letter somewhere was being treated seriously by MI5.

Im Thurn now switched his assumptions. He decided that 'C. must have only copy'. He based this assumption on his belief that 'MacDonald knew the 25th and not from Maxton'. If the premise had been right, the conclusion would have been reasonable. C was not, however, one of the diary entries referring to someone merely by the initial of their name. He was the head of MI1C, a man who has always gone by the same magic sobriquet even after the agency's name was changed to MI6 in the early thirties. ('C' originated with the founder of the overseas espionage department, a Naval officer called Mansfield Cumming.) C, at the time, was Admiral Sir Hugh Sinclair. If MacDonald had been told on the 25th, he could very well have been told by C, the man whose job it was to know everything that was happening in Europe. But MacDonald clearly did not know anything on the 25th, so im Thurn's assumption was wrong. However, he had to depend on X's information, and from this he plausibly deduced that C was the most likely possessor of the letter or a photocopy of it. Despite the inaccuracy of this assumption, im Thurn's deduction was absolutely correct.

This took him for the moment, although not, as we shall see, permanently, somewhat outside the range of his normal contacts. 'Dangerous try C.', the diary reads. There was a more approachable alternative: 'Try and draw Scotland Yard first.'

That night, therefore, im Thurn prepared for his meeting with the Special Branch. As he did so, Ramsay MacDonald was wearily opening up his boxes of Government papers in his hotel room in Manchester. He peered for the first time at the official copy of the Zinoviev letter. He did not find it remarkable. Still less did he imagine that a political trap, set up with elaborate ingenuity, was fast closing about him.

British Intelligence Authenticates the Forgery

The British administrative machine is only occasionally to be found in disarray, and most of these occasions regularly coincide with elections. Ministers are busy in their constituencies. Cabinets are difficult to call. The dying Government is in no position to take initiatives. Its response to events which have nothing to do with the campaign tends to be sluggish, and this was even truer in the 1920s, when the vast Governmental apparatus of physical and electronic communications was in its infancy. The departments are left to keep things gently ticking over. It is a time when political control over them is at its weakest. The politicians, hard at work on the stump, are in danger of not knowing what is going on.

This, pre-eminently, is what happened in 1924. One of the most significant paradoxes of the entire Zinoviev affair is the contrast between the knowledge available to politicians on the one hand and to the officials of several departments on the other. Apart from MacDonald, none of the Cabinet had even the vaguest premonition of what was to come. After it was all over, J. H. Thomas put this on the record. Neither Philip Snowden, Chancellor of the Exchequer, J. R. Clynes, Deputy Leader and Lord Privy Seal, Arthur Henderson, Home Secretary, nor Thomas himself, the Colonial Secretary, heard a single word about the letter until it was published. Yet if the Zinoviev letter had real significance, it was as a political missive. Its contents were not really frightening. The relationship between its purpose – revolution – and the actual proximity of its purpose was not nearly close enough to make it of paramount interest to the military or even the intelligence services. Throughout the next few days, however, it was they who, almost independently, became more and more involved, while their political masters remained outside the scope of the action, in the wings.

Certainly MacDonald took no steps to inform any of his colleagues. He shouldered the burden of deciding what to do with it and never seems to have thought of sharing it. Not that he viewed this as a particularly onerous task. As he studied the letter for the first time, on 15 October, he quickly decided on a virtually routine treatment. Before eventually going to bed, he added his own minute.

He made three points: that the Foreign Office must make sure that the document was authentic; that he favoured in principle publication of such things; and that a letter of protest to the Russian chargé d'affaires in London, so worded as to carry conviction, should be prepared for his consideration. As he argued later, defending himself against the charge that he intended to delay publication of the letter until after the election, he could easily have written: 'Please bring this up when I return to London.' The fact that he did not do this is a telling argument in the case which suggests that he behaved quite properly throughout.

MacDonald's minute reached the Foreign Office on 17 October. Meanwhile, Donald im Thurn was getting into increasingly deep waters. From his visit to Scotland Yard he emerged more confused than when he went in. The diary entry for 16 October tersely maps the convolutions of his own efforts to probe beneath the surface:

> Saw Scotland Yard to find out if Departments had seen letter. Answer No. S. would have seen it if circulated, therefore either C. has not circulated or Childs knows and is keeping it dark. Has Childs a copy or a photo. Fear only the former, otherwise circulated most certainly. Must find out. If not, must fix attention on forcing circulation.

(S., according to the diary's explanatory notes prepared by Mrs im Thurn, was a Foreign Office clerk named Bunty Saunders, an old friend of the family. Miss Saunders does indeed appear in the 1924 Foreign Office List. Her occupation is listed as Clerical

Officer (Women), and it is quite possible that she was responsible for circulating intelligence documents to other departments. She was still (in 1967) alive, living in retirement in a Thames-side village, but she invokes the Official Secrets Act to explain her refusal to reply to any questions about her role in the affair.)

The man im Thurn went to see at Scotland Yard was Major-General Sir Wyndham Childs, Assistant Commissioner and Head of the Special Branch. The Special Branch was in many ways inseparable from MI5 in affairs which affected the security of Britain itself. Both reported to the Home Secretary, and only when MI5 carried its operations into Europe was the essential difference between the two security organizations really important.

Im Thurn was now assuming that MI1C, through C himself, possessed the only official copy of the letter. He saw all initiative as resting with C. If he had circulated it, then Special Branch was sure to know – indeed, to have its own copy. But the Yard told him that circulation had not taken place: Childs, evidently, was being more open than Alexander of MI5. It appears as though he gave im Thurn the overt brush-off, rather than toying with him or appearing to offer sympathy. Yet im Thurn's deductions are entirely logical. He realizes Childs may simply be covering up, which was the most natural thing for him to do. But he tends on balance to believe that Childs is being straight with him. Something that Childs says virtually convinces him that Special Branch certainly has not got a photocopy. As an experienced agent, im Thurn appreciates that a photocopy, as opposed to a mere transcription, is the only evidence which would satisfy an intelligence officer. (In this, of course, he was more scrupulous than any of the departments which eventually did handle the letter. They never saw the original or a photo of it, and yet the Foreign Office was quite willing to commit the Government to giving it the seal of authenticity.) It was still just possible, however, that Childs had come by a copy at second-hand, or had heard on the intelligence grapevine about the letter's existence in London. But if this was all, then here was further evidence suggesting circulation had not taken place.

From this moment, im Thurn's objective became more closely defined. Having begun by trying to establish the letter's existence, and developed into an effort to discover its whereabouts, his investigation now moved into its third phase. It was vital to ensure that it was actually circulated among as many departments as possible. The reason for this is obvious. Until there was circulation, a doubt would hang over the letter's authenticity. Circulation was a preliminary requirement to formal Government recognition of the document and its eventual publication. The Younger-im Thurn agreement about publication in *The Times* was unlikely to be fulfilled otherwise. The paper would be certain to want some indication of authenticity. At the moment im Thurn was not even in a position to give *The Times* a copy. Circulation would put him in a better position to do this; but it would also give *The Times* an opportunity, through its own contacts, to confirm his story.

That evening im Thurn had another meeting with Alexander of MI5. They, too, had not been notified. Alexander said that his boss, Sir Vernon Kell, under whom im Thurn had served during the war, was still waiting to hear something from C. Alexander had evidently told im Thurn's story to Kell, and Kell, significantly, had agreed that, if it was true, the letter ought to be made more public: at least circulated among relevant departments, if not published at large.

At this meeting Alexander made a stronger commitment to im Thurn than he had made before. Previously he had been wary. Now a sort of bargain was sealed. The MI5 man offered to give im Thurn the document, if it came into his hands: 'A. offered publish it through me in a perfectly safe manner. K. (Kell) interested.'

By the 17th, as the official copy of the letter, unknown to Donald im Thurn, was arriving back at the Foreign Office from MacDonald's electoral caravan, he had become suddenly more desperate. Even though he had enlisted the aid of MI5, the prospect of not forcing the letter into the open in time for the election now confronted him. 'Decide risk everything as time was getting close,' he wrote. He was convinced, now, that C must have the letter, but he still felt he could not make a direct approach. Instead, he decided to tackle yet another branch of the intelligence service, Naval Intelligence at the Admiralty. He resolved, moreover, that if the Director of Naval Intelligence told him nothing, he would go straight to the Director of Military Intelligence, Kell himself.

85

The DNI at the time was Rear Admiral Hotham. But before frontally approaching him, im Thurn devised an elementary ploy which would enable him to go ahead and fulfil his bargain with the Tories even if he failed to get hold of the letter itself. He decided, in short, to try to outfox a man whose job it was to outfox others.

Im Thurn knew, or thought he knew, the date on the Zinoviev letter. This was 15 September, unrecorded in the diary but given to him earlier by X. One of the oldest tricks in any form of investigation is deliberately to get a detail wrong, in conversation with an adversary, and hope that his natural vanity will force him to display superior knowledge by divulging it. In im Thurn's dilemma, such a device could have a twofold effect. A correction, if it came, would simultaneously confirm that X's information was correct and that the DNI had seen the letter. This, in turn, would constitute final proof to im Thurn that the letter had been received by the Government.

When he saw the DNI on the 18th, therefore, im Thurn described the letter as dated 5 September. The trick worked with devastating simplicity. Hotham duly corrected him when he mentioned the 5th: 'Saw D.N.I.,' the diary says. 'Got date of letter out of him and deducted that it could not be original.'

From this moment, the entire balance of power between im Thurn and his intelligence contacts shifted in his favour – and he knew it. He now felt sure enough to begin issuing gentle threats rather than asking urgent questions. He would feel obliged, he told Hotham, to pass on his information to contacts who might give it more publicity if Whitehall delayed publication of the letter. It was a brilliant deception. By this single threat, the professional con-men of the intelligence service were themselves conned into an attitude which came perilously close to panic.

At midday, soon after he left Hotham, im Thurn received a telephone call from the harassed DNI. It was a request that he should meet a subordinate in Naval Intelligence, identified in the diary as MAW. The full identity of MAW is the only one which has not been disclosed either in the im Thurn family papers or by a close examination of the 1924 Navy List. (There seems to have been only one officer with the initials MAW in the List for 1924 and he was an officer in the New Zealand Navy, in

Britain to take a course – an unlikely candidate.) All that we know, and all that we need to know, is that he was close to Hotham.

At lunch that day, MAW promised im Thurn that he would do his best to get the letter circulated. But he also unwittingly told im Thurn more than he knew for certain: 'Made discoveries,' im Thurn recorded that night. '. . . C. has only copy. No good publishing my news unless I can get the letter circulated departmentally.' He was evidently told: 'That will make it authentic.' The reason for this confident indiscretion on the part of MAW was extraordinarily simple: 'D.N.I. seems to think I have copy. MAW spoke as if I have.' Im Thurn, not slow to catch the atmosphere of collusion over the claret, genially dispensed a gobbet of information on his own account. He told MAW that the most likely place the intelligence people might start to look for the original was in the files of the Soviet chargé d'affaires, Christian Rakovsky. MAW's information was a great deal closer to the point than im Thurn's.

Before the end of lunch, however, the man from Naval Intelligence offered a warning and a promise. He strongly suggested that im Thurn should hold his hand and not publish yet. Let it rest until after the weekend, he suggested. He was going to talk to his chief that afternoon, and he would be in touch again on Monday afternoon.

That night im Thurn was exultant. 'All X's reports seem to be true after all,' he wrote, his last vestige of scepticism finally banished by the confidences of Naval Intelligence. He also lapsed from his normal skeletal style as if to gloat once again over his vital breakthrough at the start of the day: 'Today both D.N.I. and MAW asked me if the date of the letter was the 5th and not 15th, so it is proved they have knowledge of 15th letter.'

Foreign Office procedures could scarcely be called precipitate at the best of times. In the 'twenties, an election imposed additional burdens on their speed of action. With the Foreign Secretary out of London, his instruction to prepare a Note of protest about the Zinoviev letter took some time to complete its route through the department.

However, before the week-end, Don Gregory, the head of the Northern Department, drew up a draft protesting fairly firmly to the Soviet representative in London. Then Crowe, the Permanent Secretary, having once again reviewed his position on the letter's authenticity and satisfied himself of it, submitted the amended draft to MacDonald with the observation that it could be published as soon as it had been delivered to Rakovsky.

On Monday the 20th, the draft was sent off to MacDonald's election headquarters at Aberavon. It was received there the next day, but predictably MacDonald had moved off again, this time to the Midlands and his son's constituency of Bassetlaw. He only returned to Wales later on the night of the 22nd. Thus, yet another delay impeded the official progress to final action in the case of the Zinoviev letter.

These repeated delays were later to form the core of the Conservative charge that Ramsay MacDonald never intended to publish the letter before the election. This was the focus of their self-righteous air of triumph in the few days between actual publication and polling day: that if it had not been for the patriotic tenacity of the Press in general and the *Daily Mail* in particular, this scandalous document, exposing the Socialists for the Bolshevik fellow-travellers that they were, would never have been brought before the British electorate. There was a strong element of humbug in this accusation at the time. It can now be seen to be categorically false insofar as it rested on the length of time which intervened between receipt of the letter at the Foreign Office and the actual decision to respond to it. This was caused by the difficulties of trying to run a Government and an arduous election campaign simultaneously. In the final analysis, it is not possible to be certain what MacDonald would have done had he not been pre-empted by events. But clearly the contemporary charge, by Curzon, Birkenhead, Baldwin and other leading Tories, that he had kept the letter dark for anything from a fortnight to a month was recklessly inaccurate.

The intelligence services, of course, were another matter. While the letter was making its orthodox, if stumbling, way through the Foreign Office, they were still trying to find out the truth about a document which it was surely their job to know all about. Donald im Thurn's diary conveys a persuasive impression of top intelligence men hopelessly at sea: out of touch with their political superiors, uninformed by their colleague who was likely to know most about it, and thrown into confusion by the activities of their former operative, im Thurn himself.

Over the weekend, the attitude of Naval Intelligence seemed to have altered completely. On Friday they were garrulous, by Monday, silent. MAW failed to make his promised call to im Thurn. The DNI refused to see him. Im Thurn badly wanted the interview because his own weekend had not been idle. He had evidently paid a visit to his paymasters, the Tories, and told them that their electoral bombshell was about to burst. He wanted Sir Stanley Jackson to meet the DNI for himself. The reason why the DNI refused became fairly evident: 'A. rang up told me enquiries being made about me re my activities. . . . D.N.I. apparently seemed nervous because I had information and meant to publish.'

The faithful Alexander, however, felt quite unrestrained. He kept a rendezvous with im Thurn at 5.30 that evening, and produced two items of news. The first was that his boss, Kell, had retired to bed. Whether his illness was diplomatic is unknown, but his putative promise of co-operation certainly seemed to have been withdrawn. The illness, Alexander said, meant that his own assistance in the adventure would be curtailed: 'He could not see what he could do to help.' But before falling ill Kell had talked to C. C had evidently resisted pressure from Kell to get the letter circulated: 'C. had asked K. to leave letter with him one week.'

There are a number of possible explanations for C's reluctance to draw his colleagues into the affair. One may be pure inter-departmental rivalry, of which the various intelligence agencies were – as they have been ever since – the most diligent exponents in Whitehall. Whether it was MI5, MI1C, Naval Intelligence or the Special Branch, they liked to keep their coups to themselves. C, at MI1C, need not have been any more immune to this than anyone else. But there is an alternative possibility, namely that C, being in regular contact with the Permanent Secretary at the Foreign Office, was acting on a shrewd assessment of that department's best interests. He probably knew what the others did not, that the office had the letter well in hand. He might also guess – as turned out to be the case – that any further circulation would jeopardise Sir Eyre Crowe's measured handling of the situation. In any case, since a verdict had been given, very possibly on his own authority, on the letter's authenticity, it would merely have muddied the waters if other departments had been given their own chance to pass judgement on it. All these speculations may have contributed to C's irritating failure of communication and his final request, when Kell eventually did confront him, for a week's grace.

However, as Alexander pointed out to im Thurn, C was no longer entirely in control of events. He now knew that his information was not exclusive: indeed, that there was a strong possibility that another copy of the letter was circulating: 'A. thought that as C. knows outside person knows about letter he could cut short the week.'

Alexander's instincts were uncommonly prescient. It was not a week but mere hours which intervened before C moved decisively. The very next day, Tuesday, 21 October, Donald im Thurn received the most flattering overture of his entire career as a regular and irregular secret agent. He received a telephone call from no less a personage than C himself. The diary is unfailingly laconic: 'C. rang up tell me about circulation. It would take place. At least, he meant me to understand that.' But the message was shattering: im Thurn had won. The only thing im Thurn did not know was how C would conduct the operation.

He lost no time in telling the Tories. He saw Lord Younger this time, and told him that there was no longer any need for qualms. This news meant that the carefully-laid plans of Central Office could now be brought into action. Since im Thurn first went to them on the 15th, the Conservatives had not simply sat back and waited to see what luck he would have. They had an investment to protect. When the moment came to cash in, they had to be ready.

The Central Office publicity machine, already finely geared to an anti-Bolshevik campaign, was forewarned of the possibility of a specific assault on Zinoviev within hours of im Thurn's being introduced to Jackson and Younger by Major Guy Kindersley. Philip Cambray was the director of publicity at the time. He now recalls the episode in some detail. He was called in by the chief whip, Lord Monsell, ten days before the letter ultimately appeared in the Press, i.e. on the 15th. Monsell's instruction was succinct: find out as much as possible about Zinoviev. When Cambray asked why, he was told by Monsell: 'I can't tell you, but it's important.' It was decided that Cambray should produce a short biography of the sinister Soviet leader. He did not know to what purpose it was to be put, nor when it would be released. To him, it was simply part of the wide-ranging attack by the party on the Red issue. He duly produced the biography, with some expert assistance from a Russian émigré, an economist from Georgia who, Mr Cambray remembers, was chiefly informed by an unyielding hatred for the man who, he claimed, ordered that his brother be shot. (It was by the presence of this man that the Tory press was judiciously alerted to the forthcoming sensation.)

This preparation accounts for the speed with which the party was able to exploit the letter after im Thurn had paid his triumphant visit to Lord Younger. The inventory of inflammatory pamphlets was already extensive. A series of tracts had attacked the trade treaty section by section. They were followed by many more lurid sheets. 'Red Bread from Ruined Russia' and 'Reds – not Bread' attacked the Labour argument that the treaty would bring more employment to Great Britain. 'The Bolshevik Yoke – It's your money we want' read another unsubtle leaflet, shaped in the form of 'the Socialist election egg'. A doctor just back from Leningrad was eagerly given space to recount his discovery that 'about half the population of Russia would today need medical treatment', 'most Russians have had no new clothes for eight years', and 'I saw personally two cases of cannibalism'. The message was neatly rounded off: 'This is Socialism.' Now, miraculously, a rash of new pamphlets relating only to Zinoviev was about to appear round the country. At least seven remain among the Central Office archives. At the time, no one paused to discover how this defiance of the laws of the printing press had come about. Now it is only too clear.

After satisfying Younger that the letter could not now be concealed, only one obstacle remained to prevent im Thurn from feeling absolutely confident of publication. All he needed was a copy for himself.

On the evening of the 21st, he got further corroboration that C had not been lying: the faithful Alexander kept his by now daily rendezvous, and told im Thurn that circulation was indeed taking place. But his diary that night contained a hint of one last-minute panic. 'Cannot rely on getting copy,' he wrote. But the failure was not going to undo him at this late stage: 'What the hell! Must play all I can on F.O. fear of publication.'

If there is one thing in which Donald im Thurn could now claim to be an expert it was the art of playing on official fears. This was the technique which had sustained him throughout the previous ten days, during which he had been transformed from a pest to his old acquaintances into the scourge of Whitehall. However, he did make one final attempt to get a copy of the letter in his possession. On Wednesday morning he returned to where he began, Scotland Yard and its Assistant Commissioner, Wyndham Childs. He must have hoped that Childs would at least let him see the tantalizing document. It was a fruitless meeting. 'Childs no earthly,' im Thurn writes, in a distinctly aggrieved tone.

Im Thurn could wait no longer. At 1.15 he went to see the political correspondent of *The Times*, Alan Pitt Robbins. In the diary, he calls him inaccurately 'Robins', an understandable lapse which is explained by im Thurn's apparent lack of familiarity with the political, as distinct from the administrative, world. Certainly Robbins was *The Times*'s lobby correspondent at the time. It is reasonable to assume that im Thurn was put in touch with him by his own political contacts, Kindersley perhaps, or even Younger. It was, after all, part of the original plan devised on the 15th that *The Times* should be the vehicle.

At their meeting, Robbins was regaled with most of the story so far: im Thurn writes that he 'asked for assistance and explained whole situation and thought now it was safe to move as departmental circulation to C-in-C's taking place immediately'. It is simple to imagine the points which im Thurn made – that the Government had the letter but was seeking to conceal it, that he himself knew of it from a separate source, that a few discreet calls from *Times* correspondents to their respective friends in the departments would confirm what was going on and what was in the letter.

Robbins seems to have been suitably impressed. The message, in fact, could scarcely escape him. For that same day the Conservatives had started gently dropping a few hints. The *Manchester Evening Chronicle*, on the Wednesday night, obscurely told its readers to be ready for a major development in the Bolshevik issue connected with the name of Zinoviev.

The Times itself got to work on Thursday, ferreting around among its contacts. Alexander, who now emerges as not merely an informant but a fully convinced collaborator, telephoned im Thurn urging him to relax the pressure. A 'strongly advised do nothing further as all necessary steps were being taken'. The only missing information was how it was to be done, and who was to do the deed.

Publication, in short, was now inevitable. As he considered Crowe's draft of the protest Note in Aberavon that Thursday morning, Ramsay MacDonald was not to know that, whatever minute he chose to write, the die was cast.

One final irony surrounds that decisive morning. At last copies of the letter were reaching the departments outside the Foreign Office. As the senior intelligence men at the Home Office, the Admiralty and Scotland Yard began to scrutinize the document which they had heard so much about but which had eluded them for so long, they seem all to have been struck with a similar thought. Later attempts by newspapers to reconstruct the truth about the Zinoviev letter were to hint at this uniform response. But at the time it was one which the Foreign Office did not share. It was most fully expressed by the man at Scotland Yard, Wyndham Childs. In his memoirs he writes with some indignation of MacDonald's failure to seek the views of departments outside the Foreign Office. He notes the fact that no one ever saw the original of the letter, and records his disapproval of the Foreign Office's allowing the Prime Minister, 'or possibly inducing him – I do not know', to send the protest Note without having the original in his possession. And he adds: 'There was absolutely no reason to think that this particular effusion was genuine. I can conclude by giving it as my opinion that if Mr Zinoviev sent it, he was, in colloquial language, a blithering idiot.'

8

The Daily Mail *Joins the Plot*

The Times, however, did not have the news to itself. On Thursday night Thomas Marlowe, the editor of the *Daily Mail*, must have felt bemused. To be approached by one source with the information that there was a sensational document exposing relations between the Russians and the Labour Party which the Government was trying to censor, was a rare stroke of journalistic luck. To be visited by another source who had the letter in his pocket was a ludicrous piece of good fortune. That evening Marlowe had not yet actually seen a copy of the letter, but he seems to have had little doubt about his ability to get one the following day, and he had no doubt at all about his intention to publish once he had obtained a copy of the document. Even without an election campaign in which the first Labour Government was desperately defending its brief record in office, it would have been a good story. During an election campaign, especially for a vigorously Conservative newspaper whose publisher – Lord Rothermere – proudly proclaimed his uncritical support for the Opposition, it was a rare opportunity. For an editor whose loyalty to his proprietor's opinions was unqualified, it was an unforgettable episode.

Three-and-a-half years later Marlowe, no longer the *Mail*'s editor, wrote for publication a self-congratulatory letter to the editor of the *Observer* explaining how he had obtained the Zinoviev letter. He told the story only in selective outlines. No names were mentioned, but Marlowe's account does complement im Thurn's diary, and some jotted notes in his scrap book of newspaper clippings. (The scrap book, like the explanatory notes written by Mrs im Thurn, was given to Major Guy

Kindersley when he undertook his own investigation into the origins of the Zinoviev letter. It was among the documents made available to us by his son.) From the two sources it is possible to piece together a plausible explanation of the process preceding the publication of the letter by the *Daily Mail*.

Marlowe first heard of the letter when he arrived at the office on the morning of the 23rd. A telephone message, which had arrived late the night before, was on the writing table in his office. It was from 'an old and trusted friend', and read:

> There is a document in London which you ought to have. It shows the relations between the Bolsheviks and the British Labour leaders. The Prime Minister knows all about it, but is trying to avoid publication. It has been circulated today to Foreign Office, Home Office, Admiralty, and War Office.

The old and trusted friend, whom we shall call for the moment H, did not tell him what was in the letter or where to get a copy. But this did not worry Marlowe. 'The problem thus put to me was a comparatively simple one. The last sentence of the message was almost a solution of it,' he wrote confidently in his *Observer* letter. The implication was that he had good enough contacts in the four departments to persuade one of them to divulge the contents of the letter.

Marlowe began to telephone these contacts, and soon reached another 'friend', whom he invited to come to his office 'without delay'. The friend (we will call him Z) was evidently an obliging man; he appeared at Marlowe's office shortly after lunch. At first his journey seemed to have been fruitless; he knew about the letter but, even though he 'was disposed to be indignant at the Government's reluctance to allow publication', he did not think he could help Marlowe get a copy. This encouraged Marlowe to begin bullying his contact. He insisted that he must have the letter and eventually Z promised that – if he could obtain the approval of a third person – he would send a copy to the *Mail* through the post.

Only half an hour after Marlowe's pliable friend left his office, yet another friend (B) arrived. He was, it seems, uninvited. He actually had the letter in his pocket, according to Marlowe's account, and he wanted the editor of the *Mail* to advise him on the best method of publication. Marlowe's answer was naturally unequivocal. He told this second friend that he should give the letter to him – Marlowe – and unselfishly promised not only to publish it himself, but to give copies to all the other London papers.

But Marlowe was to be tantalized yet again. 'It seemed,' he wrote, 'that he also had a friend to consult, whose decision could not be made known till the following midday.' Marlowe, possibly feigning disappointment to provoke an immediate transaction, for there is no other conceivable reason why he should have said what followed, told his friend (B) that he 'should probably receive a copy from another source before then, and that if it came during that evening he should certainly publish it the next morning'. Marlowe made an appointment with his second friend just in case: it was for midday on Friday, 24 October.

When Marlowe's contacts consulted their respective friends on Thursday night, they both, it seems, independently agreed that the *Mail* should get the letter. Marlowe reports that, after his midday meeting on Friday, he returned to the office with the letter in his possession, 'and there on the table was another copy which had just come by post'. The editor sent for the printer, for these were the days when editors could still send for printers (now they tend to make nervous approaches through subordinates), and ordered him to set the letter in type. He was still determined to share the story; proofs were to be sent to all other newspapers. The Zinoviev letter was very shortly to electrify a huge, unsuspecting public.

Marlowe's account seems straightforward enough, ingenuous even. But an attempt to discover the confusing identity of his friends makes the story a good deal more complicated than it superficially appears.

The primary source of material for speculation is Donald im Thurn's diary, and the book of clippings which he so assiduously kept, and occasionally annotated. These implicate the Conservative Party as being among Marlowe's sources and they are an explanation for the misleading nature of the only other public reference to what is supposed to have happened. In a statement im Thurn gave to Stanley Baldwin on 19 March 1928, which the Prime Minister triumphantly read to the House of Commons hours later, im Thurn was decidedly enigmatic about the transaction. 'I handed a copy of the letter, not to the *Daily Mail* direct, but to a trusted City friend, whom I knew to be in close touch with that newspaper, and requested him to arrange for its publication.'

The diary is more forthcoming, but confusing nevertheless, since it introduces a completely new element into the situation. On Wednesday, 22 October, as we have seen, im Thurn wrote: '1.15 saw Robins at the 'Times'. Asked for assistance and explained whole situation and thought now it was safe to move as departmental circulation to C-in-C's taking place immediately.' The only mention of *The Times* in Marlowe's account was a passing reference to a telephone call he made to its editor early on Friday afternoon. 'It occurred to me,' he wrote, 'that it was most important that there should be a leading article in *The Times* next morning. The afternoon was getting on, and I was afraid that before the proofs were delivered *The Times* might have arranged for leading articles on other subjects. So I telephoned to the editor, and found myself speaking to Mr Brumwell, the acting editor. I told him what he might expect to receive in the next hour or so.'

There is no hint here that *The Times* knew anything about the letter, or that Marlowe knew that *The Times* might have some information about it. Yet it is clear from the diary that *The Times* not only knew about the letter before the *Mail*, but that there was active collusion between the two newspapers about the method of publishing it.

From the entry for Wednesday it ostensibly seems possible that im Thurn's approach to Robbins was wholly personal – a request for advice. Journalists still act as private citizens, sometimes in conflict with the interests of their newspapers. But in the case of Alan Pitt Robbins, who is clearly the subject of this entry, this seems unlikely. He was an experienced journalist, used to evolving methods of converting information he received privately into news for his paper. Thursday's entry proves that this was the real basis of their meeting. (Although Robbins, who later became director of the International Press Institute, was still alive in 1966, he was, sadly, too ill to recall and explain his role in the affair.)

The Thursday entry reads:

A. rang up. Strongly advised do nothing further as all necessary steps were being taken. Evidently 'Times' getting busy. Saw Browning morning, suggested him moving. Browning thought he knew the very man. Saw Jackson 3.30. Leave it now for 'Times' and Browning's friend. Appointment 5.30 'Times', better break it off today. They will do the needful without interference.

It is clear from this that *The Times* was involved as a newspaper; Robbins was not acting alone. The entry also implicates Conservative Central Office in the sequence of events leading to the publication of the letter. 'Jackson' was F. S. Jackson, chairman of the Conservative Party, who was already fully informed of, and involved in, the activities of im Thurn's fellow-conspirators.

What the diary does not clarify is who left the telephone message for Marlowe on Wednesday evening, or who came to see him the next day. For clues to the identity of this perplexing network of friends it is necessary to turn to im Thurn's book of newspaper cuttings. Fortunately, the page on which he stuck a clipping of Marlowe's letter is one of those which is annotated. It does not offer categoric evidence of identity, but it is the most suggestive source available for logical speculation.

The first annotation is beside the mention of 'the old and trusted friend' who first informed Marlowe of the existence of the letter in that cryptic message on Wednesday night. This, wrote im Thurn, was 'R. Hall'. There can be no question of identity here. It is a clear reference to Vice-Admiral Sir Reginald Hall, the legendary war-time Director of Naval Intelligence. With stark blue eyes, and a twitch in his eyelid, he was commonly known as 'Blinker' Hall.

Few people who knew anything of his intelligence activities (and they are better chronicled than those of any other British intelligence man, with the exception, of course, of Ian Fleming) express less than unqualified admiration for his skill. Walter Hines Page, the American Ambassador in London during the war, later told President Woodrow Wilson: 'The man is a genius – a clear case of genius.' Page had reason to know, for Hall's powers reached their zenith at the time of the affair of the Zimmerman telegram in 1917. A decoded intercept from the German Foreign Office to its Mexican ambassador suggesting that plans be laid for a joint German–Mexican invasion of the United States was released at exactly the moment to make it a vital influence on America's decision to enter the war on the side of the Allies. What characterized this episode was Hall's superb sense of timing: the Zimmerman telegram was released at the time and in the way which would create least suspicion about its authenticity. (Although it was, unlike the Zinoviev letter, completely authentic, the powerful pro-German lobby in the United States did its best to demonstrate otherwise.)

After the war, the Foreign Office, jealous of Hall's power and influence, squeezed him out of the intelligence services, and Hall went, less happily, into politics. Elected naturally enough as a Conservative M.P. in 1922 (intelligence men, like criminals and sportsmen, tend to be Tory) he took party politics seriously. Shortly afterwards the Tories tried to utilize his organizing ability by appointing him Principal Agent. But Hall was a seaman in a landlubber's job, and he left it shortly after losing his seat in the 1923 election. One of the junior officials at Central Office in the early 'twenties, Philip Cambray, who was Director of Publicity during the 1924 campaign, remembers Hall as 'a genial, pleasant chief whose peculiarity was to give an instruction but not to explain the reason for it. Later one might be told "Well, my boy, that was a good job of work" – but for what purpose or end was not disclosed.' But Hall's formal departure from the Central Office hierarchy did not terminate his relationship with it. He had worked closely with Jackson, the Party chairman, and Lord Younger, the ex-chairman, and it would have been logical for both to turn to Hall for advice when they heard from im Thurn about the letter's existence. He was the obvious man to employ in a conspiracy designed to ensure that publication of the Zinoviev letter occurred in the right place at exactly the right moment.

Hall did retain his contacts with Naval Intelligence following his departure from its Directorship in 1919, and was in a perfect position to discover when the Foreign Office began to circulate the letter to other departments for their comments. Sinclair, the head of MI1C, had been a subordinate officer of his during the war. According to im Thurn's diary, the letter was circulated on Wednesday, 23 October, providing the Conservatives with the essential knowledge that they could shift any blame for the leak from themselves to the civil service. It was surely not coincidental that the former head of Naval Intelligence, who had also been a senior official at Central Office, should have been the man to phone Marlowe late on the Wednesday evening.

The next person to be identified is the shadowy friend whom Marlowe 'invited to come to see him without delay'. At this point the notations in im Thurn's scrap book become more speculative. Beside this section of Marlowe's account he wrote 'ed of *Times* or Fred B?' The possibility of the editor of *The Times* answering a summons of that kind, and submitting himself to the sort of gentle bullying that Marlowe inflicted on his visitor, is remote. Im Thurn knew *The Times* had been brought into the plot, and probably speculated on this basis alone.

The suspicion falls, then, on 'Fred B', who was clearly the Browning im Thurn mentions in his diary. However, the diary also suggests that, in his speculative jottings in the margin of the Marlowe account, im Thurn did not get Browning's role quite right. He put 'Fred B' down as the visitor whom Marlowe effectively summoned to see him immediately after getting Hall's message on the Thursday morning. In fact, the most convincing evidence is that Browning was not Marlowe's first visitor, but his second – the man who arrived half-an-hour later with the letter in his pocket.

This conclusion rests on several pieces of evidence. First, the diary – written contemporaneously, unlike the annotations which were made in 1928 – records for Thursday morning: 'Saw Browning morning, suggested him moving.' This establishes that any move made by Browning had already been considered, either at im Thurn's prompting, or at the suggestion of his colleagues. It is very unlikely that he responded to a summons from Marlowe.

Beside Marlowe's description of his second visitor, im Thurn has pencilled the initial 'J'. This seems most likely to be Jackson, the Tory chairman. But again the reference is speculative. The friend whom this second visitor said he had to consult is identified as 'Y or ME'. If J was Jackson, Y, logically, would be Lord Younger, the ex-chairman of the party and Jackson's closest counsellor at Central Office. However, the addition of 'or ME' emphasizes the considerable uncertainty with which im Thurn analysed each reference in the Marlowe account, except the reference to Hall, about which he is unequivocal. For 'or ME' can only be interpreted as a reference to himself: there is no other principal with the initials M.E. to whom it could possibly have referred. Thus, im Thurn, having imagined that this second visitor was Jackson, plausibly deduced that Jackson might have told Marlowe that he had to consult an anonymous friend, who would, naturally, have been im Thurn or Younger.

We know from the diary that im Thurn was not, in fact, consulted in any phase of the *Mail*'s decision to publish. Hence we also know that the annotations about Jackson are speculative rather than factual: they were reasonable hypotheses, made some years later, but not with certain knowledge.

That they were in reality misconceived we can now deduce from the next entry in the diary. Reporting the events of the next day, Friday, it begins: ' "Daily Mail" knows something. Believe "Times" "Daily Mail" met late yesterday afternoon, and will play the same bluff as mine about the copy.' The implication is that there was collusion between *The Times* and *Mail* the day before. But with hindsight, it is also clear that Marlowe's account, far from being the straightforward record it affects to be, was more likely a disingenuous effort to distort the facts. At any rate, the last entry in im Thurn's diary, on 27 October, makes clear that Browning was one of Marlowe's visitors on the Thursday afternoon. Browning 'told me', it reads, 'that on Thursday afternoon he had passed information on to the "Daily Mail".'

If Browning was, as seems likely, the second visitor, could Jackson have been the first? Considering the terms in which Marlowe claims to have spoken to his first visitor, this is possible, though unlikely. Was Jackson, then, involved at all? Thursday's diary entry – 'Saw Jackson 3.30.' – suggests he was a decisive figure. But it need not have been as a link with the *Mail*; he could for example have been a contact with *The Times*. For there is certainly no reasonable doubt that he and Conservative Central Office were in intimate communication with the press.

But if Browning was the second visitor, and a personal visit from Jackson is not to be deduced from Marlowe's letter, who was the first visitor? Browning and the editor of *The Times* seem to have ruled themselves out, although both were in

101

contact at other times with Marlowe. Could it have been an anonymous civil servant, as the Labour Party suggested in 1928, when they called for an inquiry into the Zinoviev letter affair?

There is a small piece of evidence to suggest it might have been. Philip Cambray recalls that gossip in Whitehall in the week following publication of the letter implied strongly that a civil servant from the Home Office had given a copy to the *Mail*. He had, so the slightly ludicrous story went, gone for a drink in the St Stephen's Tavern, which is just across the road from the House of Commons and was known in the 'twenties as a local for the Special Branch men working in Scotland Yard across the street. He had approached one of the Special Branch men whom he recognized (the Home Office then, as now, was responsible for Special Branch). He is then alleged to have told the policeman that he was appalled by the Government's failure to act, and to have asked for advice about leaking it to the press. The Special Branch man is said to have told him to take it to the editor of the *Daily Mail*. The civil servant in question, says Cambray, was a private secretary to Arthur Henderson, the Home Secretary.

Besides the anonymity of this story's source – Cambray heard it during a welter of political speculation during the week of the election, and political stories are often even more unreliable than fishermen's – it emerged after the election that none of MacDonald's Ministers had seen the letter. Yet, if the letter really had reached Henderson's private secretary, the likelihood is that it would also have reached Henderson himself, despite the difficulties of communication imposed by the election.

There is, however, one other shred of evidence which suggests that Marlowe's second source might have been a civil servant. It appears as a passing reference in a biography of Sir Ronald Waterhouse by his wife, Nourah Waterhouse. Waterhouse was principal private secretary to MacDonald in 1924, and his wife's book is gossipy and often unreliable. Its section on the Zinoviev letter, obviously constructed by Lady Waterhouse herself, is hopelessly wrong about the sequence of events preceding the *Mail*'s publication of the letter, but it does contain one important reference to the *Mail*'s sources which must have been in Waterhouse's papers and around which his wife placed her own historical narrative of the affair. Waterhouse, it states, was rung up at 10 Downing Street by MacDonald and asked to discover how the *Mail* had obtained a copy of the Zinoviev letter. He 'put the question point blank to a very senior person on the *Daily Mail*'. The answer was oblique 'I cannot tell you,' Waterhouse was told, 'but find out who was dining with Marlowe at the Savoy on Friday night.' Waterhouse later obtained a description of Marlowe's guest: he had a disability 'unique in the official world' which, Nourah Waterhouse claims, made him easy to identify as a 'high official, quite unconnected with the Foreign Office'. Unfortunately she did not elaborate.

Whoever was Marlowe's second source for the letter – Jackson, a civil servant, or even another intelligence operative – neither the *Mail* nor *The Times* had to use the bluff im Thurn referred to in his Friday diary entry: they 'will play the same bluff as mine about the copy.' Im Thurn had boldly given the impression that he possessed a copy of the letter throughout the previous two weeks, when in fact he did not. It would have been a worthwhile risk for the *Mail* and *The Times* to pretend that they had a copy of the letter, and to blackmail the Foreign Office into releasing the letter officially. But Hall's telephone tip and Browning's unexpected visit made this unnecessary.

Who, then, was Browning? There are no clues in the diary itself. The only evidence offered by im Thurn was in his statement to Baldwin four years later, when he referred to a 'City friend' who was his contact with the *Mail*; but there is no evidence that any man named Browning belonged to the slightly bizarre group of City friends im Thurn had at the time. In any case, the contents of the Baldwin statement can now be seen to have been both misleading and inaccurate.

Suspicion naturally falls on the intelligence service, and there is a clue in the Army List for 1924. There was then one Capt. Frederick Arthur Montague Browning – but he was adjutant at the Royal Military College, Sandhurst. (He later married Daphne du Maurier and in the Second World War became a General, commonly known as 'Boy' Browning.) It would have been difficult for Captain Browning, fully occupied at Sandhurst, to devote himself to intrigue in London. Nor, indeed, was he in intelligence.

One curious fact emerged from our inquiries about 'Boy'

Browning. His father was also called Frederick, and during the war had achieved the rank of Lieutenant-Colonel. And it is from this sliver of information that it is possible to determine accurately the identity of the Browning who saw Marlowe. This also leads circumstantially to the source of one of the *Mail*'s copies of the Zinoviev letter. Fortunately, Lieutenant-Colonel Browning's daughter, who lives in retirement in Dorset, was in 1967 able to confirm that it was indeed her father who was involved in the conspiracy to leak the contents of the letter to the *Mail*. She recalled his coming home during that week, in a state of some excitement over something he had got hold of 'from one of his old contacts'. The essential fact about Lieutenant-Colonel Frederick Browning is that by the end of the War, he had become second-in-command of MI1C.

In 1924 Browning was aged fifty-four, living comfortably by managing the family firm of wine merchants, and off the proceeds of his directorship of the Savoy Hotel (to which he had been introduced by Lucas D'Oyly Carte, an Oxford friend who shared Browning's passion for the theatre). Before the outbreak of the World War he spent the leisurely Edwardian days going to the theatre and distinguishing himself primarily by his skill at rackets and cricket, which he played competently just below county level. But like many wealthy young men of his generation, he also had a voluntary job which pushed him almost inexorably towards positions of administrative power. Browning's employment was with one of the military heroes of the Boer War, Lord Roberts, whom he helped run the National Service League. With the outbreak of war he automatically became Roberts's ADC, with the acting rank of Captain. When Roberts died in France late in 1914, Browning returned to England and interested Lord Northcliffe, then publisher of *The Times* and the *Daily Mail* – to whom Roberts had introduced him – in the munitions scandal. He also tried his hand at censoring letters from Holland: he had discovered that no one else was doing the job, and it was quite natural in those days, it seems, that he should simply be given the powers to start it. When the Ministry of Munitions was established in 1915, Browning was one of its first officials.

Shortly afterwards he joined Sir Mansfield Cumming, who had founded an espionage department which was to operate in

104

nations outside the Empire (Kell's MI5 controlled espionage within the Empire). The Department was precariously situated in wooden huts on the roof of Whitehall Court, a warren of flats and clubs which overlooks the Thames behind Whitehall. It was called MI1C. (It became MI6 – which was the intelligence translation service in the 'twenties – after a particularly humiliating court case in the 'thirties involving Sir Compton Mackenzie, who was a first World War intelligence operative as well as novelist. The 'C', it was decided, was too easily translated into 'comedians'.)

During the War Cumming still ran the department he had created in 1911. (He continued to run it after the war until his death in 1923, after which his successors retained his own code name – 'C'.) As his deputy, Browning came to respect him, and to know many of his colleagues in intelligence. One of them, however, he had known long before the war. Sir Reginald Hall, Director of Naval Intelligence, was a boyhood friend and a constant visitor to Browning's home in Lowndes Street behind Belgrave Square. Another visitor was a man whose acquaintance Browning had made through Lord Northcliffe – the editor of one of his papers, Thomas Marlowe. After Northcliffe's death and Rothermere's take-over of the *Mail*, Marlowe remained its editor and continued to visit the Browning household. He was, says Browning's daughter, 'a nice fatherly man'. There were many other visitors in the 'twenties, including the odd spy and intelligence officer. Browning was a gregarious and popular man – 'He knew everybody,' his daughter says.

The three friends – Browning, Hall, and Marlowe – provided an ideal network on which to base a plot to distribute the Zinoviev letter. The Tory Party and the network of retired intelligence officers were linked through Browning with the editor of the largest newspaper in the country. This would explain how Marlowe got his copy of the letter. But it does not explain how Browning got the copy which he passed to Marlowe at lunchtime on Friday, 24 October, or which particular 'friend' Browning had to consult before transmission took place.

It could have been Hall who gave the original tip to Browning, and therefore Hall whom Browning had to consult. But once again, the most valuable clues to a solution of the problem are contained in im Thurn's diary. As early as the previous Thursday, 16 October, im Thurn's hopes were being raised by the intelligence services. He was told that C – by now Sir Hugh Sinclair – 'thought that it should be more public'. Then im Thurn records the extraordinary remark: 'A. [Alexander, the MI5 officer] offered publish it through me in a perfectly safe manner. K. [Sir Vernon Kell, head of MI5] interested.' The implication is that the head of MI5 was willing to use im Thurn to get the document published. After that Kell's interest seems to have waned, as it became increasingly clear that Sinclair was intent on masterminding the operation himself.

On Friday, 17 October, im Thurn decided that Sinclair must have the only copy of the letter. The next day the correctness of his deduction was confirmed by the Naval Intelligence Department. By Monday the situation had crystallized. Sinclair had asked Kell to leave the letter with him for one week, but Alexander of MI5 believed that now Sinclair knew im Thurn was trying to engineer publication, he would not wait for a week. The following day Sinclair actually rang up im Thurn to tell him that circulation would take place.

Sir Hugh Sinclair was deeply implicated by the middle of the week. But more than that, he had, by circulating the letter to other intelligence departments, protected himself from accusations of leaking the letter himself. Five potential sources of information make it immeasurably more difficult to locate the source of a leak to the press. Is it then possible that Browning's source of the Zinoviev letter was the head of the Government's own overseas espionage department? That he had agreed with Kell's interest in publishing the document 'in a perfectly safe manner', and actually done something about it? Remarkable as it seems, the answer, on the basis of circumstantial evidence, is yes.

Sinclair had taken over MI1C after Cumming's death the previous year. He was known as 'Queux' Sinclair (after the hero of Pinero's play *The Gay Lord Queux*), and was considered an amusing companion for colleagues intelligent enough to evade his biting wit. Among those colleagues was Reginald Hall, whose second-in-command he had been during the war. When Hall left the service in 1919, Sinclair was promoted into his place. It is inconceivable that he would not have continued to see Hall in the small world of the intelligence men who inhabited London in the 'twenties.

It is also distinctly possible that Sinclair knew Browning. They acted in similar capacities at MI1C and Naval Intelligence during the war, and they must have liaised – probably closely. There is also one more, slightly eccentric, link. One of Sinclair's greatest passions was food; and he liked not only to eat it but to cook it too. Among his favourite restaurants was the Savoy, where he was welcomed in the kitchens after his meal to discuss its preparation with the chef. He knew the management well, and it is almost inconceivable that he should not have known the director who had also been a senior intelligence officer, Frederick Browning. So it is possible that Sinclair – who had declared to colleagues his interest in making the contents of the letter public – should have connived with his ex-chief, Hall, and with a man who had preceded him at MI1C, Browning, to transmit the letter to the *Mail*.

(There is another circumstantial deduction from Nourah Waterhouse's strange piece of gossip: that Marlowe's guest at the Savoy at the meeting at which he received the letter was unconnected with the Foreign Office and had 'a disability unique in the official world'. Sinclair's predecessor at MI1C, Sir Mansfield Cumming, did have a disability. He had a wooden leg – which might well have been unique in the world of senior Government officials. And he had died only months earlier. It is possible that the man who gave Waterhouse the clue had heard that the source was 'C', and assumed that 'C' was still Cumming. The mistake would not be startling, since the identity of the head of MI1C is known to only a small circle of very senior officials. This deduction is, however, as flimsy as Lady Waterhouse's own grasp of historical fact.)

The reasons for the involvement of each of the three known conspirators are straightforward enough. Hall, the Tory, saw the political advantages to be gained from publication of the letter. Marlowe, the editor of a loyal Tory paper, knew a scoop when he saw one, and would not have been particularly keen to question its authenticity. Browning, like many other men of his class and experience, tended to believe the worst of the Bolsheviks, and a call to revolution would not have astonished him. He would have seen it as a betrayal of his duty as a patriotic gentleman had he not agreed to act as intermediary. According to his daughter, he did not question the authenticity of the letter either.

But what could be the reasons for Sinclair's involvement in a plot to distribute a letter whose authenticity was questionable, and which would almost certainly destroy the electoral chances of the Government which was actually responsible for intelligence? The most likely explanation is disarmingly simple.

During 1924 Sir Eyre Crowe, permanent secretary at the Foreign Office, had become convinced that the Labour Government intended to abolish the secret service structure. It was still young and vulnerable, and it was naturally anathema to Socialists, whose idealistic internationalism was based on a principle which lay in unalterable opposition to the principle on which intelligence is based: that other countries aim to undermine the security of the British state. Two Cabinet Ministers, Lord Parmoor, the Lord President, and C. P. Trevelyan, President of the Board of Education, were notorious for their opposition to the intelligence services. According to men who served under him, including Sir Clifford Norton, later Ambassador to Greece, Crowe sensed a similar tendency in MacDonald. Once his conviction that Labour was opposed to intelligence had taken root, it would have been obvious for him to assume that foreign espionage services – those controlled by MI1C – would be the first to go. It would have been natural for him to warn the head of MI1C to activate every defensive mechanism he controlled to prevent his service from being broken up.

In these circumstances it is unlikely that MI1C would inquire too carefully into the origins of the Zinoviev letter: its authenticity would have been accepted rather than proven. The Foreign Office would have been more inclined to suspend its disbelief of a document of this kind if it was being told by MI1C that it was, indeed, genuine. And once a small, but powerful group of threatened men had convinced themselves that the letter was genuine, their incipient institutional paranoia made it almost inevitable that they should become equally convinced that Ramsay MacDonald was secretly plotting to prevent the letter's publication. It is entirely logical that they should have put the freemasonry of intelligence and ex-intelligence men to work.

Grigory Zinoviev, President of the Third International

The Labour Cabinet, 1924
From the left, back row: Sidney Webb, John Wheatley,
F. W. Jowett. Middle row: C. P. Trevelyan, Stephen Walsh,
Lord Thomson, Viscount Chelmsford, Lord Olivier, Noel
Buxton, Josiah Wedgwood, Vernon Hartshorn, Tom Shaw.
Front row: William Adamson, Lord Parmoor, Philip Snow-
den, Viscount Haldane, Ramsay MacDonald, J. R. Clynes,
J. H. Thomas, Arthur Henderson.

Дружеские шаржи.

Тов. Зиновьев произносит речь...

Рис. на обложке худ. ДЕНИ

Zinoviev's speeches prompted even the Moscow *Pravda* to a 'friendly cartoon'. This one depicts the embarrassment of Chicherin, the Foreign Minister.

Arthur MacManus, British representative on the Comintern

Christian Rakovsky, Soviet chargé d'affaires in London

Alexis Bellegarde, the forger, and his daughter

The room, today, where the letter was forged

The Berlin flat where the letter was forged (window marked with a cross): 117 Eisenacherstrasse

Donald im Thurn, secret agent in World War I

ADMIRALTY TEMPORARY PASS.

Visitor's own Name

Representing, or on behalf of

IF BY APPOINTMENT.

Name of Official with whom appointment was made

IF NOT BY APPOINTMENT.

Name of Official with whom
an interview is desired

Nature of Enquiry or Business

Unless this pass is produced on leaving the building, th
holder may be detained for enquiry.

Im Thurn's pass for his visit to the DNI, 18 October 1924

The London Steamship and Trading Corporation: office
party, 1923 (Donald im Thurn standing fifth from left)

Major Guy Kindersley, Conservative M.P.

The cigarette case: im Thurn's present to Kindersley after it was all over

Consorting with the Bolsheviks: a Red Scare poster from the 1924 Election

Stanley Baldwin and Lord Younger, party leader and party treasurer

Sir Stanley Jackson, party chairman, and Sir Reginald Hall, former Conservative M.P., Chief Agent, and Director of Naval Intelligence

Colonel Vernon Kell, head of M I 5

Captain Sidney Reilly, the 'master spy'

Sir Eyre Crowe, Permanent Secretary, Foreign Office

J. D. Gregory, Head of the Northern Department

Red Letter Day: the *Daily Mail*, 25 October 1924

One of im Thurn's letters to Kindersley, October 1924

BROTHER MAXTON:
"IS THE SPIRIT WITH US?
KNOCK ONCE FOR 'YES', TWICE
FOR 'NO' — BUT BE SURE TO
KNOCK THE RIGHT PARTY."

ZINOVIEV GHOST

THE ZINOVIEV SÉANCE.

Low's cartoon on the eve of the debate

Im Thurn acknowledges the Tory payment, April 1928

2nd April, 1928.

The Conservative & Unionist Central Office,
Paris Chambers,
S.W.1.

Dear Sirs,　　　Zinovieff Letter.

I beg to acknowledge the sum of five
thousand pounds (£5,000) on behalf of X.

For a period of ten years X will
additionally receive two hundred and fifty pounds
(£250) a year, paid on the 1st June to him by our
Agent in the Argentine. At the end of ten years
this payment will cease and he will be paid the
sum of two thousand five hundred pounds (£2,500).
In case of death this arrangement will cease unless he should have remarried when his widow will
b e entitled to this arrangement.

He will be given Argentine papers and
will therefore be to all intents and purposes
Argentine National, which he will never dare to
dispute in after life as the punishment in the
Argentine for living under false papers is very
severe. He will sail as deck hand and on
arrival will present himself to out Agent who
will only know him under his new name and will
know nothing further about him, except that he
will pay these yearly sums over to him for the
said period of ten years.

Yours faithfully,

Copy No.
3 Copies.

Thomas Marlowe, editor of the *Daily Mail*

Major Joseph Ball, Conservative Director of Publicity

8

THE ZINOVIEFF LETTER.

HOW IT REACHED THE "DAILY MAIL."

MR. MARLOWE'S STATEMENT.

In a letter published in the *Observer* of yesterday Mr. Thomas Marlowe, editor of the *Daily Mail* at the time of the publication of the Zinovieff letter on the eve of the General Election of 1924, explains how the MS. came into his possession. He states:—

The Zinovieff letter was published in the London newspapers on the morning of Saturday, October 25, 1924. I first heard of it on the Thursday, October 23, when I found on the writing table at my office the following telephone message, which had been received late on the preceding evening. Wednesday, October 22:—from an old and trusted friend :—

There is a document in London which you ought to have. It shows the relations between the Bolsheviks and British Labour leaders. The Prime Minister knows all about it, but is trying to avoid publication. It has been circulated to-day to Foreign Office, Home Office, Admiralty, and War Office.

The problem thus put to me was a comparatively simple one. The last sentence of the message was almost a solution of it. Telephonic soundings soon put me in touch with another friend, whom I invited to come and see me without delay. He called early in the afternoon and although he knew of the document and was disposed to be indignant at the Government's reluctance to allow publication, he did not think he could help me to get a copy of it. I insisted that I must have it, and at length he promised that if he could obtain the approval of a third person he would send me a copy through the post.

Half an hour after he had left me another friend called. He had the thing in his pocket, and what he wanted was my advice as to the best method of publication. I had no doubts on this subject, and gave him my opinion promptly. It was to the effect that he should hand his copy of the letter to me, whereupon I would give it the widest publicity and bring it to the other London newspapers. But it seemed that he also had a friend to consult, whose decision could not be made known till the following midday. I told him that I should probably receive a copy from another source before then, and that if it came during that evening I would certainly publish it next morning. I arranged in any case to meet him at midday, and early on the Friday afternoon I had the letter in my possession.

I returned with it to my office, and there on the table was another copy which had just come by post. I compared the two copies and found only such trifling differences as would arise from any lengthy documents being transcribed by different hands. The only important difference was that in one copy the name of McManus, to whom the letter was written, appeared immediately under the name of Zinovieff, as if McManus were the co-signatory.

I sent for the printer and ordered him to get the letter into type at once and pull a sufficient number of proofs to supply all the other newspapers. I then wrote a circular note to the various editors, informing them that, as they would no doubt wish to satisfy themselves as to the authenticity of the letter, they might do so by inquiry at the Foreign Office, Home Office, Admiralty, or War Office.

have been over. Mr. MacDonald would have succeeded in delaying the publication until it could do his party no harm.

Mr. Marlowe recalls that Mr. MacDonald "agreed with Sir Eyre Crowe as to the desirability of publishing, but said they must make certain that it was authentic." He adds :—

I was told simply that he had sent the letter back to Crowe for further evidence of its authenticity, and that this was regarded by his officials as an indication that he desired to shelve it, as they were already satisfied that it was authentic, and they would not have wasted his time and their own by putting it before him if they had had any doubt on that point.

After recounting the circumstances, already known from official statements and from the recent Report on the "francs case," in which the decision of the Foreign Office to publish the Zinovieff letter was taken, Mr. Marlowe proceeds :—

How in these circumstances could Mr. MacDonald believe that Mr. Gregory had played him false ? There can be no doubt that he did think so. He ordered an official or departmental inquiry to find out how the Zinovieff letter came to be published. He invited me to attend this inquiry, but I declined to do so, replying that I had nothing to add to what I had already published. In addition he ordered a personal inquiry concerning Mr. Gregory, and I was told that he informed his inquiry agent that I had paid Gregory £5,000 for the document, and that Gregory had sold it for reasons which the Prime Minister stated in plain language, but which I will not particularise beyond saying this : that they had nothing to do with speculation in foreign currency or with political partisanship. I know nothing about Mr. Gregory's circumstances. I have never seen him, to my knowledge, or had any communication with him, direct or indirect, and I did not pay him, or any other person, £5,000, or any other sum, for the Zinovieff letter. The men I dealt with were gentlemen to whom I could not offer money, and who would have been gravely affronted if I had done so. The Zinovieff letter did not cost me a single penny.

In a concluding passage Mr. Marlowe states :—

Knowing as he [Mr. MacDonald] did that the letter was no forgery he consoled himself with hinting that it had been published with his own "unauthorized" protest attached to it—as the result of some dirty trick at the Foreign Office.

"A CONSPIRACY."

FURTHER STATEMENT BY MR. MAC DONALD.

Mr. MacDonald, after he had considered Mr. Marlowe's letter yesterday morning, made a statement to a representative of *The Times*, in which he said he regarded the letter as a confession that the Zinovieff document was probably faked, and that its use was a fraud. Mr. Marlowe's intervention made it all the more necessary that the Government should give an inquiry into the whole subject of the Zinovieff letter.

The opening paragraphs of Mr. Marlowe's letter, Mr. MacDonald said, showed conclusively that there was a conspiracy. A friend it seemed came to Mr. Marlowe and showed him a certain document. When Mr. Marlowe asked to be allowed to use it, he was told that this could not be done, because there ...

An extract from *The Times* of Marlowe's letter to *The Observer*, with annotations by Donald im Thurn

Mme Irina Bellegarde, the witness to the forgery

Hall's motives for taking part in the plot are just as logical, though slightly baser. He had personal experience of the effect of an intelligence coup on a political situation: his department's brilliant work deciphering the Zimmerman telegram, and Hall's careful timing of its release to the Woodrow Wilson Administration in Washington had been the most significant single episode in the process which brought America into the war in 1917. The Zinoviev letter arrived at exactly the right moment to influence another Governmental decision which seemed crucial to the Conservative Party: whether Britain should forge close links with the Bolshevik revolutionaries or dismiss them as a Red rabble whose existence threatened Conservative democracy in Britain. As a former Tory Member of Parliament, Hall did not question the correctness of the Conservative decision to oppose the 'Red rabble'; as an ex-intelligence officer why should he not, therefore, use his rare knowledge and experience to swing the voters against Labour's pro-Russian policy? The whole operation bears unmistakable signs of his intuitive skill at timing an intelligence operation. There is no better time to astonish an electorate than five days before an election. The floating vote is vulnerable, yet the main force of a party's campaign has been dissipated. In the short lull before polling day an electoral bombshell will invariably have its greatest effect, a rule of which the Zinoviev letter's impact on the 1924 campaign is the most significant illustration. Hall performed his role in the plot flawlessly.

At the end of the machinations of the last full week before the election, only one thing was lacking which would make this the greatest election stunt in the memory of Conservative politicians. That was the air of respectability which would be given to the letter if the Foreign Office were to invest it with official status. Fortunately for the *Daily Mail*, and the Conservative Party, a hurried conference was taking place in the Foreign Office, on that same Friday, 24 October, which was to give the sensational exposure those trappings of authenticity of which the plotters dreamed.

9

The Foreign Office: Culpable or Inefficient?

On the morning of Friday 24 October, Sir Eyre Crowe, at the Foreign Office, received from Aberavon MacDonald's revision of the draft Note of protest to Rakovsky, the Soviet chargé d'affaires. This was to be sent as soon as the authenticity of the Zinoviev letter had been established. The draft, prepared by J. D. Gregory, the head of the Northern Department, came back with extensive handwritten alterations in the wide margin of the foolscap paper always used for the preparation of minutes and notes.

At a meeting in Crowe's room that same morning, it was decided to send the protest Note to Rakovsky immediately. Crowe had no doubts about the authenticity of the letter. It had already been established to his satisfaction. Within two or three hours he had also decided to publish the texts of the letter and the Note. That decision was to embitter relations between the Foreign Office and the Labour Party for years. The suspicion that either Gregory, who signed the protest Note to Rakovsky in MacDonald's absence, or Crowe had deliberately sabotaged Labour election chances was actually to be investigated by a civil service inquiry in 1928. Certainly the publication of the letter and the Note with such alacrity was out of character with the normally cautious behaviour of the Foreign Office. One of the most inexplicable anomalies of the affair in the years since the letter was published has been the behaviour of the Foreign Office: was it culpable, or just plain inefficient? It was clearly one or the other.

110

The official explanation for publication was that the Foreign Office had learned that the letter was about to be published by the *Daily Mail*: it was released to save the Government from the embarrassment of being accused of deliberately withholding the letter. According to the report of the civil service Board of Inquiry four years later – headed by the permanent secretary to the Treasury, Sir Warren Fisher – Crowe believed it would actually strengthen the hand of the Government. It was probably the greatest miscalculation of his career.

There is a description of the warning given to the Foreign Office in Marlowe's letter to the *Observer*. But this is a curiously unsatisfactory part of Marlowe's narrative: it appears to contain a niggling contradiction. Describing the hectic activity in the *Daily Mail* office on Friday afternoon, immediately after he had ordered that proofs of the letter be distributed to other Fleet Street newspapers, Marlowe writes:

> Of course I had not gone very far before the Foreign Office was informed of what was happening, and it seems that Sir Eyre Crowe promptly decided that it would be better for everyone concerned that the Foreign Office should publish the document officially, with the draft of the Prime Minister's reply to Mr Rakovsky, the Soviet Minister, rather than permit the disclosure to be made by the newspapers.

The suggestion is clear: the Foreign Office did not move until after Marlowe had received a copy of the letter at lunch time. Yet the Fisher Report said later that Crowe had made his decision to send the protest to Rakovsky before lunch. And from the speed with which the office acted it is possible that the decision to publish was also made at that time. Marlowe himself noted this speed of action, but he did not draw the conclusion that the decision could have been made before he received his copies of the letter. He comments:

> In publishing the documents the Foreign Office acted with so much energy that the official paper reached one or two of the newspaper offices before my proofs were delivered to them. Nevertheless it was obvious that the official publication had been forced by my action.

It is, in fact, not obvious at all. Again im Thurn's diary offers a clue to what is more likely to have happened. The entry for

111

Friday reads: 'Believe "Times" "Daily Mail" met late yesterday afternoon and will play the same bluff as mine about the copy. Press forces 3.45 F.O. who gives up letter after "Mail" asked "Times" to approach "Times" F.O. official. Looks alright for us.' That *The Times* should try to bluff the Foreign Office into officially authenticating the letter is not surprising. The trick is much used by even the most scrupulous journalists. All im Thurn offers is the time at which the Foreign Office finally released the letter, not the time at which Crowe, possibly misled by information from the mysterious ' "Times" F.O. official', decided on publication. It is also possible that the head of MI1C whose department had become responsible to the Foreign Office in 1922, had tipped Crowe off about the *Mail*'s possession of a copy. With this knowledge Crowe could well have decided on publication before lunch, and before the *Mail*'s request for official authentification.

There are other important peculiarities about the Foreign Office's behaviour. For example, no one in the Foreign Office seems to have thought of communicating with the Foreign Secretary before despatching and publishing the Note. Nor, apparently, did they consult Ponsonby, MacDonald's junior Minister, who had remained in London. Admittedly the telephone service was not extensive in 1924, and there were no special links between the Foreign Secretary and his office. But MacDonald was contactable in Aberavon; some of his colleagues were to phone him the next morning, and MacDonald himself was to make an anguished call to Whitehall asking how the letter and the Note had reached the press. One quick conversation could have prevented one of the more acrimonious disputes on record between Ministry officials and their Minister.

MacDonald claimed that he had not initialled the draft received by Crowe on the Friday morning. Without that initial, he argued, Crowe had no authority either to despatch the Note to Rakovsky or to publish its text. The informal Foreign Office rules concerning draft statements were clear. When a draft was amended by a Minister he would initial it at the foot of the statement. Once this had been done, an official could act with the full authority of the political head of the department. What happened in the Foreign Office, during the hectic few hours in which the draft protest Note was received, transcribed on to

112

official notepaper, signed, and sent off, obviously broke the rules. Sir Neville Bland, Crowe's private secretary in 1924, recalled in 1967 that MacDonald had placed his initial in the margin – below his amendments – but not at the bottom of the complete draft.

In 1924 William Strang was a second secretary in the Northern Department, the section headed by Gregory which dealt with northern and eastern Europe, including Russia. He described the events of that day and the following week-end in his autobiography, *Home and Abroad*.

When the draft protest was returned from South Wales there were no specific instructions from MacDonald accompanying it. The decision to despatch it was based on the Foreign Secretary's earlier agreement-in-principle to Crowe's minute suggesting that, once he had satisfied himself that the letter was authentic, a protest should be sent and immediately published. The design, according to Strang, was to expose Soviet 'methods'.

Strang was in Gregory's office when, because of the Foreign Secretary's absence, he was about to sign the protest Note. 'I remember remarking . . .' he recalls, 'that the draft was not initialled. He [Gregory] replied that he couldn't help that: Crowe had said the Note was to go off.' Strang writes that he could only suppose that Crowe had somehow assured himself of MacDonald's intentions. Of course, he had not.

Crowe learned of his mistake on the Saturday, again from Strang, when he was considering what to do about 'an alarmed query' from the Prime Minister. 'I showed Crowe the paper and drew his attention to the absence of an initial,' writes Strang. 'He said, "I hadn't noticed that. I must now wait for the storm to break upon my devoted head".' Crowe's problem did not, however, impair his feeling for the niceties of the bureaucratic life. As Strang left him late at night, he thoughtfully reminded his junior official that he was allowed to charge his taxi home on expenses.

During the week-end, Crowe had more time to reflect than he had had on Friday. His failure to check with MacDonald was one indication of haste, but not the only one. The text of the protest Note itself also suggests that the senior officials in the Foreign Office had rushed the document out at the first available opportunity.

113

Despite his advanced state of exhaustion MacDonald does not seem to have deviated from his normal pattern of behaviour when drafting the protest to Rakovsky. The pattern is described in a book about MacDonald (called simply *J. Ramsay MacDonald, 1923–1925*) published in 1925 and written under the pseudonym 'Iconoclast' by a journalist named M. A. Hamilton. MacDonald, it seems, customarily made various revisions to any draft, whether it was a speech, a statement or a diplomatic protest. He had been known to make five or six revisions in which the process of insertion and deletion in his neat handwriting could actually be traced. This was due to his strange habit of rarely scoring out a paragraph of which he disapproved. The replacement paragraph was simply written next to it. 'I noted specially when once working with him on a committee which had to knock a draft constitution into shape,' Iconoclast wrote, 'an offending paragraph was left in a copy supposed to be completely overhauled. "I leave it in there to remind me of a point I want to fight," MacDonald explained.'

Careful study of paragraphs three and five of the published Note to Rakovsky suggests that this is exactly what happened in this case. Paragraph three begins: 'No one who understands the constitution and the relationships of the Communist International will doubt its intimate connection and contact with the Soviet Government', and later the International is described as 'a propagandist body organically connected with that foreign Government'.

Paragraph five is in almost complete contradiction to paragraph three. It describes the International as 'a political body as powerful as itself' [the Soviet Government], and goes on to berate the Soviet Government for failing to exercise some control over the International and preventing it from breaking Anglo–Soviet anti-propaganda agreements. 'If it has not this power, and if responsibilities which belong to the State in other countries are in Russia in the keeping of private and irresponsible bodies . . .' the paragraph runs. The suggestion is clear. Paragraph five assumes that the Communist International *is* independent of the Soviet Government. Paragraph three assumes that it is not.

This is the most startling contradiction between the two paragraphs, but there are others. The tone and language of the two paragraphs are quite different. The style in paragraph three is littered with phrases like: 'No Government will ever tolerate an arrangement with a foreign government by which the latter is in formal diplomatic relations of a correct kind with it . . .' The later paragraph is less tortuous in style and, although firm in tone, noticeably more conciliatory. Paragraph three suggests a breakdown of the Russian Treaty; paragraph five suggests that the British Government is still convinced of its importance.

'Iconoclast' commented on the paradox implicit in the two versions as follows: '[Paragraph five] breathes a spirit different, and states a view of facts at once different from, and irreconcilable with, the earlier paragraph to which it is discordantly attached. Paragraph five asks questions which M. Rakovsky might answer. Paragraph three makes statements to which an answer is hardly conceivable except in the form of a rupture. Paragraph five although firm is not – paragraph three is – an ultimatum. Paragraph five implies that the Treaties stand; paragraph three makes that assumption almost impossible.'

'Iconoclast' concludes that MacDonald wrote paragraph five and that the earlier paragraph had been written in the Foreign Office. (It was almost certainly Gregory's work.) But, as usually happened, he had not scored out the third paragraph. Obviously, if this analysis is accepted, MacDonald expected to receive the draft protest back from the Foreign Office. It was indeed, as he claimed in a speech after the week-end, at Kenfig Hill in Glamorganshire, 'something written in my own hand which I wanted to see back.'

But the Foreign Office failed to notice the internal inconsistencies. What is unclear is whether its senior officials failed to notice them because they did not wish to notice them, or whether the lapse was genuinely a result of the haste in which Crowe felt it necessary to move. As the dispute festered on in the years following publication, and as Gregory's reputation gradually became tarnished, the conviction took root among Labour plot theorists that the Foreign Office had deliberately sent and published the letter and the protests despite MacDonald's orders to the contrary with the sole purpose of destroying Labour's election chances. There is evidence to support a plot theory – the uncertainty about the time at which Crowe decided on publication, the failure to notice either the lack of an initial at the bottom of the draft or the internal contradictions in the draft protest. Is this enough?

Gregory's own account of the affair is contained in his autobiography (which was misleadingly titled *On the Edge of Diplomacy*; he was, of course, in the thick of it). It reveals a little. If Gregory was involved in a plot, he regarded it more as a schoolboy jape than an effort to unseat a Government. His own attitudes towards the authenticity of the letter itself are ambivalent. 'A specimen of this hero's [Zinoviev's] lucubrations – or a copy or a facsimile or a clever imitation (it doesn't matter in the least which),' is the way he describes the letter in his flirtatious account of the episode. Indeed, the one event which seems to stimulate his memory of the affair took place after the significant Friday, when he was despatched with Strang to give an account of the Foreign Office's role in the distribution of the letter and the Note to MacDonald in Cardiff.

Describing the mission as being as incoherent as some of the Labour supporters they met on arrival in Cardiff, Gregory does not bother to record what he actually said to MacDonald. He does, however, devote about 1,000 words to a frivolous description of the exhausted MacDonald having something urged on him by his agent. 'No,' MacDonald finally replied, 'if you do that they will say I murdered her.' Gregory, with his tongue firmly in his cheek, refers to this inexplicable remark of a tired man as: 'this epoch making statement'. It is, to say the least, a marginal contribution to the affair.

In the period between the publication of the letter and the election, it was Gregory who provided Labour backbenchers with their most identifiable villain. E. D. Morel, a devoted fighter for improved Anglo–Russian relations, epitomized their feelings at an election meeting in Dundee. 'The act of treachery by the man Gregory at the Foreign Office is unparalleled in the history of the country. The state of affairs disclosed by his act is absolutely intolerable,' Morel thundered.

But Gregory, in his autobiography, deliberately tries to play down the importance of the Zinoviev letter. 'Why this particular rag should have been considered such a singularly tasty morsel I have never to this day been able to explain to myself. People

116

could at any time have had a whole meal off Zinoviev letters, if they had wished. But the October 1924 brand seems to have been a real delicacy: and it has been responsible for a vast amount of indigestion.'

It was, finally, to cause Gregory himself a good deal of indigestion. In 1928 his role in the affair came under close scrutiny from Fisher's inquiry. There was a suggestion that he had attempted to benefit financially from the chaos wrought by the letter's publication. But the inquiry concluded that even if Gregory had been determined to unseat the Labour Government, Crowe would of necessity have had to have been a party to the plot. 'The decision to despatch the letter was, we are satisfied, the decision of Sir Eyre Crowe alone,' the Fisher inquiry reported. It added:

> Apart from the fact that he was not a man to allow himself to be overruled or overpersuaded by a subordinate, we are able to state on the authority of one of our own number, as well as on the unimpeachable evidence of other witnesses, that Sir Eyre Crowe acknowledged his entire responsibility for the action taken.

The 'one of our own number' was almost certainly Fisher himself, who was a friend of Crowe's. Fisher did not, of course, study the evidence from Poland. It was unavailable at the time.

The Polish evidence is certainly damning. The diary of the speaker of the Polish Parliament, Maciej Rataj, states that General Sikorski, the Polish Prime Minister, had said: 'Gregory of the British Foreign Office, a Conservative and candidate for the office of Minister Plenipotentiary in Warsaw was helpful in exploiting the forgery.' This, combined with the justifiable suspicions which surrounded Gregory's currency speculation, suggests strongly that he was one of the conspirators.

But it would be a mistake to read too much into Sikorski's revelations. Analysis of the sentence referring to Gregory does not necessarily implicate him in a plot. His signature on the note to Rakovsky, and the speed with which he appended it, was indeed 'helpful in exploiting the forgery'. It was, of course, common gossip that he was a Conservative, and the head of the Northern Department would naturally be considered for the post of Minister Plenipotentiary in Warsaw. Gregory is, from a superficial reading of the published evidence, a natural candidate for the role of plotter, but although the weight of evidence against him is considerable, there is no final link which conclusively implicates him in the plot. It seems as though the curious role of J. D. Gregory is, in fact, a red herring, and that Crowe did take the vital decision to officially authenticate the Zinoviev letter on his own responsibility.

But if it was, as Fisher suggested, characteristic of Crowe to make the decision and to take full responsibility for it, it was uncharacteristic of him to make the hasty decision that he did. There are, however, some clues towards an explanation of his behaviour. The first of them is in a letter Crowe wrote to MacDonald (a copy of which went to the King) on 25 October, publication day:

> What would have been the impression [he said] if – as would inevitably happen – it was discovered that the Foreign Office had been in possession of the incriminating document for some time, but had concealed this fact and refrained from action? Would it not have been said that information that vitally concerned the security of the Empire had been deliberately suppressed during the elections, which were meanwhile to be affected by Bolshevik propaganda? I thought it would be wrong to allow my Government, and my Prime Minister personally, to be exposed to such a calumnious charge. This was one of my motives in so strongly urging a public and instant protest.

It is impossible to avoid the suspicion that Crowe might, in fact, have been more interested in the reputation of the Foreign Office than in that of the MacDonald Government. Certainly he was already deeply worried about the future of the espionage organization, MI1C, which supplied his office with information and for which he, as permanent secretary, was responsible. When they supplied him with a copy of the Zinoviev letter – as it seems very likely that they did – he would have regarded it as a coup, a justification for their existence. In the circumstances it is possible to imagine Crowe suspending disbelief and accepting the authenticity of the letter. Once he had accepted its authenticity, the reputation of the Foreign Office was obviously at stake. To be accused of harbouring an important document for political purposes would have been deeply injurious to Crowe's sense of the rightness of things.

The decision was easy to rationalize on other grounds. Mac-Donald was worried about alleged Russian interference in Britain's internal affairs, and had stated that if reliable evidence of any Soviet propaganda activity was discovered a protest Note should be sent off to Rakovsky, and published. He regarded publicity as a sure method of counteracting potentially insidious propaganda. This, Crowe argued, was confirmed in MacDonald's specific instructions regarding the Zinoviev letter.

Crowe also attempted explicitly to rationalize his decisions. Shortly after Labour left office he wrote to Lord Haldane, the ex-Liberal who had been Lord Chancellor, claiming, in the strictest confidence, that the authenticity of the letter had been established. Zinoviev, he wrote happily, had admitted to the Soviet Government that he was indeed the author of the letter.

'We got this piece of information on Thursday evening,' Crowe told Haldane (referring to the Thursday before 9 November), 'and I just had time to tell MacDonald before he went off to make his speech that evening. He thanked me, and I believe that in his heart of hearts he was convinced, though he – perhaps naturally – did not say so. At any rate he allowed me to warn him against committing himself any further to the alleged forgery of the letter.'

Crowe was naturally anxious to bolster his own belief in the letter's authenticity, and equally anxious to try to dampen down political speculation about it. He had, after all, taken a decision based on his acceptance of its authenticity. But it brought him more personal trouble than any other decision he took during his term as permanent secretary. For despite the careful efforts of his friends and admirers, Lord Strang among them, to show that MacDonald's instructions were confusing and unclear, the fact remains that this devoted bureaucrat had failed to check them.

'It has been asked,' the Fisher report commented, 'why the letter was handed to the press and why there was no telephone communication with Mr MacDonald during the 25th [a misprint for the 24th]. The answer to the first question is that Sir Eyre Crowe directed it. The answer to the second question appears to be that, as Sir Eyre Crowe seems to have satisfied himself as to the wishes of the Secretary of State, there was no occasion to telephone.' MacDonald and the Labour Party naturally believed that there was.

The precipitate behaviour of the Foreign Office startled not only the Labour Party. Rakovsky was just as surprised. He received the Foreign Office protest in the presence of a reporter from the *Daily Express,* whose news editor had already received his copy. Rakovsky, justifiably, found the whole episode decidedly undiplomatic. 'I quite understand that the Foreign Office is very careful that the election should have no foreign intervention but I am surprised that the Foreign Office, before even waiting for a reply from us, has given the alleged communication publicity,' he told the reporter.

While Crowe was taking his premature decision first to send and then to publish the protest, however, Marlowe's ex-intelligence friends – Hall and Browning – were making quite sure that the letter would get into the newspapers anyway. And Marlowe's actions, together with those of im Thurn, the Tories and the intelligence services, ostensibly reduce the blame for the letter's distribution which must be placed on the devoted head of Crowe. Nevertheless, the Foreign Office's decision to publish was critical to the plot's success. Its behaviour may not have been the root cause of Labour's embarrassment, but it certainly ensured that this would be total and irremediable.

There is one other possibility, although it completely evades proof. Crowe could have agreed to distribution of the letter to the *Mail* by the head of MI1C. He would, of course, have told Sinclair that if the scheme failed he would deny all responsibility. Indeed he would have almost certainly added that even if the scheme succeeded he did not want to know any of the details which preceded its success. But if he had known a plot was afoot, his awareness would explain his insistence that the Northern Department take the letter seriously; his determination not to question the authenticity; and the speed with which copies reached Fleet Street on the Friday afternoon. Decisions of this sort are never minuted. In fact, plots of this kind are often initiated by an oblique suggestion from a senior official, who never sullies his innocence with actual knowledge of the machinations of the plot. It is possible to use this speculation – that Crowe was a party to the plot – to explain his passive behaviour during the week-end following publication. But if he was involved, only he and Sinclair would have known it, and both would have taken the secret to their graves. No documents will ever be discovered to justify this particular speculation.

The most reasonable speculation is Strang's mature judgement in *Home and Abroad* : the Foreign Office over-estimated the embarrassment which would have been caused had the *Daily Mail* published before the letter was officially released, and MacDonald himself should have been asked personally to sign so important a diplomatic Note

10

The Press: a Credulous Response

When the *Daily Mail* and *The Times* threatened publication, and forced the Foreign Office to dispense with its customary caution and to authenticate the letter, they put the seal on the press's role in the 1924 election, which was probably more significant than it has been in any general election before or since. Usually the influence of the press on politics, and particularly on elections, is grossly exaggerated. Politicians inflate its importance when they need a scapegoat for a poor campaign. But a campaign, more than most other essentially short-term political activities, is a pre-planned exercise in which newspapers merely report and reflect the opinions of politicians. There is too little time for newspaper reports to influence a party's policies. Indeed, the influence of the press in the years since 1924 has deteriorated to such an extent that its primary function has now become the publication of opinion polls. Politicians are genuinely more interested in the impact of their television performances. So, it often seems, are the newspapers themselves.

This was not so in 1924. Television was not much more than a dream in the mind of John Logie Baird. Radio was still a gimmick in its infancy; not until the General Strike two years later was its impact really felt on a political situation. This limited the field of public communication, and gave the newspapers potentially far more power to influence opinion than they now have. So, in 1924, the Labour politicians who complained bitterly about the power of the newspapers did not, for once, inflate it. Publication of the Zinoviev letter, and the press's treatment of it, seemed to give a brief reality to the allegations of a right-wing plot inspired by ambitious newspaper proprietors to undermine the Labour Party.

There were two other factors of particular significance which made it possible for newspapers to exploit the letter in the 1924 election in a way they would find difficult in the 'sixties. For one thing, far less reporting was inspired by informed scepticism. The balance of power within newspapers between proprietors and reporters only began to swing in the reporters' direction many years later. In the 'twenties, reporters on all newspapers, including the quality papers, had far less freedom to publish facts which might undermine the firmly held opinions of their proprietor. The last single-minded proprietorial campaign was Lord Beaverbrook's against Britain's attempt to join the Common Market in 1962, and by then its principal interest was as a journalistic throwback. In the 1920s, however, this kind of campaign was the rule rather than the exception.

The other significant factor was the overwhelming predominance of the Conservative Press. It was only after the 1924 election that the *Daily Herald* – deciding that the Labour Party's cruel mauling by the other newspapers could only be balanced by making the *Herald* a mass circulation newspaper – began to compete for new readers. And it was not until the 'thirties that it succeeded in becoming a really popular paper. (Then it became the first to push its circulation above two million.) Nor did the *Herald* have any influential allies until the 'thirties when the *Daily Mirror* first began its deliberate effort to become a mass circulation, Labour-supporting daily paper.

The extent of Labour's communications problem is illustrated remarkably well by the estimated circulations of six leading newspapers in October 1924:

Supporting the Conservatives:	*Daily Mail*	1,790,057
	Daily Express	804,319
	The Times	180,000
	Daily Telegraph	120,000
Supporting the Liberals:	*Manchester Guardian*	50,000
Supporting Labour:	*Daily Herald*	300,000

These statistics (management figures in the case of the *Mail* and *Express* and estimates in all other cases) show that the sales ratio of anti-Labour to Labour newspapers was almost 10:1.

The total circulation of the Conservative *daily* press listed above was 2,894,376, as against the Herald's 300,000. The ratio would, of course, become even more unbalanced if the Sunday and provincial circulation were included; these two groups were, if anything, even more solidly pro-Tory.

The Labour leaders were well aware of the effect on the morale of a party whose supporters read the outpourings of a viciously biased press every morning. But all they could offer were very long term palliatives. Just before the election campaign began MacDonald told delegates to the 1924 Labour Conference that they should not be discouraged about the long-term influence of the press. He was, of course, right; within twenty years the *Daily Mirror* was running a campaign which was to help Labour gain its first overall Parliamentary majority. But his philosophical view of the press cannot have allayed the fears of many of the delegates. In the previous election, in 1923, they had observed in the constituencies that at the beginning of the campaign the papers seemed to conspire to say as little as possible about Labour's progress. When Labour's success became disquieting to the Tories the Press turned a conspiracy of silence into a conspiracy of misreporting. Even so, MacDonald remarked that: 'there is some comfort that there is a limit to the influence of tricky conspiracies and resourceful demagogues.'

Within three weeks the party had discovered that this 'limit' was a good deal further out than most of them could have imagined. A campaign dominated by the Red scare had been completed by the publication of the Zinoviev letter. The effect had frightened some commentators. 'From papers totalling nearly three million circulation came as fervent a challenge as has ever been launched against a democratic Government in the English language,' writes Charles Higbie (from whose unpublished thesis much of the material in this chapter is drawn). It is not surprising that the plotters in the Tory Party and intelligence should have chosen to channel the forged letter through the *Daily Mail*. It was the obvious choice; during the previous three weeks it had proved to be outstandingly loyal to the Tory Party, and the most stridently effective promoter of the Red scare.

No reader could have been in any doubt about where the

Mail's proprietor, Lord Rothermere, placed his loyalties. The *Mail* printed each day 'an outstanding Unionist campaign poster released today from that party's headquarters'. The pattern had been firmly established in an editorial five days before Parliament was dissolved. Attacking the Russian treaties, it wrote melodramatically: 'It is the fact that a British Government . . . is preparing to use the British taxpayer's credit and cash for the purpose of financing a gang of thieves and murderers who repudiate all social and financial morality. The wrong is graver because this gang of alien criminals who have usurped power in Russia wish to destroy the British empire and our civilized system of credit.' There was going to be no tortuous intellectual vacillation from the *Daily Mail* after that.

In producing facts to support its editorial case, the *Mail* went to lengths which astonish anyone who has experienced only the papers of the 'fifties and 'sixties. On 10 October it carried a report, alleged to be circulating in Paris, stating that six members of MacDonald's Cabinet 'had been induced to accept Russian jewels concealed in chocolates and then had been blackmailed into prevailing upon the Prime Minister to back the Treaty in spite of his earlier objections'. (This story, like most effective propaganda, has a faint element of truth: the Comintern probably did use boxes of chocolates to smuggle fragmented pieces of the Imperial jewels to finance overseas Communist Parties.)

The *Mail* concentrated its venomous editorials and election news stories on the Red scare – with only one digression, in which a series of pictures of dole queues were printed, with the message that Labour was responsible for unemployment – long before its editor, Marlowe, first heard about the existence of the Zinoviev letter. Even a book review, published on 17 October, detailed alleged Bolshevik atrocities, and concluded: 'It tells the truth about our Prime Minister's friends.'

With the publication of the letter on 25 October, the tone changed from strident to hysterical: 'Moscow issues order to the British Communists. . . . British Communists in turn give orders to the Socialist Government which it tamely and humbly obeys,' said the editorial on the day of publication. On the following Monday, the last deck on its screaming seven-decker headline said baldly:

125

THE ONLY THING LEFT TO DO IS
VOTE CONSERVATIVE

And just to make quite sure, its slogan on election eve, printed clearly on the front page, was remarkable even for the *Mail*. 'Get rid of our shifty Prime Minister,' it said. The voters did; and the Tories were delighted, if ungrateful – for Rothermere never got the political power he sought.

The *Express* lacked the advantage offered by the *Mail*'s 'discovery' of the letter. Although no less strident in its deliberate propagation of the Red scare it was, therefore, somewhat less hysterical. Apart from an excursion into a scare story affecting to show how the League of Nations could direct the British fleet against Australia ('every vote for the Socialists is a vote for robbing Britain of her Fleet and handing it over to foreigners,' its analysis proclaimed), it concentrated on demonstrating 'that the Socialist experiment has failed'.

Possibly by design, but probably by coincidence, Zinoviev's name appeared twice in the columns of the *Express* before 25 October. The first mention is in a report of an alleged speech at Riga in which Zinoviev is said to have claimed that Mac-Donald, of all people, was becoming a Russian agitator in spite of himself. The second is in a claim that the treaties strengthened the hands of Russian extremists 'like Stalin, Bucharin and Zinoviev'.

The *Express,* however, was fully capable of vitriolic prose. It atacked Shapurji Saklatvala, the Indian Communist standing at Battersea, in these terms: 'Imagine a little dark skinned Indian Communist, harsh voiced, with a curious little "clip" in his accent, the fire of fanatic frenzy always leaping from queerly bright eyes, hatred of almost everything seeming to consume his nervously moving body, and a great cataract of words always spouting, frothing, foaming from him in a never-ending stream.' And as its own contribution to the proper electoral mood, the *Express* resurrected, on 24 October, an ex-War Minister, Major General Seely, to claim that Bolshevik propaganda had undermined the morale of a group of soldiers in a YMCA hut during the First World War. It was not Beaverbrook's fault that the Zinoviev letter, published next day, somewhat diminished the impact of the outraged General Seely.

Perhaps because it was jealous of the *Mail*'s scoop, the *Express* did not prosecute the charges of Government treachery with quite so much vigour. By election day it frankly admitted that the letter could have been a forgery, and the day after publication the *Sunday Express* actually included Rakovsky's denial of the letter's authenticity in the second deck of its headline; and its story posed a whole series of embarrassing questions. But these tentative efforts at journalistic propriety were quickly obliterated by the message which was splashed in suitable red ink across every page of the *Express* on election day: 'Do Not Vote Red Today.'

In response to all this the *Daily Herald* was forced from aggression to desperate defence. It was, in fact, no more objective in its presentation of news than the pro-Conservative papers ('Labour Marching On: Do Your Bit' was one of its campaign headlines). It is, however, impossible to read its files without feeling some sympathy for the way in which it tried each day to combat the influence of its bigger popular rivals. It ran stories whose only object could have been to raise the morale of the faithful; like the one which attempted to demonstrate that eight of the states in the United States were worse defaulters on international bond issues than the Soviets. And after publication of the letter, the *Herald* tried hard to put a brave face on the whole affair. But the paper could only fight a defensive battle against the *Mail* for another three days. It was, however, the only paper to declare outright that the letter was a forgery.

The *Herald* conceived its main task as being a corrective to the *Mail*. It did not have the resources to fight the misconception perpetrated by the quality papers, although there was certainly plenty to rebut. During October *The Times* devoted over twenty of its broad columns to news items reflecting badly on Russia. It reached its nadir on 24 October, when it ran a story headlined:

SOVIET SHIP AT PORT TALBOT
Communists In Close Touch With Crew

Port Talbot was in MacDonald's own constituency, and *The Times* heavily insinuated that, as a result of the presence of the Russian ship, Liberal speakers had been subject 'to serious

127

interruption when they referred to the **Russian Treaty**'. Its report of the letter's publication the next day was predictably uncritical. It suggested that publication had been deliberately delayed by MacDonald for political reasons. On polling day *The Times* rubbed in the message with a story headlined: 'Another Red Plot in Germany', and muttered unhappily about talk of resignations of high officials at the Foreign Office.

The tone of the *Daily Telegraph* was, perhaps, less fulminating than it would have been had its merger with the *Morning Post*, scourge of the British Communist Party, already taken place. But it showed an increased interest in news from Russia during the campaign. Indeed, its news from Moscow was turning over at such a rate that on 27 October it reported that three of Zinoviev's secretaries had been executed for their part in the affair. Zinoviev, it reported, had denied writing the letter, and had expressed amazement at the letter's cleverness. This report deserves some mild admiration. Although the possibility of its being true is severely reduced by the fact that Zinoviev was on holiday miles away from Moscow that week-end, it was one of the few attempts to try to discover what was the reaction of the Bolsheviks in Moscow.

The *Manchester Guardian*'s case was different. Like all other newspapers, apart from the *Herald*, it was opposed to the Government. But it did not support the Conservatives either; it still supported the Liberals. It was therefore highly critical of MacDonald's handling of the letter, if dubious about its authenticity. James Bone, the *Guardian*'s distinguished London editor, actually elicited the exclusive information that both the *Mail* and Tory Central Office had been in possession of the letter before the Foreign Office officially released it for publication. But the *Guardian*, like other papers, did not use this small, but significant, snippet of information to initiate large scale investigations into the letter's origin and authenticity. Only the *Herald*, after the election was over, seriously attempted to discover more about the letter. It is symptomatic of the press at the time that the *Herald*'s motivation, just like that of its rivals in their coverage of the affair, was primarily political.

This degree of political commitment was the single most significant feature of the newspapers in the 'twenties. Political prejudice, and sometimes political ambition, was the motiva-

128

tion underlying the opinions of most proprietors, and expression of prejudice was almost the *raison d'être* of their papers. Reporting an approximation of the truth was subordinated recklessly to a determination to get some message across. The guardianship of democracy was often proclaimed as a justification of their excesses. But it was very rarely displayed.

Although political prejudice is still discernible in the news columns of contemporary papers, it is inconceivable that their treatment of a modern Zinoviev letter would repeat the blunders of forty years ago. A modern editor, receiving the news which Thomas Marlowe received, would pass it immediately to his resident Kremlinologist for detailed textual analysis. He would set his reporting teams to try to discover the location of the original and the evidence on which the Foreign Office based its actions. He would be in touch with Moscow. He would take the elementary step of discovering the reaction of the alleged addressees, the British Communist Party. He would, in short, not have been satisfied by the assurances of shrewd intelligence agents and unscrupulous politicians.

That some of these services did not exist in 1924 was, obviously, not Marlowe's or any other editor's fault: it has taken time to develop the business of Kremlinology into a lucrative full-time profession. But equally, the failure to conduct even rudimentary investigations was a reflection of the spirit of the 'twenties.

A great majority of the readers of the *Mail* and *The Times* did not wish to have their illusions destroyed by facts. They believed the Zinoviev letter to be genuine, and they were not going to be disabused by their newspapers.

It was *almost* a case of the journalist behaving as Arnold Bennett, one of their contemporaries, described them in *The Title*. 'Journalists say a thing that they know isn't true in the hope that if they keep on saying it long enough it will be true.' In the case of the Zinoviev letter, the journalists did not know that what they were saying was not true. But, just as important, they did not want to find out.

11

MacDonald Mismanages the Affair

On the night of Friday, 24 October, Jimmy Thomas, the garrulous Colonial Secretary, had been speaking for Philip Snowden, the Chancellor of the Exchequer, in his Colne Valley constituency. He stayed the night there – an unexpectedly fortunate decision since it produced the briefest and most pertinent comment on the effect of the Zinoviev letter on Labour's election chances. Snowden, in his autobiography, writes: 'On Saturday morning, the 25th October Mr Thomas . . . came hammering at my bedroom door early, and shouted: "Get up you lazy devil! We're bunkered!"'

Neither Snowden nor Thomas had known anything about the letter. Their consternation was complete. They immediately telephoned MacDonald in Aberavon to find out about it. His reaction was extraordinary, and there can be only two explanations: either he mistrusted Snowden so much that he refused to speak freely, or he was so exhausted by the campaign that he was quite unable to focus his attention on the political repercussions of publication. The latter is more likely, for Snowden reports: 'He did not seem to be very much concerned about it, and said that he did not know whether it was fake or genuine. But he was making enquiries, and would refer to the matter in a speech.' Both Snowden and Thomas automatically assumed that he would make the speech that Saturday.

So did the newspapers. On Saturday morning their reaction was automatic: the most important story of the day was to discover what MacDonald in South Wales thought about the letter. But the publicity machine in an election campaign was primitive in the 'twenties. There were no morning press conferences at which the party leaders subjected themselves to potentially embarrassing questions, and no organized communications system connecting the party headquarters with the party leaders. On that Saturday the newspapers, and Snowden, and hundreds of anxious candidates throughout the country, were both astonished and disappointed. MacDonald had absolutely nothing to say about the Zinoviev letter. The Sunday papers, unable to print quotes from the Prime Minister, did the only thing left to them. Their story was that he had said nothing. 'STRANGE SILENCE OF RAMSAY MACDONALD' was the *Sunday Express's* headline. Next morning the *Daily Mail* was even more emphatic: 'MOSCOW BOMB SILENCES PREMIER' it proclaimed. The implication was straightforward: MacDonald, recognizing that the letter was genuine, was too embarrassed to comment.

His colleagues were less evasive in their Saturday speeches, though their reactions were confused and confusing. There had obviously been no overnight consultations to establish a party line on the letter. J. R. Clynes commented rather sadly: 'Frankly, this document, if authentic, would imperil any arrangement with Russia.' But the strangest reaction was of perverse pride in the episode. 'If it is not a fake,' cried Thomas, 'then it shows that the British Government immediately pulled up the Russians.' Josiah Wedgwood, Chancellor of the Duchy of Lancaster, betrayed the same paradoxical pride in the affair. Even Snowden spoke in similar tones in an effort to salvage what little political advantage was left in the wreckage. But he was expecting a major policy statement from MacDonald in South Wales.

Other members of the Government were less interested in salvage, however, and went straight into the attack. Trevelyan spoke of the letter being 'the usual white lie from Russia', after declaring: 'I shall assume the letter is a fake until I know for certain.' Even more significant was the reaction of the Under-Secretary of State at the Foreign Office, Arthur Ponsonby, who had been in the office during the previous week yet had been ignored by the officials. Ponsonby thought it 'not unlikely' that the letter was a forgery. Sir Patrick Hastings, the memory of the Campbell Case all too uncomfortably fresh in his mind, cautiously asserted that the letter 'might' be a fake. And, as if to demonstrate that the Cabinet's reactions could cover the spectrum, Stephen Walsh, the War Minister, asked casually: 'What does it matter to us whether the letter is a forgery or not?'

It mattered to the *Daily Herald*, which carried bold headlines claiming: 'ZINOVIEV LETTER DECLARED FORGERY'. According to the *Herald*'s political correspondent the great question was: 'how did such an obvious forgery come to be planted on the Foreign Office?' But when MacDonald did finally break his silence, in Cardiff on the Monday afternoon, he reacted with notably less conviction than the party's journalistic mouthpiece. The three-day delay certainly did him harm, since it provided the predominantly Tory press with two more days in which to hammer home the implications of the letter without having to trouble to use space to print the reply of the Labour leader. What did even more harm was the perversely equivocal attitude which MacDonald struck when he eventually spoke about the letter.

Like Thomas, Wedgwood and Snowden, he seemed determined to convince his audience that the Government had acted with commendable speed. The Government had been accused of delaying publication. Rumours suggested that the Foreign Office had received the letter in September. 'Why,' the *Sunday Express* had thundered the day before, 'was the correspondence published only yesterday?' MacDonald revealed that the letter had reached the Foreign Office on 10 October, been registered on the 14th and reached him on the 16th.

MacDonald seemed so proud of the slickness of the procedure that he tried to turn the episode against Labour's enemies. 'Although, my friends, I have not been one single hour in London since the letter came under my notice,' he said, 'only nine days have elapsed from the first registering of the letter and the publication of the despatch last Friday.' According to *The Times* reporter, the loyal audience cheered at the suggestion that this was efficient Government at work. And MacDonald, spurred on by their applause, continued: 'As a matter of fact, I make safe to say that, had the Foreign Office been in either Tory or Liberal hands, that letter would have taken weeks to go through the various sieves through which it had to go. Rapidity of action, a business way of handling, a

132

determination on the part of the Government to stand no nonsense, if there is any nonsense, is a conspicuous example of the new way in which foreign affairs are being conducted.'

This curious defence of the Government's behaviour came at the end of the speech; it was never to be used again. The peroration contrasted oddly with the opening, during which MacDonald had considered his own role in the publication of the letter. Here he implied, though no more, that he, as Foreign Secretary, had not been convinced by his officials of the letter's authenticity before its text was published.

'If it was authentic, it had to be published at once, and in the meantime, while investigations were going on to discover the authenticity of the letter, that draft letter to Rakovsky would be prepared, so that when authenticity was established no time would be lost in making our protest to the Soviet Government,' MacDonald said, before explaining how he had written a minute explaining this, and received a trial draft of the protest on the 21st. 'On the morning of the 24th,' he continued, 'I looked at the draft. I altered it, and sent it back in altered form, *expecting it to come back to me with proofs of authenticity,* but that night it was published.'

At this implication there were cries of shame from the audience. MacDonald had clearly been duped by his civil servants into premature publication of the letter before its authenticity had been satisfactorily established. This was the interpretation offered by Conservative papers the following morning: MacDonald had added insult to injury, they argued, by blaming his civil servants for publication. And although MacDonald went to unusual lengths to defend his civil servants ('I make no complaints. . . . They honestly believed that the document was genuine, and on that belief they acted'), the damage had been done. Snowden, an enemy of MacDonald's, reported that a friend of his on the platform was so distressed by the leader's performance that the platform party 'fervently prayed that it would open and swallow them up'. *The Times* on the other hand claimed that the faithful cheered.

This confusion was, however, incidental to the major inconsistency in the speech. It was cruelly spotlighted in a *Manchester Guardian* editorial the following morning. MacDonald claimed, it observed, that the Foreign Office had failed to prove the

133

authenticity of the letter to him before officially sanctioning its release, yet he had simultaneously boasted that the Government had acted with greater decision than either their Tory or Liberal opponents would have done in a similar situation. Not even the relatively sympathetic *Manchester Guardian* would let him have it both ways. Asquith, the Liberal leader, was even harsher: he could, he said, 'not remember to have read a more distracted, incoherent and unilluminating statement in the whole of his political experience.'

In retrospect, the most interesting feature of the Cardiff speech is not what MacDonald said but what he left unsaid. At no point did he adopt the only attacking position that was open to him: declare that the Foreign Office had made a mistake, and that the letter was a forgery.

There was evidence to support this position. MacDonald must have found it slightly distasteful, however, to realize that all the most convincing evidence, based on textual analysis of the letter, originated within the Communist Party. On the Saturday of publication, John Ross Campbell and Harry Pollitt, both members of the Communist Party's political committee, had woken up in Dundee to discover that the newspapers were full of a Red scare. 'It was,' Campbell recalled in 1967, 'the first time we had ever heard of a Zinoviev letter.'

Campbell and Pollitt read through the text of the letter in Dundee, and immediately dismissed it as a forgery. It was what might be expected of them, since they were being accused of taking part in a conspiracy. Yet their immediate reasons for believing the letter to be forged were relevant to Labour's election case.

The first irregularity, also seized on by Rakovsky in his reply to the Note on 25 October, was the heading of the letter itself. This read: 'Executive Committee, Third Communist International.' There was, as Campbell, Pollitt and Rakovsky were quick to point out, no such thing as the 'Third Communist International' since there had been no First or Second 'Communist' Internationals. The first two had never called themselves 'Communists'. The second oddity was the description of Zinoviev himself at the foot of the letter: 'With Communist Greetings, President of the Presidium of the I.K.K.I., Zinoviev.' In fact Zinoviev regularly signed himself 'President of the

Executive Committee'. It is also unlikely that he would have used the form I.K.K.I. rather than the English version E.C.C.I., meaning Executive Committee of the Communist International. The third mistake was in the signatures. The British representative on the Presidium of the International was Arthur MacManus. His name was spelt McManus in the Zinoviev letter released by the Foreign Office. (This particular argument was, however, diminished by the fact that at the end of MacManus's repudiation of the letter, issued officially by the C.P. on 25 October, his name was spelt McManus.) More serious, however, was the use of 'Zinoviev' instead of the usual 'G. Zinoviev' and 'Kuusinen' instead of 'O. W. Kuusinen'. And Kuusinen was not secretary of the International, as the letter claimed, but merely a member of the secretariat. On the day of publication in the newspapers Rakovsky ended his own superficial textual analysis of the Zinoviev letter with a comprehensive indictment: 'The whole of the contents of the documents are, moreover, from the Communist point of view, a tissue of absurdities.'

Closer analysis reveals a number of these. The Trades Union Congress delegation which examined the files of the Communist International at Zinoviev's invitation in November and December 1924 produced a detailed account of them. Their textual analysis on its own convinced them that the letter was forged.

The first two paragraphs of the letter contain nothing unusual, except perhaps the initials S.S.S.R. for Soviet Russia. The English form, then as now, was U.S.S.R. The paragraphs point out that the Anglo-Soviet treaties were due to be put before the House of Commons for ratification, and that a fierce campaign was being mounted by bourgeois and reactionary circles which had no desire to see the proletariats consolidating their interests and normal relations between the two countries restored. 'The proletariat of Great Britain . . . must show the greatest possible energy in the further struggle for ratification and against the endeavours of British capitalists to compel Parliament to annul it,' the second paragraph concluded. It was the sort of conventional message the British Communist Party might well expect to receive from the International.

The third paragraph contains the first peculiarity. 'It is indispensable,' it read, 'to stir up the masses of the British proletariat to bring into movement the army of unemployed proletarians, whose position can be improved only after a loan has been granted to the S.S.S.R. . . .' The T.U.C. delegation found the sub-clause reading 'to bring into movement the army of unemployed proletarians' a strange one. 'An interpolation is obvious from sense and syntax,' it reported. The sentence certainly reads more clearly and naturally without it.

The paragraph goes on to state that the group in the Labour Party which sympathized with the treaty should bring increased pressure to bear on the Government in favour of ratification. Again, this was hardly an incendiary passage; it reflected the perfectly normal operation of pressure-group politics. Likewise the next passage, stating the Bolshevik distaste for MacDonald's foreign policy, which, it said, 'already represents an inferior copy of the policy of the Curzon Government.' The order to 'organise a campaign of disclosure of the foreign policy of MacDonald' was not likely to send a shiver down the spine of the middle class. They might even have been comforted by the thought that the Communists believed MacDonald to be a class traitor.

It was in the fifth paragraph, however, that the language departed from normal. It began with the incorrect use of the initials I.K.K.I., instead of E.C.C.I., and then referred quite suddenly to 'wide material in its [Moscow's] possession regarding the activities of British Imperialism in the Middle and Far East'. There was nothing essentially strange about this, since the argument formed a common part of the Communist International's anti-war propaganda. But juxtaposed between one sentence about the treaty, and another calling on the British CP to 'strain every nerve in the struggle for the ratification of the Treaty,' the anti-war propaganda appears illogical and suspicious.

In the next sentence, another sub-clause incurred the suspicion of the TUC investigators. The sentence read: 'A settlement of relations between the two countries will assist in the revolutionising of the international and British proletariat not less than a successful rising in any of the working districts of England, as the establishment of close contact between the British and Russian proletariat . . .' The inclusion of 'not less than a successful rising in any of the working districts of

England' in the sentence destroys its internal logic; the interpolation, said the TUC, makes the sentence almost nonsense.

The sentence ended by referring to the extension of the propaganda and ideas of Leninism in England and the Colonies. Since the colonies had not been previously mentioned, and were to be introduced later as offering a quite different challenge, their inclusion at this point in the letter seems slightly eccentric. In the next sentence, however, the tone of the letter becomes thoroughly revolutionary. 'Armed warfare,' it says, 'must be preceded by a struggle against the inclinations to compromise which are embedded among the majority of British workmen, against the ideas of evolution and peaceful extermination of capitalism. Only then will it be possible to count upon complete success of an armed insurrection.' It was at this point that the newspapers became excited. The idea of armed warfare was radical and frightening. It was also strange when considered in relation to the next sentence. 'In Ireland and the Colonies the case is different; there there is a national question, and this represents too great a factor for success for us to waste time on a prolonged preparation of the working class.' The Colonies were, of course, much more fruitful ground for militant revolution. And in the next paragraph the letter seems to recognize this; its intention seems to be to boost the morale of the leaders of the British Communist Party. 'But *even* in England, as other countries where the workers are politically developed, events themselves may more rapidly revolutionise the working masses than propaganda. For instance, a strike movement, repressions by the Government etc.' This is far removed from the idea of the armed insurrection referred to only three sentences previously.

But at the end of that sentence the tone of the letter alters completely. 'The style and character changes to secret instruction to a Communist conspiracy,' the TUC reported. 'From your last report,' the letter said, 'it is evident that agitation propaganda work in the army is weak, in the navy a very little better. Your explanation that the quality of the members attracted justifies the quantity is right in principle, nevertheless it would be desirable to have cells in all the units of the troops, particularly among those quartered in the large centres of the country, and also among factories working on munitions and at military store depots.' Then, having established a conspiratorial atmosphere, the letter peters out in the next paragraph into conventional anti-war propaganda, and obvious suggestions about propaganda slogans.

The revolutionary tone returns, however, in the conclusion, which said:

> The Military Section of the British Communist Party, so far as we are aware, further suffers from a lack of specialists, the future directors of the British Red Army. It is time you thought of forming such a group, which, together with the leaders, might be, in the event of an outbreak of active strife, the brain of the military organization of the party. Go attentively through the lists of the military 'cells' detailing from them the more energetic and capable men, turn attention to the more talented military specialists who have for one reason or another left the Service and hold Socialist views. Attract them into the ranks of the Communist Party if they desire honestly to serve the proletariat and desire in the future to direct, not the blind mechanical forces in the service of the bourgeoisie, but a national army. Form a directing operative head of the Military Section. Do not put this off to a future moment, which may be pregnant with events and catch you unprepared.

Zinoviev himself, in a refutation of the letter published in *The Communist Review* in December 1924, rested his case on this one passage. He scoffed at the idea of there being a Military Section of the British Communist Party. 'Everyone knows,' he said, 'that the CP of Great Britain today has far more urgent business than the creation of a British Red Army. The British Communist Party, supported by the "Minority Movement" in the trade unions, is seeking to propagate the views of the Communist international among the masses of ordinary English workers.' Zinoviev concluded that the forged letter was proof of their success.

This theme was continued in an analysis of the sentence demanding that 'talented military specialists' be found in the party's military 'cells' to form a directing operative head of the Military Section. 'The thing is an absurdity from beginning to end,' Zinoviev wrote harshly. 'At present there exists no Military Section in the CP of Great Britain. . . . It has more important tasks: the winning of the majority of English

138

workers by means of agitation and the propagation of the ideas of Marxism.'

The TUC made one small but fascinating excursion into really detailed textual analysis. Noting the use of the phrase 'national army', it concluded that this was a mistranslation of the Russian word 'narodny'. Any Communist would have translated this 'People's Army', the delegation claimed. If a Communist had meant to say 'national army' he would have used the word 'nazionalny', not 'narodny'. The clear implication was that the sentence had been written by Russians but not by Communist Russians. And although the Labour Party drew that broad implication, they never used this small but significant mistranslation to support the suggestion that the letter was a White Russian forgery.

Zinoviev's most dramatic point was connected with the date of the letter he was alleged to have sent. It was headed 'Presidium, September 15th, 1924, Moscow.' The forger, Zinoviev commented, has shown himself to be very stupid in his choice of date. 'On the 15th September, 1924, I was taking a holiday in Kislovodsk, and therefore, could not have signed any official letters.'

That suggestive piece of information was not, of course, available to MacDonald in South Wales during the week-end of 25–26 October. Nor was MacDonald to know that there was a strange and unexplained contradiction between the two copies the *Daily Mail* had received the previous Friday. Marlowe, the *Mail*'s editor, in his letter to the *Observer* in 1928, revealed, as an important part of his narrative, that there was an 'important difference' between the copies. 'In one copy the name of McManus [the incorrect spelling was his], to whom the letter was written, appeared immediately under the name of Zinoviev, as if McManus were the co-signatory,' he stated. (He did not say whether MacManus's name appeared as addressee, or not at all in the other copy.) There were, Marlowe reported, other trifling differences which would inevitably occur in 'any such lengthy documents being transcribed by different hands'. But he dismissed them as unimportant. A politician, on the other hand, could have made details like this part of a devastating attack on the authenticity of the letter. And although MacDonald may not have had information of this kind available in

139

South Wales on 26 October, there was still enough in the *Mail's* version to undertake a textual analysis which could have tarnished the Conservatives' self-righteousness. But even if MacDonald had felt inclined to declare the letter a forgery (and he persistently maintained later that this was not the point) he had neither the assistance nor the energy to perform the elementary, but time-consuming, detection work. The result was the Cardiff speech, which did little to relieve the gloom which had fallen on many Labour candidates. Two days later, when the election results were declared, gloom swallowed most of them quite completely.

When the Cabinet met on the morning of 31 October, two days after the election, it was confidently believed that MacDonald would resign immediately. The only problem was that the King, to whom MacDonald had to return the seals of office, was in Sandringham. Preliminary arrangements had already been made for his return to London; unlike his predecessor, Edward VII, George V did not believe in making his Prime Ministers trail obediently to whichever resort he was staying in. But the arrangements had to be scrapped. The Labour Government did not resign straight away, and the sole cause of its lingering in office was an understandable desire to use the last driblet of political power to investigate the authenticity of the Zinoviev letter.

The decision followed a discussion which had begun conventionally enough with an analysis of Labour's election campaign. Something had gone very wrong to prevent the party gaining seats: one member of the Cabinet had expected a gain of around twenty seats, another more than that. Thomas talked of being 'frankly disappointed'. They all agreed one thing, however. The campaign had been going well until the previous Friday night. The slump did not begin until the Zinoviev letter was published. 'The people lost confidence in us; the women were frightened; speakers felt themselves paralysed,' commented one of the Cabinet sadly.

Then MacDonald was asked to explain his own position. He called for the Foreign Office dossier on the letter and used it to explain to the Cabinet what he had told his audience in Cardiff only four nights previously: namely that when he rewrote the draft protest to Rakovsky he had not initialled it, and expected

140

to see it again for signature before it went off. But the explanation did not satisfy all his colleagues. One group, led by Haldane and Snowden, took up the criticism of MacDonald for blaming his civil servants. It was not unreasonable, they argued, that once he had sent a minute favouring publication of the protest the civil servants should authorize publication of the complete re-draft which they had received in MacDonald's own handwriting. MacDonald tried to defend himself by switching the argument. He was not told formally by the Foreign Office that the protest Note had been dispatched. A *Daily News* reporter had contacted him in South Wales, and asked for his comment. 'I felt like a man sewn in a sack and thrown into the sea,' he said. The explanation for his weekend silence was equally unforthcoming. He said he had been without adequate data on which to base a public explanation.

None of these excuses seemed to satisfy Haldane and Snowden, but they provoked a passionate response from another group in the Cabinet, led by Parmoor. He was supported by Trevelyan, Lord Thomson and Josiah Wedgwood. They were a predictable collection of middle-class Socialists who believed that the Labour Government had been defeated because of a carefully conceived plot. Parmoor, certain that the letter was a forgery, demanded an inquiry which would sift all the available evidence. This would inevitably lead, Parmoor believed, to an exposure of the role of the secret service. Parmoor had a well developed sense of the dramatic. He actually introduced evidence of forgery. Lord Beaverbrook, he said, had assured him that the letter was the work of a well known forger named Williams. But the mention of Beaverbrook's name – a man with few friends in politics, none of them in the Labour Party – did not help his cause.

Haldane, obviously horrified at the prospect of a Parmoor inquiry into the Foreign Office (it would lead to the assassination of some of the agencies of the Foreign Office, he claimed) resisted the idea of a broadly briefed inquiry. MacDonald seems to have lost control of the Cabinet, and Arthur Henderson tried desperately to restore the initiative to the Prime Minister by suggesting that he, as head of the Foreign Office, should make whatever inquiries he thought fit into the Zinoviev letter. But it had no effect. Parmoor immediately started to clamour for a public inquiry. Snowden, sensing disaster for the Foreign Office, replied that any inquiry must be secret. Thomas then suggested the appointment of an ad hoc Cabinet committee to go through all the documents.

At this point, MacDonald finally intervened as decisively as he did at any stage of the meeting. He tried desperately to persuade the Cabinet to distinguish between two questions: first, the conduct of the civil servants, and second, the authenticity of the letter. Much to Parmoor's annoyance, he urged that the first question be dropped. Tempers were becoming frayed, and Thomas seemed convinced that Parmoor and Trevelyan were willing to sacrifice the Foreign Office for an opportunity to get rid of the secret service.

MacDonald again attempted to silence the disputants by backing Thomas's proposal for a secret inquiry by a Cabinet committee. He suggested that its members should be Henderson, Thomas and Haldane. But this trio was too right-wing for the plot theorists; Wedgwood and Trevelyan insisted on Parmoor being included. Finally the Prime Minister agreed that Parmoor should have Thomas's place. His last significant act was to inform the assistant secretary to the Cabinet, Tom Jones, who was responsible for the minutes of the meeting, that no reference should be made in the records to the role of the civil service in the affair of the Zinoviev letter.

The significance of MacDonald's rejection of any inquiry into the civil service is clear. Only a thorough investigation into the origins of the letter, a study of secret service personnel and their methods and an examination of the relationship between the secret services and the Foreign Office could have revealed enough about the letter to support suspicions that it was forged, and that it had been deliberately used to embarrass Labour in the middle of an election campaign. The behaviour of civil servants was central to any inquiry, yet MacDonald was unwilling to penetrate beyond the fringes of the episode.

The explanation is probably straightforward. MacDonald conformed rigorously to well-established codes of behaviour (conformity was one of his characteristics which appealed to the King, who admitted to his private secretary, Lord Stamfordham, that he would not be pleased to lose him). The code then, as now, was that civil servants must not be attacked because they cannot answer back. It is a ingenuous attitude towards a body which wields such great power. But it gripped MacDonald and reduced to impotence the Cabinet committee's efforts to discover what had happened before the letter was received in the Foreign Office on 10 October. Crowe's letter of regret at the premature publication of the letter and Note so moved MacDonald that any imputations of bad faith, or even less damaging suggestions that Crowe might have been misled by the secret service, were simply not entertained. This, together with MacDonald's rejection of evidence of forgery from Communist sources, made Labour's efforts over the next four years to demonstrate the extent to which they and the electorate had been cheated more sterile than they need have been.

12

1924-28: Labour's Struggle to Revive the Issue

Most of the men sitting round the Cabinet table at its last meeting on 4 November 1924 were depressed. Power had come to them so quickly, and been lost so soon. They were experiencing for the first time the gloom which enshrouds all retiring Cabinet ministers: they were about to lose their Red Boxes, their easy access to information, their teams of efficient, ubiquitous secretaries, their offices. It was not an atmosphere conducive to rigorous examination of the available facts relating to the letter's publication and it is not surprising that the tone of the Cabinet committee's three-paragraph report on its authenticity, published after the Cabinet's last meeting, carried with it an air of bitter helplessness: 'Unfortunately, in the short time available, the committee find it impossible to obtain evidence throwing further light on the matter,' it concluded.

When the Conservatives took over, their first problem seemed straightforward enough. The issue of the Zinoviev letter had to be anaesthetized, and the best way of doing it seemed to be with a Cabinet committee of their own. Moreover, since the Labour Party was certain to attack the letter in the House, they themselves would welcome some evidence to support their emotional conviction that it was genuine. But first the new Government had to define a policy towards Soviet Russia, and, more particularly, towards the Bolshevik representative in London, Christian Rakovsky. This was less simple than it might seem.

The Russian issue caused the first split among members of Baldwin's new Cabinet. The source of the division was an unpredictable politician who had not even been a member of the Conservative Party at the beginning of 1924, yet who ended the year as the Tory Chancellor of the Exchequer – Winston Churchill. (His sudden burst surprised him as much as anybody. When Baldwin offered him the Chancellorship, Churchill assumed that it was of the Duchy of Lancaster.) His stance on the Russian issue was somewhat paradoxical even on his record: coming from the Liberals he adopted a position on the Bolsheviks which symbolized the Conservative right. And it caused the new Foreign Secretary, Austen Chamberlain, considerable trouble. By the third week in November, Chamberlain, a cautious and thoughtful Foreign Secretary, had begun to doubt the wisdom of the Churchill appointment to the Treasury.

Churchill's broadside on the Zinoviev affair was fired in a letter to Chamberlain on 14 November, a copy of which he carefully sent to Baldwin to guard against it being conveniently pigeon-holed by the Foreign Office. It is a classic example of inter-war Churchilliana, worth quoting in full.

I cannot help feeling [he wrote] that the decision about Russia involves a very critical issue for the Government. When millions have been so excited on the subject during the election, it would be dangerous to disappoint their reasonable expectations and to lead them to suppose that now we are in office we have receded from the views we expressed during the campaign. Failure on the part of a Government to respond to the mandate given to them by the electors would immediately cause widespread dissatisfaction. The Labour Party would be swift to point the moral, i.e. that we had only used the Russian bogy to frighten the electors into giving us their votes, and that the moment we were ourselves responsible we made very little change in the policy of our predecessors. Such an impression would affect the prestige of the Government from the very outset. Moreover, we shall in all probability state that we believe the Zinoviev letter to be authentic, and that it is only part and parcel of the propaganda increasingly pursued by the Soviets. If we say this it follows that we believe the Bolsheviks have broken their solemn agreements under which they were admitted into this country both in the days of the Krassin mission and in those of Rakovsky. If they have thus broken their engagements, and attempted to stir up rebellion in our midst, what grounds are there that can justify our proceeding to allow them to remain here? The representatives of no other country would be permitted to remain if convicted in our opinion of similar offences. I am certain that no mere Note or answer will by itself be sufficient to satisfy either justice or public opinion. It is essential that *action* should follow a declaration of the authenticity of the Zinoviev letter. The question is what action. The more I reflect on the matter, the more I am sure that we should revoke the recognition of the Soviet Government which was decided upon by MacDonald.

Churchill's bombast was extreme by any standards, though it is notable that even so fervent an anti-Communist was unwilling to face the commercial consequences of a break in diplomatic relations. 'The trade delegation could remain,' he wrote later in his letter to Chamberlain. But Rakovsky should not. The break, however, was not meant to last for ever. 'It would not be an irrevocable act,' Churchill concluded, 'because if, after a few years, it was found that the Soviet Government had desisted from propaganda in the British Empire, recognition could again be extended.'

Chamberlain was also under pressure from others. The Home Secretary, Sir William Joynson-Hicks, wrote on the same day demanding a decision. His posture was less militant, however. 'I assume,' he wrote to Chamberlain, 'the Treaties are so dead that we shall not put them before Parliament for ratification.' The Foreign Secretary was non-committal. 'I'm afraid I can't give you any enlightenment at the moment on the course we shall pursue as regards our Russian policy,' he replied. 'I am busy studying the problem, but am not as yet ready to make proposals to the Cabinet.' With Churchill he remained cautious, but the implication of his reply on 17 November was that he would strongly oppose the Chancellor's militancy when the issue was discussed by the Cabinet: 'I do not wish that either I myself or my colleagues should form any precipitate decision, but the step you propose, which amounts, I suppose, to handing Rakovsky his passport, and recalling our representative in Moscow, is a very grave one. Clearly this is not a matter to be decided without grave thought.'

Equally clearly, however, Chamberlain's grave thoughts were being produced with some haste. Within five days he announced that the Treaties would go, but that Rakovsky would stay. The peremptorily worded note to Rakovsky on 21 November ('I have the honour to inform you that after due deliberation his Majesty's Government find themselves unable to recommend the treaties in question to the consideration of Parliament or to submit them to the King for His Majesty's ratification'), was, in fact, a victory for his own relatively moderate policy.

It was a victory which seemed to please most shades of political opinion. The exceptions were the Labour Party, which saw in it the destruction of the policy on which they had lavished most time and energy in the previous ten months, and the small, Churchillian wing of the Tories. On 22 November, Lloyd George actually wrote to Chamberlain to congratulate him on his victory. 'May I say how delighted I am that whilst you have sent a very firm communication to the Soviets you have not listened to the wild counsels that would urge the expulsion of their representatives.' The wildest counsellor of them all, frustrated by his defeat on the Government's Russian policy, turned his attention to intelligence cables: he felt the Chancellor ought to see them, he complained. But he lost that battle too.

In December, Labour's spirits began to revive. Their fragmented and bewildered reaction to the letter was replaced by approval for one explanation of it: that they had been the victims of a plot of wicked complexity.

The Labour Party has always had an institutional weakness for plot theories. In their present dilemma this suited them admirably. The notion of a plot provided a straightforward rationalization for a bad defeat which was easily assimilated by the faithful. The need to find proof for this explanation of the affair was first fuelled two weeks before Christmas when the subject was discussed in the Commons.

In the early 'twenties, the contacts between the Labour Party and the Trades Union Congress were closer than they are now. Similarly, the contacts between the TUC and the Russian Bolsheviks had not yet been diminished by the excesses of the Cold War. In November a TUC delegation visited Moscow, and it conceived its duty to be to help its Labour and Soviet friends by conducting an investigation into the authenticity of the letter.

Zinoviev himself suggested that they examine the Comintern's files to see if they could see any sign of the letter he had

147

supposedly sent to Britain. The delegation did so, and in an interim report published on 9 December, duly stated that there was no evidence that any such document had been despatched at the relevant time. In fact, 'no document even remotely similar in character to the allegedly Zinoviev letter left Moscow, or any Soviet or other department, bearing Zinoviev's signature, during the period referred to in the [British newspaper] report'. The letter, they concluded, was without doubt a forgery.

Admittedly, if Zinoviev actually had written the letter, it would have been uncommonly foolish of him to leave it in the Comintern files for the TUC delegation to discover. But his open-handed invitation was similar to a whole series of desperate efforts by the Russians to persuade the British to start a serious inquiry. As early as 8 November, Rakovsky urgently requested Chamberlain to submit the case to an impartial arbitration court. Just before Christmas, after skirmishes in the Commons during which the Home Secretary had claimed that proof of authenticity could not be made public because it would endanger the life of the person who supplied the letter to the Government, Chicherin, the Soviet Foreign Minister, blandly offered 'the person' a guarantee of unhindered departure from the Soviet Union.

Armed with the TUC's evidence, the Labour Party was able to manufacture a considerable volume of outrage when Stanley Baldwin made his first Parliamentary statement about the letter on 10 December. The authenticity of the letter had been considered by a Cabinet committee, he said, which had reached the unanimous conclusion that there was no doubt about it. The Prime Minister curtly rejected demands that documentary evidence to support the decision be given to the House.

Labour's attack was led by Clynes. It is not enough, he said, that the Conservatives should ask the Labour Party to believe their conclusions without revealing any of their evidence. The taunt was answered not by Baldwin but by Joynson-Hicks, one of the more fervently anti-Communist Tory diehards, once described as that rare specimen, an intelligent backwoodsman.

Joynson-Hicks solemnly revealed the names of the Cabinet committee. It comprised the Lord Chancellor (Viscount Cave), an ex-Lord Chancellor (Lord Birkenhead), the Foreign Secretary (Chamberlain), the ex-Foreign Secretary (Lord Curzon),

148

and Lord Cecil, the Chancellor of the Duchy of Lancaster. The idea of a group of socialist upstarts wanting elaboration from so imposing a group of Tory peers obviously upset the Home Secretary. 'We who were not on the committee were prepared to accept the statement they made to us that they, as men of *business*, were convinced that the letter was a genuine letter and not a forgery,' he said [authors' italics]. The suggestion that the 'men of business' might have produced a whitewash induced in him intensely righteous indignation.

But his touching faith in his colleagues was not enough to close the matter. Five days later Chamberlain spoke mysteriously about the involvement of the secret service. 'It is the essence of the secret service that it must be secret,' he said. But then he disclosed some of its alleged secrets to support the Cabinet committee's conclusion.

This is the fullest account the Tories were to give of the letter's origins for three and a half years, and since 1924 it has been produced as one of the most convincing arguments in favour of the letter's authenticity:

> The letter was first received by the Government from one source. We know its whole course of origin until it reached our hands. The next thing that happened was, that information was received by the Government of the existence of this letter from another source, wholly independent of, and wholly unconnected with, the first source, and which did not know that we had any prior indication that there was such a letter at all.
>
> The next stage was that from a third source, independent of both the others, not knowing either of the others and unknown to them, we got further evidence confirmatory of the authenticity of the document; and the last stage was that from a fourth source, independent of the first three, we got further confirmatory evidence.
>
> I would like to add that the sources from which we obtained this evidence were not casual visitors to the Foreign Office who arrived with a document to sell, but were people who were known to us and whose trustworthiness we have been in a position to prove over a space of time longer or shorter in the different cases.

But not one of these alleged sources was to be named until 1928 (and even then the name was unsatisfactory). This was certainly not enough to assuage the opposition's anger.

Although MacDonald still vacillated ('my own position is – authenticity is not proved'), Clynes and Thomas continued to press the case for an inquiry by bluntly and repeatedly claiming that the letter was forged.

The Government, however, refused to be drawn into another round of dispute by Clynes's claim that if the letter was really genuine they ought to charge MacManus with treason. And after the Christmas recess Labour could find no way of forcing the subject on to the floor of the House again.

Earlier in the month there had in fact been another disclosure which was to quicken Labour's hopes of an inquiry, although members of the Parliamentary Party knew nothing about it during the December debates. The *Daily Herald* had received a telephone call from a Labour Party agent in Islington. A young woman had come to him with an extraordinary story about none other than J. D. Gregory, head of the Northern Department at the Foreign Office. Was the *Herald* interested? the agent asked. Obviously it was, and the young woman was brought to the *Herald*'s office and introduced to the Foreign Editor, W. N. (Trilby) Ewer.

The girl said her name was Violet Digby, and she had worked as a servant for a woman named Mrs Dyne who lived in Earls Court. Ewer, by luck, recognized the name instantly. During the breakdown of the Anglo–Russian trade talks in August, he had been asked by Gregory to meet him for a drink. When they met Gregory was with a woman: 'She looked like all the glamorous spies I had seen on the films,' he recalled in 1967. The woman was introduced as Mrs A. Bradley Dyne, and Gregory was completely unconcerned by her presence while he leaked confidences about the treaty negotiations to the Foreign Editor.

Violet Digby confirmed Ewer's own opinion of Gregory's relationship with Mrs Dyne; it was obviously intimate. (Later, in 1937, it emerged in a court hearing about a financial dispute between Mrs Dyne and Gregory, that Mr Dyne had considered suing his wife for divorce, and naming Gregory as co-respondent.) But the relationship was financial as well; the girl told the *Herald* that the two were heavily involved in financial speculation in French francs with a firm named Iremonger's. Mrs Dyne had told her they had lost a lot of money, and that

Gregory would have to leave the Foreign Office, and get a job elsewhere. That, the girl claimed, was about 21 October 1924.

The statutory declaration which Ewer persuaded her to sign on 11 December concluded quite dramatically:

> On Saturday, October 25 Mrs Dyne called attention to Mr Gregory's photo in the paper. . . . On the same day Mrs Dyne spoke to her bank manager on the telephone and asked if he could wait. She mentioned the sum of 60,000 francs, and said it would be alright. About this time Mrs Dyne said Mr Gregory did it when the Prime Minister's back was turned. On Monday, October 27, Mrs Dyne said that MacDonald would get thrown out, and Mr Gregory had made his name. Mr Gregory should have come to London, but Mrs Dyne said he had phoned up to say that he had gone to Cardiff to see Mr MacDonald. On Tuesday night, October 28, Mr Gregory came with a man aged about 40, a foreigner. Mr Gregory said laughing 'Come into the plot.' They went into the room together, staying until about 9 p.m., when the Russian left. They appeared to be very pleased and coming out Mrs Dyne said 'Come, we are fifty-fifty in this situation.'

The implication to be drawn from the dates and names was obvious to Ewer. Gregory, with the help of a White Russian, had tricked MacDonald into permitting the certification and publication of the Zinoviev letter. His motives might have been financial gain, but even then Ewer suspected that Gregory was more interested in the destruction of Anglo–Soviet relations.

The *Herald* decided they could not publish Violet Digby's testimony. There was no corroborating evidence to support a plea of justification in the libel action which would inevitably ensue. So Ewer gave the declaration to MacDonald. Even with his record of evading the Zinoviev issue, MacDonald's reaction was remarkable. He dismissed the evidence as the unreliable backstairs gossip of a discharged servant girl. But he decided that the honourable course would be to send it to the Foreign Office so the rumours could be tested by officials instead of misused by politicians.

What followed emerged in an article by Lord Castlerosse in the *Sunday Express* which, from internal evidence, was based on an off-the-record interview between Gregory and Castlerosse.

Castlerosse, incidentally, rejected the conformist journalistic belief that there is no story in the method a reporter uses to get a story. He reported on how Gregory's butler opened the door and said hoarsely: 'Mr Gregory left for the country this morning.' 'Barnes,' Castlerosse replied, 'it grieves me to hear you telling an untruth in such a hoarse voice. Is Mr Gregory in his drawing room or his study?' Barnes looked at him reprovingly. 'Mr Gregory is in the drawing room, and as for my loss of voice, it has been caused by overmuch telephoning,' he replied.

According to the article, Gregory was told by Crowe of the accusations made by the Labour Party. Crowe, it seems, did not take the accusations seriously, but suggested that Gregory go to see MacDonald. But when Gregory did so, MacDonald refused to discuss the situation. Castlerosse's report states laconically: 'They parted on bad terms.' And although he later denied it, it seems that Sir Austen Chamberlain saw Gregory too. 'I assume this is servants' tittle-tattle,' he is reported to have asked Gregory. Gregory agreed without hesitating.

Gregory had a slightly more troublesome interview with Thomas, who taxed him for forty-five minutes with all the details of the Digby declaration. Thomas himself described the occasion during the Commons debate in 1928. 'Now look here, Gregory,' he began, 'this is the kind of thing that is going about, and it is only fair you should know it, and I'm taking the straightforward course of showing it to you right away.' Gregory's reaction to the statutory declaration was just as simple. 'There is not a vestige of truth in it, it is not only absurd and ridiculous, but the facts are that Mrs Dyne's husband was a college chum of mine, and I merely visited his house.' 'I accept that unreservedly,' Thomas replied pompously.

The next attempt to revive the issue was in May 1925. The Parliamentary Labour Party decided that since the Government would do nothing, they would conduct their own inquiry. Thomas was one of the 'inquiry's' three members. He was balanced by the appointment of Maxton. The third member was an obscure back bencher named W. Graham.

It was a futile exercise. Declarations were received from Mac-Manus and Zinoviev swearing that the letter was a forgery. The inquiry, naturally, accepted their denials, but its own conclusion that the letter was forged did not carry conviction outside the haunts of the party faithful.

From Labour's point of view, in fact, there was only one positive outcome from the Zinoviev affair in the two years following the 1924 defeat. At its Conference in 1925, the party took the opportunity to hack away its last ties with the British Communist Party, thereby removing at least one pretext for anyone ever again to accuse the Socialists of truckling to Moscow.

Without stretching causation too far, it is possible to see the impact of the Zinoviev affair on the whole broad future of democratic socialism in Britain. The decision to refuse Communists the Labour umbrella in electoral politics was a critical moment in the transformation of the Labour Party into the mass democratic organization which permanently replaced the Liberals in the two-party system. No one would suggest that the Zinoviev affair was a sole cause of this. But it was, emotionally at least, a significant factor in the ostracism of the CP.

The 1925 inquiry temporarily ended Labour's attempt to prove the letter a fraud. By the following year there were far more important events to perturb the party. On 4 May 1926 the class war was concentrated into the nine days of the General Strike. The Conservative Government took on the Labour movement and defeated it. And in doing so they managed to whip up the fury among their supporters about Bolshevik interference. In an atmosphere of hysteria, the report that Soviet money was being used to finance trade unions seemed a predictable element in a pattern which began with the Zinoviev letter and would end, unless right-minded men did something to combat it, in bloody Russian-style revolution.

The atmosphere was tense enough to encourage the Tory Government in the following year to raid Arcos, the Russian trading mission in London. It was suspected of concealing Soviet espionage in Britain. Scotland Yard's special branch found long lists of British seamen who had served in Russian ships. But the tone of the comments on these lists hardly conjured up a convincing picture of hell-bent revolutionaries. 'Good agitator, bad stoker' was about the extent of the inflammatory material uncovered. Nevertheless, the Arcos raid gave the Conservative Government the flimsy excuse for finally demolishing the diplomatic links between Britain and the Soviets so lovingly built up by Labour in 1924. Diplomatic relations were cut off completely; even trade relations, which were still highly prized by any British industrialist with any stake in them, were severely damaged.

In 1927 came the Moscow trial, in which the Soviets produced tentative and, as it has turned out, accurate evidence of a man who admitted that the letter was forged by 'two Russian exiles'. It aroused astonishingly little interest in Britain. It seemed that Labour, like MacDonald when he was in office, was drugged by a conventional scepticism of Soviet evidence. Only Clynes, of the leaders, kept worrying away at the letter's authenticity. And when he conscientiously tried to persuade readers of *The Times* correspondence column that the letter was a forgery, A. P. Herbert, a regular contributor even then, found it only too easy to make him look silly.

The most curious episode of 1927 was the publication in collected Foreign Office papers of Gregory's Note to Rakovsky. What startled the Opposition was the presence of Ramsay MacDonald's signature at the bottom of the text. When the error was pointed out, in a Commons question from Ponsonby, the Foreign Office admitted its mistake. There were no accusations of skulduggery; it seemed too trivial a point on which to reopen the whole controversy yet again.

However, on 30 January 1928 the affair was suddenly transformed into an irresistible political issue again. The event responsible for this transformation took place in the unlikeliest of locations. In the King's Bench Division of the High Court, a seemingly simple case was heard involving a firm of bankers called Messrs Iremonger and Co., and a currency speculator named Mrs Aminta M. Bradley Dyne. It would normally have rated only two or three paragraphs in newspapers, even though it involved the considerable sum of £39,000. What made the Dyne case so different was that it implicated her Foreign Office friend, J. D. Gregory.

In the opening speech for the defence, Sir Henry Maddocks mentioned that Mrs Dyne had actually been introduced to Iremonger's by Gregory. Not only had he introduced her, Sir Henry continued, but he had speculated in the market value of French francs (the object was to buy them cheaply on credit and sell them at a profit before actually paying any cash when the value of French currency on the International exchange markets rose). Nor was the indiscretion relieved by the fact that Gregory's losses amounted to £9,000. 'Mr Gregory knew less than I did about selling what you hadn't got,' said Mrs Dyne naïvely when she gave evidence. 'In fact he knew less about business than anyone I know. It sounds very extraordinary, but it is so.'

To the Foreign Office it was an unforgivable breach that Gregory should have speculated at all. As soon as news of the evidence reached the FO, around tea time on the 30th, Crowe's successor as Permanent Secretary, Lord Tyrell, outraged that even an unproven suspicion of scandal should be directed at one of his most senior officials, peremptorily told Gregory to leave the office at once. It had all the makings of a dreadful scandal, and Tyrell did not want sly newspaper reporters loitering the corridors in the hope of interviewing Gregory.

But the affair was more than an inconvenience. Gregory seemed to have trodden all the tenets of civil service behaviour into the ground, as had Maxse, a member of his department, who had also been named as a speculator by Mrs Dyne. Within two days the Prime Minister's office announced that an inquiry would be held into the statements given in evidence in the law courts. The august investigating team was led by Sir Warren Fisher, Permanent Secretary to the Treasury, who was joined by the Comptroller and Auditor General, Sir Malcolm Ramsay, and the Treasury Solicitor, M. L. Gwyer.

At this point there was no suspicion that the inquiry was to revive the issue of the Zinoviev letter. Except among a few Labour politicians for whom the names of Gregory and Dyne rang a loud and persistent bell, the mention of the Foreign Office official who had played such a controversial role in 1924 was regarded as purely coincidental.

Fisher was scandalized at the thought of a Foreign Office official with access to the confidential cables speculating in foreign currency, and set about the task of rooting out any other offenders with considerable zeal. All members of the FO were circulated and asked if they had done the same thing: a couple had and were censured, but the only other name of importance to emerge during Fisher's hearing was that of Owen O'Malley,

155

another member of the Northern Department. The idea of speculation, so Fisher alleged, was actually initiated by him. Gregory had merely followed his example, though he eventually committed more and lost more.

But the inquiry's probe into currency speculation suddenly and unexpectedly changed course when two new witnesses asked to be heard: Ramsay MacDonald and J. H. Thomas. Both explained how they had come into the possession of Violet Digby's statutory declaration a little over three years earlier. Fisher immediately broadened the scope of the inquiry to discover whether Gregory had been involved in a conspiracy to defeat the Labour Government.

When the Fisher inquiry reported on 27 February, after only four weeks' work, Gregory was dismissed from the Foreign service. O'Malley was permitted to resign but he was allowed to return to the Foreign Office only a year later, after privately convincing Fisher of his innocence. He is still alive to describe the meeting at which he changed Fisher's mind. After it, Fisher went to endless trouble to clear O'Malley's name. Maxse was severely reprimanded and forfeited three years' seniority.

The politically stimulating section of the report was in its tail, which contained a brief and occasionally illuminating section on the Zinoviev letter. Despite the accuracy of Violet Digby's assertions about Gregory's currency speculation with Mrs Dyne, and Gregory's false denials to MacDonald, Thomas and Crowe that he was involved in speculation, the Fisher committee brusquely dismissed charges that there was a plot to publish the letter. 'We say frankly that we do not believe that Mrs Dyne ever said on October 25 or at any time that "Mr Gregory did it while the Prime Minister's back was turned" unless she was merely repeating current gossip.' As for the mysterious Russian, he was, 'we are satisfied, not a Russian at all but a foreign diplomat of another nationality who had long been a personal friend of Mr Gregory and his family.'

MacDonald's immediate reaction to the report was another masterpiece of equivocation. He would not cast any doubt on Sir Eyre Crowe – 'the soul of personal honour and official rectitude' – nevertheless, he added, all the hullabaloo over the letter in October 1924 was 'a stunt'.

The Parliamentary Labour Party acted less hesitantly, however. On the 28th, they demanded a new inquiry, and Mac-Donald agreed to ask for a House of Commons debate on the section of the Fisher Report dealing with Zinoviev. The weight of the forthcoming attack, begun by the faithful *Daily Herald*, was in fact at a slight tangent to the report. The mysterious link was still unsolved: 'How,' the *Herald* asked, 'did the *Daily Mail* get the Red Letter?' On 29 February Baldwin granted Labour time for a debate on the Fisher report, and on Sunday, 4 March, Labour was provided with the material which gave it potential control of the debate. Marlowe's account of how as editor of the *Mail* he got his copies was published in the *Observer*. We now know how selective his disclosures were. But at the time it was ostensibly the authoritative account of a transaction which, by implication, involved civil servants. It filled news columns for several days.

Marlowe refuted the natural allegation by the Labour Party that the whole affair was a classic example of cheque-book journalism. He also dealt with the widespread belief that Gregory was involved. He said that MacDonald told private detectives assigned to investigate the affair that Gregory had been paid £5,000 for the document. It was a possible deduction from the circumstantial evidence: Gregory was obviously in need of money in October 1924. But Marlowe dismissed the allegation with considerable indignation:

I know nothing about Mr Gregory's circumstances. I have never seen him to my knowledge, or had any communication with him, direct or indirect, and I did not pay him or any other person £5,000, or any other sum for the Zinoviev letter. The men I dealt with were gentlemen to whom I could not offer money, and who would have been gravely affronted if I had done so. The Zinoviev letter did not cost me a single penny, and I may add that in forty years of journalism every bit of important news I ever had was obtained on the same terms.

But Marlowe's account failed to satisfy the curiosity of the opposition. MacDonald responded by stating that the integrity of civil servants was now at stake: there must be an inquiry. Later in the week Baldwin announced that the debate would be on the 19th. All demands for an inquiry should wait until then.

But pressure for an inquiry was building up in a way which must have disturbed the Tories. They began to search for a fuller explanation. They did not share the complacency of Lord Rothermere, publisher of the *Daily Mail*, who wrote an article in the *Sunday Pictorial* stating that the public was being 'bored to tears by incessant demands for inquiries and investigations which can reveal nothing new'. The Tories, perhaps believing that there was something new to reveal, took the 19 March debate rather more seriously.

13

The Debate: How Baldwin Destroyed MacDonald

The debate fixed for 19 March was on the following motion: 'That, in the opinion of this House, certain disclosures contained in the Board of Inquiry appointed to investigate certain statements affecting civil servants, and other disclosures made subsequently, regarding what is known as the Zinoviev letter, are of national importance and concern and should be made the subject of an inquiry by a body empowered to take evidence on oath, to send for witnesses and papers, and to report.'

The specific question revived by the Fisher report was the circulation of the letter rather than its authenticity. This was the aspect which MacDonald himself, in his ambivalent way, always seemed to think the most important. As he repeated yet again in his response to Marlowe's disclosures, he had never formed a definite conclusion as to authenticity. The significant point was 'the use to which the document was put'. Nevertheless, the forgery question could not be excluded. As the issue hit the headlines during March 1928, this was what Labour M.P.s remembered even more vividly than the question of how the *Daily Mail* got its copy.

The *Morning Post* was quick to scoff at Labour's inquiring zeal: 'Like some unhappy ghost, condemned to expiate a sin on earth by continually re-enacting its misdeed, the Labour Party returns to the Zinoviev letter.' And the party was certainly in a tricky position. It was not oversupplied with ammunition.

After all, if there were errors of judgement at the Foreign

Office they came when Labour itself was in power and Mac-Donald himself was the responsible Minister. From the beginning he had vacillated on the question of authenticity and straddled an awkward fence on the question of circulation. He had defended his civil servants, notably Crowe, from all charges of disloyalty. He had, in effect, forced such an exoneration through the last Cabinet of the 1924 Government. He had accepted Crowe's own defence of Gregory. He had even felt obliged to repudiate Marlowe's implication that Government servants had made confidential documents available to the press. Yet despite all this, he was trying to raise suspicions that somehow the letter had fallen improperly into the hands of the *Mail* and the Tory Party. Admittedly, new information had appeared, in the form of Violet Digby's statutory declaration. And a new pretext had arisen from the appearance of the Fisher report itself. But these together scarcely constituted an irresistible new case for an inquiry.

Labour did make one curious new attempt to equip itself more richly. It is described by Hugh Dalton, in his memoirs, *Call Back Yesterday.*

A week before the debate, MacDonald received a 'confidential letter' from Paris, from a man called Dombrovsky. It offered to put at the party's disposal some real information about the true origin of the letter. 'The English of the Dombrovsky letter is so bad,' Dalton remarked in his diary at the time, 'that we can't make out whether the suggestion is that the document is forged or genuine.' Nevertheless, determined to leave no stone unturned, the Parliamentary executive sent Tom Shaw, former Minister of Labour, to Paris by the next train. 'Quite like a film story!' thought Dalton.

On the 15th, Shaw returned to tell the executive what he had found. Dombrovsky turned out to be a professional forger, and also, incidentally, a 'tuberculous degenerate'. His real name was Riczevsky. He and a companion claimed to Shaw that they had forged the Zinoviev letter themselves, and sold it to a person whose photograph they had kept but whose name they did not know. The purchaser, they claimed, said he was acting for the British secret service.

This pair certainly had the credentials for the job. They said that they had often dealt with the Spanish and Portuguese

Governments, for example, and forged documents to order. In 1925 they were denounced by the Soviet Ambassador in Paris, and in fact found guilty of forgery by the French police. By nationality they were Russian. They had once worked, they said, for the White Russians, who had now dropped them.

Their proposal to Shaw was this. They offered him 'an exact copy of the forged Zinoviev letter, including the signatures and a dossier showing how the business was handled by them'. In return they wanted the princely sum of £20 – although Shaw had already paid them several hundred francs for the privilege of meeting them.

At one point, the Labour leaders seriously contemplated taking up the offer. Dalton writes, on the 15th: 'At a meeting this morning of J.R.M., J.H.T., and Maxton – the speakers in Monday's debate – with Shaw and Ponsonby, it was agreed that Shaw ought to go back to Paris and pay £20 for this dossier.'

However, desperate as it was for evidence, the party had second thoughts, stimulated mainly by Thomas. Thomas realized that 'if these rascals are double-crossing us, and the Government here know what is happening', it would be embarrassing to be challenged with the fact that the party had just sent a former Cabinet Minister to Paris 'to pay £20 to bribe two White Russian spies'. A second meeting was called, at which Thomas, seconded by Dalton, proposed that further action be postponed until after the debate. Trevelyan, Tom Johnston and Sidney Webb supported this. It was opposed by Snowden, Lansbury, Shaw and one other, with MacDonald himself absent. Thus, by five votes to four, they backed Thomas's instinct. Dalton describes this as 'certainly right' and adds: 'Apart from all else, how convenient for the Tories to be able to sidetrack the whole debate from the leak to the *Daily Mail* back to the authenticity of the letter!'

(After the debate, Dalton was to note: 'Baldwin, in the course of his speech, said that he understood we were going to produce an affidavit by the real forgers of the Z. letter. At this point Uncle [Henderson] nudged me on the bench and winked. Weren't we wise to stop Tom Shaw before he had committed us too far!')

Not that the Conservatives felt any more sanguine about the

161

forthcoming debate. At Palace Chambers a new generation of party managers had taken over the machine. Baldwin himself was still the leader, but the principal engineers of the Red scare which was now about to be re-examined had moved on. In particular, Younger had retired and Jackson was Governor of Bengal. Thus, the two key men who had negotiated the agreement the Tories had reached with Donald im Thurn – and almost certainly the only two in Central Office who knew of it at the time – were not available to help Baldwin devise his strategy.

In their place had come two men of a very different colour from the wily, unscrupulous Scottish brewer and the English cricketer. As chairman, Baldwin had appointed in 1927 J. C. C. Davidson, his right-hand man and closest intimate. Davidson's brief was to clean up the party, and bring it out of the era of the sale of honours and related scandals which had tainted the Younger regime.

In addition, one of Davidson's first acts as chairman was to introduce into Central Office a man who was to prove one of its most potent officials for the next ten years, Major Joseph Ball. Ball had spent the war in intelligence, and they had met in the course of Davidson's duties as Bonar Law's link with the secret service. Ball stayed in the service throughout the early 'twenties, but in 1927 Davidson succeeded in seducing him away to be the party's new Director of Publicity. A burly, slightly sinister figure, Ball was a highly experienced behind-the-scenes operator, who throughout his life succeeded in keeping remarkably well clear of the public eye. He was, in fact, the classic Tory *éminence grise*.

From the start he was quite clearly Davidson's man, and undoubtedly the most unusual Tory publicity director before or since, not least because he was so much more than a routine public relations officer. Moreover, in March 1928 he was joined by another top public servant, Sir Patrick Gower, who had served successively Bonar Law, MacDonald and Baldwin in the private office at No. 10. This appointment caused a minor furore. Snowden talked of the 'impropriety, if not the indecency' of a transaction by which a trusted prime ministerial servant left government for party. But, whatever the irregularity, the combination in office of a former senior secret service

162

officer and a former private secretary to three premiers was a coup which no party has repeated.

Ball was later to become the first Director of the Research Department, and, in the Second World War, deputy director of the Security Executive. In 1928, one of his first tasks was to take over and if possible eliminate a situation which, as a recently discharged intelligence officer, he was perhaps uniquely well qualified to master: the embarrassment of the Zinoviev letter.

Shortly before the 19 March debate, Ball received a visit from an obscure Tory backbencher who – as no one at Palace Chambers was in a position to remember – was the only man besides Younger and Jackson who had witnessed the transactions of 1924. This, of course, was Major Guy Kindersley, the City friend of Donald im Thurn and the man who introduced him to the party leaders at the beginning of the 1924 election.

Kindersley, it will be recalled, later wrote his own account of the Zinoviev affair as he saw it. This is especially valuable in its description of what happened in 1928. Kindersley, believing throughout that the letter was authentic, was not, of course, able to do more than sketch the surface of the episode. But he told more of the truth than at least some of the participants, including Ball himself, thought desirable. The evidence of this is that, after he had completed his history in 1956, Kindersley sent copies to both Ball and Davidson inviting their comments. He told them that he proposed to offer it to the *Daily Mail* for publication. Ball's reply survives among the Kindersley papers. In it, Ball claims that his own memory of some of the 1928 details differs from Kindersley's. He accordingly appends his own revised version which, oddly enough, does little else but exclude every reference to Ball himself. The timetable of events is not queried, merely the disclosure of Ball's involvement. (Moreover, in an interview in 1966, Lord Davidson told the authors that it was Ball who persuaded Kindersley not to publish even the revised version.)

In view of the nature of Ball's excisions, it is reasonable to assume that Kindersley's original account was in fact all too accurate. Therefore, the original, rather than the revised, Kindersley history is the one to depend on.

It describes how, having called on Ball for another purpose,

Kindersley was told by him that the party was 'rather worried' about the approaching Zinoviev debate. 'And I could see,' Kindersley goes on, 'after one or two exploratory questions on my part that nothing was known in the Central Office about im Thurn's part in producing the letter. . . . I therefore told Ball that I thought I could put him in touch with somebody who would be able to throw a good deal of light on the matter.' In due course, the account says laconically, 'I introduced him to im Thurn.'

The Tories could not move fast enough to embrace this unheralded saviour. On the morning of the debate, he was duly produced by Kindersley at an exclusive little lunch arranged by the chairman, Davidson, at his house in North Street. Together with Ball, the party included Sir Douglas Hogg, the Attorney-General, and Baldwin himself.

If Kindersley is an accurate reporter, the first conversation between this obscure backbencher and his incredulous Prime Minister strained even the true Conservative gentleman's inborn facility for nerveless understatement. 'On my arrival,' he writes, 'I was shown upstairs to the drawing-room to find the Prime Minister already there and alone. He greeted me with the words: "Kindersley, this is the most extraordinary thing." I replied: "Yes, Sir, it is very interesting." He replied: "I don't mean that, but that you have kept your mouth shut all these years." "Well, Sir," I replied, "these sort of things are far too dangerous to talk about." ' Writing with hindsight Kindersley adds in a rare burst of melodrama: 'I always remember this, because it showed me in a flash that Stanley Baldwin never realized the full enormity of the Soviet system and the lengths to which its rulers are prepared to go to attain their ends, and how dangerous it is to cross their path. Had he done so things might be different today.'

Over lunch the conversation focused on how to make best use of im Thurn's disclosure. One suggestion was for Kindersley himself to make a statement about his and im Thurn's part in the affair. This was rejected on the grounds that the Opposition were certain to submit him to a possibly awkward cross-examination. In the end, it was decided that the Prime Minister should read a written statement prepared by im Thurn. The Conservatives, backed by a violently Tory press which was all

164

too keen to get rid of the issue, were poised to kill the Zinoviev issue and remove it from British politics for forty years.

The House was packed for the start of the debate. Peers and diplomats jostled for places in the galleries. The attendance of members was the largest for many months, and their mood was bitter.

MacDonald opened with a long justification of his handling of the letter as Foreign Secretary. Bearing in mind that an election was on, and he was out of town, it had been dealt with, as he had specified at the time, punctiliously. The normal Foreign Office procedures had been followed. Far from there ever having been any intention to suppress the letter, he had fully intended to publish once authenticity was established. The Tories had wilfully misled the public at the time. They had pretended that MacDonald had worked to conceal the letter, and that the Foreign Office had wilfully released it in order to embarrass MacDonald. When he had shown this to be false, and the FO action to be due to a mere 'misunderstanding', there had been 'still not a word of explanation and not a word of apology'.

MacDonald, in short, did not change his line. He still sought to claim, without precise specification and despite his own defence of his civil servants, that the letter had somehow entered the 1924 election by a fraud: 'This was a case of a successful conspiracy of a few people, some of them foreigners, including the controllers of their own [sic] newspapers, to influence the public mind, possibly by forgery, certainly by fraud, and to have the House of Commons elected in proportions that would have been very different but for that fraud.'

But in the end, to give his demand for an inquiry any force at all, MacDonald was forced to come out with the issue which he had all along been so reluctant to grasp. If Marlowe's story of how he got two copies of the letter was true, it meant that there was a 'systematic leakage of important State documents to certain newspapers from public offices'. MacDonald handled this implication by insisting on a distinction between the administrative and the intelligence sections of Whitehall. The letter had been circulated to the intelligence sub-departments of the Home Office, the War Office and the Admiralty, by their secret service colleagues at the Foreign Office.

MacDonald seemed to imply that, because of this, the Government of the day was relieved of responsibility; but that it was up to the present Government to establish that this diagnosis was correct. 'The position has gone so far,' MacDonald concluded, 'that it demands an inquiry, and, therefore, we would like to know how the letter came into the country, into whose hands it went, and who gave it to this newspaper.'

Despite the cheers from his own side, MacDonald had been diffuse and ranting. The insinuation, insofar as one can be picked out from the morass of tired oratory, seemed to be that someone in intelligence had delivered the letter to the *Mail*. But all MacDonald's familiar contradictions were there. Yet again he refused to commit himself to saying the letter was forged; but this did not deter him from using the argument that it might be, in order to goad the Government into setting the record straight. Yet again he dismissed the possibility of dishonour among his own civil servants; but Marlowe was castigated for his contacts among them, and the grounds for an inquiry were presented as being that 'rumours and tales . . . have shaken public confidence in the Civil Service'. Also, the spurious distinction between 'intelligence' and other Government servants had been made.

None of this made Baldwin's task any more arduous. In any case, with im Thurn's statement up his sleeve, the Prime Minister could afford some playful toying which enchanted his own backbenchers. He ridiculed MacDonald's handling of the episode in 1924, his failure to establish an inquiry then, and his folly in demanding one now. Marlowe, Baldwin said, could not be forced to divulge his sources. He could refuse to answer a Parliamentary committee, and could be put in the Clock Tower for it. But that would make Parliament a laughing stock, and would mobilize public opinion against it. After half-an-hour of easy laughs, Baldwin was firm: 'The Government refuse to lend themselves to an inquiry which can serve no national end and is foredoomed by its very nature to futility.'

Baldwin then played the card which made an inquiry seem not merely futile but redundant. Since the press, he said, was unable to speak, then one had to go to the man who gave the news to the press. As it happened, within the past forty-eight hours, the man who gave the news to Marlowe had come to the Government's attention. The ultimate source was from within the British Communist Party, but the news was possessed by a man unconnected with office and politics 'or with any of those things which make for conspiracy – a man in the City'. He knew about the letter forty-eight hours before it reached the 1924 government, and knew its contents in detail twenty-four hours before. 'He has made a statement,' Baldwin said, 'which I have had checked and verified so far as I have been able in the course of the last forty-eight hours. I met him three hours ago; I have never seen him before or heard his name . . . I will say before I read it that it is the statement of an honest and a patriotic man, and that I think the action of the *Daily Mail* was the action of a patriotic newspaper.'

Extracting the last drop of dramatic juice from the occasion, Baldwin read the statement without naming the man who had made it until the moment before he sat down. But nothing could have sounded sweeter to the Tories, nor more bewildering to the Opposition than the testimony of Donald im Thurn.

His statement began by saying that he had been released from his pledge of secrecy, made at the time to his own informant, and that he felt driven to come forward in order to answer the attacks being made on the integrity of the Army, the Navy and the civil service. He could now tell the country all the facts which he had known from the beginning.

On 8 October 1924, he had kept a business appointment with a man who happened to be in close touch with Communist circles in Britain. He was not a British official, and had never had any connection with any British Government service. At the end of their business, this man had told him of the arrival in this country of a letter sent from Moscow to the British Communist Party, from Zinoviev, who he knew as Apfelbaum. The statement continued:

> From his description of the contents of this letter I saw at once that the matter was serious, and in view of the incitements to sedition contained in it, I asked him if he could obtain for me the complete text of it. He said 'Yes' and gave me the complete text at approximately 9.30 a.m. on the following day, 9 October.
> On reading the letter, I was very indignant to find that at the time when the Labour Government was proposing to lend good British money to Moscow, as part of a treaty which they had

actually negotiated, Moscow was at that very moment engaged in fomenting sedition and revolution here. I was particularly incensed by their plans for conducting subversive propaganda in the Navy and Army.

I thereupon decided to do two things: (1) to bring the facts to the notice of the Government department mainly concerned, which I did; and (2) to communicate the information to the electorate of this country through the Press, as soon as my informant was able to settle his affairs here, and to get to a place of safety, for he assured me that his life would be in danger.

When the necessary arrangements for the safety of my informant had been made, I handed my copy of the letter not to the *Daily Mail* direct, but to a trusted City friend whom I knew to be in close touch with that newspaper, and requested him to arrange for publication. I would certainly do again, in similar circumstances, what I did then, and I am only too glad to think that I have been instrumental in placing the electorate in possession of the whole facts before they supported a policy of lending many millions of the taxpayers' money to a country which was, at that very moment, engaged in fostering sedition in the country.

The paragraph which seemed finally to give the lie to Labour's case was the last:

I would add that at no time did I obtain any information whatsoever with regard to the letter or its contents from any official source, and that from first to last I was solely responsible for obtaining the text of the letter and securing its subsequent publication in the *Daily Mail*. At no stage in these transactions did I receive any assistance from anyone employed in any capacity in any Government Department. I need hardly say that my action in this matter was dictated solely by patriotic motives and that at no time did I receive any payment or any other reward therefor.
signed: Conrad Donald im Thurn.

The Labour members were speechless. Their leaders retired to an upstairs room to review what remnants of a case they could still make. Against such a bombshell, there was no convincing retaliation to be made. Eventually, Thomas wound up, still gallantly pressing for an inquiry. But inevitably MacDonald's motion was resoundingly beaten: 326 votes to 132 – with every Liberal keeping out of the Opposition lobby.

The press, of course, was jubilant. The derision promised for MacDonald before the debate became gloating contempt after

Baldwin's triumph. 'An intolerable bore,' wrote *The Times*, welcoming the end of the affair. 'Mr MacDonald cut a sorry figure,' said the *Daily Telegraph* out of its crocodile tears: 'The net result of yesterday's debate on which the Opposition so madly insisted was to establish beyond all reasonable doubt the authenticity of what they declared to be a forgery.' The *Manchester Guardian* summed it up: 'Most people on the whole would probably be glad if they might never hear of the Zinoviev letter again.'

MacDonald himself, quixotic to the end, pronounced himself 'well satisfied'. The debate had proved, he thought, that every accusation made in the 1924 election was unfounded, and that the ordinary rules of political controversy were not to be applied when Labour was in office. He promised, on a final note of menace which appeared faintly ridiculous, that Labour would 'continue to keep its eyes and ears open so that in time the truth will be discovered'.

Even at the time, im Thurn's statement raised as many questions as it answered. But they were not taken up. To any observer who had kept his head, the glaring question must have been why, if the facts were so simple, innocent and honourable as im Thurn now said, were they not disclosed three years before when the rumours of conspiracy were at their height? And why should any business man living in England be forced to find a domicile where his life would not be in danger? What safer place existed? Just who, moreover, was Donald im Thurn?

On face value alone, the statement should have prompted the curiosity of its journalistic and political audience. Now, of course, it can be seen to be a tissue of lies and half-truths. But in March 1928, what was known, or might have been deduced, got lost in a cloud of public gratitude to the mysterious Mr im Thurn. All that mattered was that the issue was dead.

14

Pay-off: £5,000 from the Tories

Next day, 20 March, as Donald im Thurn left his house at 38 Eaton Terrace for the City, the inevitable group of reporters was standing at the bottom of the steps. They noted his spruce appearance and the deeply tanned features of a man who seemed to have spent long periods abroad (in fact, these were the sallowness of the invalid). They faithfully recorded that he was of medium height and less than middle age, and that he conducted 'a financial business on his own account' in St Mary Axe in the City. But considering that he was the hero of the hour they discovered remarkably little else about him, and still less about his dealings with the Zinoviev letter.

He told them that he had nothing to add to the statement he had given to Baldwin. He felt this was the end of the affair. 'I think it is in the interest of everybody that the matter should be dropped and buried. So far as I am concerned, it is done with,' he said. 'If I began talking about it now, things might be said which might be misunderstood and cause more bother.' He had no doubts about the letter's authenticity: 'Is it conceivable that a man in my position would have taken the steps I did in such a gravely important matter unless I felt definitely certain of the genuineness of the document?' Besides, he asked, wasn't it a remarkable coincidence that 'two days after I had a copy of the letter, the Foreign Office obtained one from an entirely independent source?'

Im Thurn explained that his motive in coming forward now was simply that the civil service was being submitted to 'grossly unfair attacks', which he could help to repudiate. As for his actions in 1924, it was quite accidental that he had been in a position to perform them. He had been acting entirely on his own, inspired by a patriotic belief that the letter should be exposed. Naturally he could offer no clues as to the identity of his informant, the business friend with Communist connections: 'There are the strongest reasons why it cannot be disclosed.'

With that, im Thurn hurried off to the Sloane Square underground station – and oblivion. The press penetrated no further into his past record or his present business. Few papers exhibited the slightest curiosity in him: it was enough that he had been Baldwin's confidant, and that Baldwin had vouched for his honour. Everyone seemed to understand that, of course, he could not reveal his own informant. These are delicate matters, they seemed to say, into which it is not for us to inquire too closely. Im Thurn himself avoided saying anything further. He disappeared entirely from the public eye.

The *Sunday Worker* looked for him in the Bankers' Almanac, the London Directory, and the Directory of Directors to establish precisely what he was in the City. They did not find him there, nor in the telephone directory, and they remarked on the 'queer secrecy' surrounding him. The *Daily News* reported that he was a 'lifelong Conservative with influential political connections'. But Sir Douglas Hogg, the Attorney-General, had emphasized in the House that he was unconnected with any political party, besides being in 'a very responsible position' and 'well known by the great bulk of City men'. The Press clutched eagerly at im Thurn's family connections: at Sir Everard im Thurn, his uncle and a former Governor of Fiji, at Captain John im Thurn, then commander of the Portsmouth signal school, and at Major Basil Bernhardt von Brumsi im Thurn of the Hampshires. Readers were assured that, although the name sounded foreign, the family represented the best in English public school tradition. But about Donald im Thurn himself, the little evidence dredged up was contradictory, and the rest was silence.

Despite the general atmosphere of complacency, a few of the more pressing questions were being asked. One came immediately from Chicherin, the Soviet Commissar for Foreign Affairs. How, asked Chicherin, in the course of an outright denial of Baldwin's statement, could the Prime Minister's reaffirmation of the letter's authenticity be reconciled with the known facts?

Baldwin had presented as new evidence of authenticity information which presumably came from the secret service. Baldwin had claimed that when news of publication reached Moscow on 25 October, Chicherin had told his colleagues that he had questioned Zinoviev about it. Zinoviev, according to Baldwin, had admitted sending it, but didn't know who had betrayed it to the British Government; the Soviets had decided to denounce it as a forgery, but had delayed their demand for an inquiry for a month, until they knew the original of the letter had been destroyed. As Chicherin did not delay to point out, the Soviet demand for an inquiry was made in Rakovsky's Note to the British Government of 27 October. Moscow was keen for independent arbitration from the beginning. It was patent nonsense to suggest that they didn't want an inquiry until the original had been destroyed, and equally false to deduce that therefore the Soviets had virtually admitted its authenticity.

Chicherin's statement provoked no reply. Other obvious questions received only the most cursory discussion. Im Thurn's statement explained how the *Mail* got one copy of the letter. Its other copy remained unaccounted for. The implication of Marlowe's account was that he had been able to conjure up copies merely by lifting the telephone. He had certainly had two, from different sources, available for publication on the afternoon of 24 October. So devastating was Baldwin's theatrical production of im Thurn that this anomaly was never felt to be serious. Nor was the fact, stated explicitly by Marlowe, that he had knowledge of precisely when the letter was circulated round Whitehall. He had been told by his original informant (whom we now know to be Reginald Hall) that it was distributed to the Home Office, the Admiralty and the War Office on 22 October. He had invited the other Fleet Street editors, to whom he had magnanimously circulated proofs of the *Mail* story, to check it at these departments or the Foreign Office.

Apart from the persistently sceptical *Daily Herald*, no one wondered how Marlowe knew this, or who had told him that the letter was also circulated to high officers in the Army and Navy. Had Marlowe been asked he would doubtless have refused to answer, as Baldwin foresaw in the debate, on the grounds of legitimate protection of his sources. The fact remained, however, that even in the light of the limited evidence

172

available at the time, Baldwin's speech was, as the *Herald* said, 'a curious combination of the red herring and the mare's nest'.

From the evidence now available it is clear that im Thurn's statement was substantially false, and that he himself was a far cry from the simple and accidental patriot. There are major discrepancies between his statement and his diary.

The sense of the statement is that he heard about the letter one day, got a copy the next, instantly informed a Government department, and delayed informing the *Mail* only until his informant had got out of the country. He appears as the very model of the ordinary citizen who seized the chance to serve his country. The message of the diary, of course, is very different, although it does not necessarily diminish from his patriotic motives.

According to the statement, he received a copy of the letter at 9.30 a.m. on 9 October 1924. According to the diary, he got no copy at any stage and on 9 October still had four days to wait before X told him the contents of the letter in detail. The essence of the diary, in fact, is its record of im Thurn prodding all the Whitehall levers he knew for two purposes, neither of which accords well with the thesis that he was the bringer rather than the seeker after information. His first purpose was to discover which departments knew about the letter; his second was to frighten the Government itself into publishing the letter.

The statement gives no indication of the two-week struggle to achieve this. Indeed, it tactfully pre-empts one of the main Labour charges, when it asserts firmly that at no stage did im Thurn receive 'any assistance from anyone employed in any capacity in any Government department'. Any suggestion of a co-operative endeavour, not to mention a conspiracy, was eliminated by im Thurn's assumption of 'sole responsibility' for obtaining the text of the letter and securing its publication in the *Mail*. This, again, was a laughable deception. Intelligence agents are just as much Government employees as are members of the Foreign Office, and clearly im Thurn was in contact with several of them, including C himself in October 1924. They were his vital sources of information about how the plans for circulation were materializing, and gave im Thurn, and hence the Tories, essential guidance on the matter of timing.

The story is similar on the central question at issue in the debate. The diary contains no evidence to support the claim that im Thurn, even through an intermediary, was the *Daily Mail*'s source. It is possible, on the evidence of his annotations to the newspaper clipping of Marlowe's letter, to argue that one of Marlowe's sources perhaps sought his approval before handing over a copy; but most of the evidence is against that conclusion. In any case, it is very different from saying that im Thurn himself gave the *Mail* its information. According to the diary, his only direct contact with Fleet Street was with *The Times*, not the *Mail* when he went to see Alan Pitt Robbins, *The Times*'s political correspondent. From then on, it was left to *The Times* to move. As late as 24 October, im Thurn records for the first time, in a tone which clearly indicates that his source was second-hand: ' "Daily Mail" knows something. Believe "Times" "Daily Mail" met late yesterday afternoon.' And, as has already been suggested, the *Mail*'s most likely source was MI1C.

Before Baldwin read im Thurn's apparently conclusive statement to the House he said that he had checked and verified it as far as possible in the previous forty-eight hours. Clearly his checking did not delve very deep. The events, after all, were three and a half years old. One of the principals who might have attested, for example, to im Thurn's immediate approach to a Government department – Sir Eyre Crowe – was dead. (Im Thurn had, significantly, left unnamed the specific department he went to, although he can only have meant to suggest the Foreign Office.) Gregory, the other man who could possibly have recalled this, had just been dismissed from the Service and was unlikely to welcome an approach for help from the Government. Equally, if corroboration was sought from the intelligence services it cannot have been thorough. Nor would they have had the slightest difficulty in concealing their own role.

It would also have been difficult to check with Marlowe, now retired from the *Mail*. He was in the south of France. In fact, Baldwin himself made heavy play of this in his speech, as he set the scene for im Thurn's disclosure. No one was more alert than he – unless it was MacDonald himself – to Marlowe's insinuations of misconduct by public servants in communicating information to newspapers. Baldwin dealt with this in cavalier fashion, by suggesting that Marlowe's memory, removed from his files and records in London, may have played him false. The Prime Minister noted, with more complacency than evidence, that Marlowe had got his dates wrong. He implied that any journalist might wish to embroider and exaggerate his contacts in the civil service, and concluded that there was 'absolutely no evidence of any sort that a communication of that kind was made, or need necessarily be made, by anyone connected with the public service'. Whatever the truth of this, the point is that Baldwin made a virtue out of the unavoidable absence of Marlowe, in a way which makes clear that he did not attempt to verify im Thurn's statement with the man who might have told him whether it was a true account.

In the end, the fact that Baldwin had little incentive and few means to check im Thurn's chronology of events is less important than the fact that the statement was read to the Commons in good faith. It contained one final assertion, however, which can now be seen to be more ambiguous than any which went before. This formed a satisfying conclusion to im Thurn's brief appearance on the Parliamentary scene, and a suitably rousing peroration to Baldwin's speech. But, unlike what went before, it was also an assertion which Baldwin, on the face of it, was in an excellent position to examine: 'I need hardly say,' he quoted im Thurn as saying, 'that my action in this matter was dictated solely by patriotic motives, and at no time did I receive any payment or any other reward therefor.'

When he disappeared into the Sloane Square underground on the morning of 20 March, im Thurn ended his public involvement with the Zinoviev letter. But his private activity, far from diminishing simultaneously, exhibited many of the signs of a man determined not to be robbed of his inheritance. In 1924 he had been of great, if not decisive, significance to the Tories. At least one man's life, he told them then, was put in peril by his action in getting the letter published. He had now kept the secret for three and a half years, and, with Kindersley, was the only man in London who could have given Baldwin the ideal excuse not to hold an inquiry. In 1924 he had sought and been given a 'guarantee against loss' by Lord Younger and Sir

175

Stanley Jackson, arranged ostensibly as a safeguard for his informant, X. Moreover, im Thurn had convinced himself, from an early date, that there was something – perhaps a knighthood – in it for him. Now in March 1928, the fate of that guarantee, not to mention the knighthood, suddenly acquired a new importance.

The evidence that the guarantee was given is stated quite clearly in the 15 October entry in the diary. It is reinforced by an entry on Sunday, 26 October, the day after publication: 'Saw Jackson in his private house re X.' What is not so clear is precisely when the guarantee was fulfilled.

Im Thurn revealed more details of the guarantee in a letter at the time to Kindersley. This was written very soon after 15 October, the day Younger and Jackson gave their promise. It discloses that the agreed total sum required by im Thurn was £10,000, to be supplied from two sources. 'Conditionally on (you know who) putting up not less than £7,500,' im Thurn wrote, 'a relation of mine has promised to add £2,500 making in all £10,000, and will allow me to draw up to a further £2,500 should I deem it necessary later on.'

The next paragraph was a little less mysterious: 'In approaching my relation I did not allow it to be thought that the Conservative Party had anything to do with it, in fact it was not mentioned, nor did I do further than just state a case without giving anything away, although my relation is most discreet. You will see by this that if the above is done there will be no necessity to ask —— for more than the £7,500, and the matter as far as —— is concerned is closed permanently.'

This of itself is not conclusive evidence that the Tories themselves had agreed to pay the £7,500. The 'you know who' could have been someone else. The letter goes on to indicate that negotiation over the sum was still going on. The letter appears, in fact, to be in the nature of an offer which Kindersley was to transmit: 'I think this is very satisfactory, at least it will be if I am placed in the position of being able to accept this outside offer.' Although the unnamed candidate for the £7,500 payment cannot be shown from this letter alone to be the Conservatives, it does show that the party was indissolubly linked to the deal. The 'relation' had agreed to guarantee £2,500, on condition that Kindersley's friends, whoever they were, found the rest.

While it is possible to prove that the principal guarantor was in fact the Conservative Party itself, the identity of the 'relation' referred to by im Thurn cannot be firmly established. It was obviously somebody or some organization dedicated to the anti-Bolshevik cause. It could well have been one of im Thurn's White Russian business associates. Alternatively, the Association of British Creditors of Russia or any of its component plutocrats would doubtless have been ready sources of cash for such an enterprise. The reference to the source as 'she' was all of a piece with the inverted commas im Thurn gave to his 'relation' – a facile literary disguise very likely to be employed by an agent who was, in part, re-living his cloak-and-dagger past. But whoever it was evidently paid up promptly. Another undated letter to Kindersley records that im Thurn, equally promptly, paid it over.

Again, the context of the letter supplies its date. 'Herewith a copy for your "archives"!' it begins, suggesting that it accompanied the copy of the im Thurn diary which was later found in Kindersley's papers. Im Thurn was exultant: this was clearly the day or two after 25 October. 'I wonder if you feel a few years younger today. I do! Well! the memory of these last 3 weeks, anxious as they were, will be very sweet to us both as we get older . . . My "relation" was as good as her word – bless her. I am transmitting every penny this afternoon via cable.'

That accounted for one quarter of the required £10,000. The Conservatives, however, were considerably less ready to pay. It is not clear exactly why they delayed. Perhaps it was by agreement, perhaps through guile, but the fact is that only in April 1928, a fortnight after im Thurn had got them off the hook, did they pay any money at all.

Prior agreement seems a less plausible explanation for this than base cunning. If the 'relation's' contribution could be sent to X without delay in 1924, it cannot have been transmission difficulties which prevented the Tories from sending theirs. It is conceivable that either X or im Thurn wanted the cash in instalments, but four years seems too long an interval between them. Besides, the tone with which im Thurn greeted the eventual extraction of the money indicates that the Tories were far from willing cashiers. There is, in fact, a strong implication

177

in im Thurn's correspondence that in 1924, after they had got the benefit from the Zinoviev letter, the Tories decided not to honour their apparent guarantee – presumably on the grounds that, since the letter was published anyway by the Foreign Office, they did not need im Thurn's services in the end.

In 1928, it was a different story. Baldwin was on the defensive. He had staved off a possibly embarrassing inquiry on the evidence of one man. If that man, presented as the simple hero, were now to state publicly that he had been promised money by the Tories for the gallant informant who risked his life, and that the Tories had not paid, Baldwin's position would be transformed. The party would be seen not only to have meanly cheated a brave man, but to have been much more actively involved in eliciting publication of the letter than it wanted to appear.

Im Thurn, if not the leading Tories at Central Office, knew that his statement had not told the whole truth. It had been tailored to suit the party's present embarrassment. That embarrassment could be painfully aggravated by other disclosures. If necessary, im Thurn could always give Central Office a frightening taste of what really did happen.

In any case, by the beginning of April he had been paid. A cheque stub, dated 2 April 1928, exists among the papers of Lord Davidson, then the chairman of the Conservative Party. The cheque was drawn on the chairman's personal account at Hoare's Bank, in the sum of £5,000. It was made out, in fact, to 'J. Ball'. On the stub, under the name of the payee are written in brackets the initials 'CDiT'.

Ball immediately paid the same sum over to im Thurn. This is proved by a letter of acknowledgement from im Thurn to Ball, dated 2 April. Formally addressed to Conservative Central Office, it begins: 'I beg to acknowledge the sum of five thousand pounds (£5,000) on behalf of X.' (A minor curiosity of this letter is that it was addressed to 'Paris Chambers' whereas the Conservatives' correct address was, of course, Palace Chambers. Since this seems to have been the first time any written communication was exchanged between im Thurn and the Tories, this odd discrepancy can be attributed to a verbal misunderstanding.)

This letter also specifies how the rest of the debt to X is to

178

be paid. Apart from the Tory lump sum of £5,000, he is to get from the other source £250 a year for ten years, plus an extra lump sum of £2,500 at the end of the ten years. This is to be paid to him in the Argentine, where he is to establish himself as an Argentine national, having sailed there as a common deck-hand. Im Thurn takes trouble to point out to the Tories how secure this will make them, as well as X: 'He will never dare to dispute (his Argentine nationality) in after life as the punishment in the Argentine for living under false papers is very severe.'

On the same date im Thurn also sent Ball a more personal note. 'I always knew I could trust you,' he wrote, 'and I thank you for having done your very best to fulfil the obligations to X undertaken by the Central Office in 1924.'

The obligations, however, were not completely fulfilled. Five thousand pounds was not £7,500. This was something which im Thurn promptly sought to turn to his own advantage. It provided another lever for extracting something which he had had his eye on ever since 1924: a knighthood.

This measure of his own deserts was one which had occurred to him as suitable from the moment the Zinoviev letter was published. In his triumphant note to Kindersley, reporting that his 'relation' had paid up, he mentions, with suitable modesty, that a knighthood for him was the only price the 'relation' wanted for paying over the money. 'She made me promise to ask you to try to get that KBE again last night, and as she wouldn't hand over without my promise she has as you see gained her point. It's beastly asking for anything for meself [*sic*].'

The three-and-a-half-year lapse did not diminish this zeal for recognition. On the contrary, a long letter to Kindersley just after the 1928 debate displays a refined appreciation of precisely why it was imperative, in the national interest, that both of them should be recognized. It speaks of having been 'diddled once by' headquarters, and adds that 'although I trust the crowd there now as I never trusted Jackson still they *may* not be there when the time comes'.

Im Thurn argued that only by honours could the Government affirm its own belief in his honesty and the truth of the letter.

Looking on the matter from a detached point of view it seems to be obviously the best policy to recognise publically [*sic*] at once and finish the business, you being included in Birthday Honours for political services, I could be national services – I think it would be a popular act seeing that I am snowed under from all over Europe and England with congratulations. If they don't do it now doesn't it prove to their enemies that Headquarters know it (the letter and me) to be a fraud or to have emanated from Headquarters as a political stunt.

The only reason im Thurn can see for the delay is that Central Office does not want to honour Marlowe, which it would find difficult to avoid if it honoured Kindersley and himself. But he thinks that the political advantages should outweigh this 'slight discomfort at Headquarters'. The letter ends with a complaint about how much im Thurn has suffered in the cause: 'At present my life is horrid and this affair has done me no end of harm, and many reflections from political enemies are being thrown about, and only a public recognition will prove to the public that I am worthy of the honour and a principal and not somebody's tool or agent. All I have said about myself applies to you naturally,' he magnanimously concludes. 'Please take this view in any discussions you may have.'

In the Note to Ball on 2 April he was more pointed, if less feverish. He said that, grateful as he was, the payment of only £5,000 left the party under a greater obligation to Kindersley and himself than before, 'if that were possible'. He claimed a decisive role for the Zinoviev letter not only in the 1924 election but in the ruin of the Liberals, the failure of the general strike, the elimination of possible revolution, and the permanent strength of the Tory Party. Surely, he reminded Ball, Baldwin's checking of his statement provided 'an additional reason why Kindersley and I should be given the recognition previously promised at the earliest convenient moment, say in the Birthday Honours'. Otherwise, he argued to Ball as to Kindersley, 'it might appear that on further examination the P.M. finds something questionable or wrong either with me personally or with the statement made.' He thought the services he had performed over four years had 'seldom been beaten'. As if aware that his letter might seem a little beyond the bounds of good taste, he concluded by recalling, a little disingenuously, that 'the distinction would be of enormous assistance to Kindersley and that he thoroughly deserves it'.

It was not an unreasonable case, even though put with such brazen logic. The era of the honours racket, when many men got Tory peerages for fewer services (although more money), had not yet entirely vanished. Honours were the common coin of politics to an even greater extent than they are today. Cleaning up the system was one of Davidson's principal charges as chairman, and he had set about it with an upright zeal.

Im Thurn, however, came into a different category, since he had, ostensibly, done something for his country. Moreover, Kindersley in his history writes that a day or two after the debate he met in the lobby someone who said that im Thurn should get a knighthood for his services. According to the recollection of Kindersley's son, Edmund, this was Davidson himself, although Kindersley describes him only as someone 'in a position to fulfil his promise'.

But nothing was ever done. Im Thurn's was only one form of logic. The Tory chiefs, if they thought about it, would have been impressed by another. For them to award anything to either Marlowe or im Thurn or Kindersley would have compelled an award to each of them. This could easily have been interpreted not so much as an affirmation of belief in im Thurn's story as evidence of their having performed a strictly political service. The Conservative position throughout was that the party had no direct part in the publication of the Zinoviev letter: they merely argued that it should be published, and that Labour tried to conceal it. At a time when charges of a Tory plot were still being made, it would have been a mistake for the Tories to be seen to be rewarding anyone involved in the affair. A knighthood for im Thurn alone might not have been too damaging. It could have been passed off as a legitimate reward for a disinterested public servant. But awards to the other two as well would have given the game away. Thus, it may not have been pure ingratitude which prompted the Government to deprive im Thurn of his life's ambition.

When im Thurn wrote to Ball, he excused his incontinent request for an honour by saying that no doubt the matter would be finally closed within a fortnight and they would have no more contact. He was right. After the spring of 1928, Donald im Thurn withdrew into permanent obscurity in the City. In the public eye, the Zinoviev affair was his first and last venture into politics.

In March 1929, im Thurn fell seriously ill. He had never been an outstandingly fit man. In the war he had missed active service for health reasons; this was the main reason why he ever found his way into MI5. The doctors were never absolutely certain what was wrong. It was some sort of illness, which his daughter, a doctor, later diagnosed as Hodgkin's Disease. Kindersley visited him several times, and never found out what the exact complaint was. One of the more lurid tales of the time, born of romantic ignorance, was that he had been poisoned by Bolshevik agents. This can now be totally discounted.

In a year he was dead. Mystery pursued him to the end. On 21 March, the night of his funeral in Somerset, his house in Eaton Terrace was empty. That night it was broken into, by people who searched only his desk and clothing. They took nothing of value, and, apparently, nothing specific was missed from among his papers. If they were searching for light on the Zinoviev letter, they were almost certainly disappointed. He had long before made sure that none of his confidential documents were kept at home. Everything, if it was anywhere, was at his office in St Mary Axe.

Three days after the death of Donald im Thurn, his wife received a letter which was seen, at least by Kindersley who inspired it, as a conscientious recompense for the knighthood he did not get. It said:

Dear Mrs im Thurn,

Though I only had the pleasure of meeting your husband once, may I offer you in all sincerity my truest sympathy? He was a man who was always ready to give himself to the service of his country.

> I am,
> Yours sincerely,
> (sgd) Stanley Baldwin.

15

The Spy who Never Made a Mistake

The mystery is not, even yet, quite over. Two unanswered questions remain. To recall them, it is necessary to return to the beginning of the story, and the moment at which copies of the letter entered England. We know how the letter was forged. And we know how it was circulated to the press and published by the Foreign Office. What we have not fully considered is the third conspiracy: the conspiracy by which the letter reached the Foreign Office and news of it reached Donald im Thurn. Who was im Thurn's confidant, the mysterious Mr X? Who was the informant on whom the Foreign Office relied so implicitly? It seems certain, at least, that they were not the same man.

A sketchy portrait of X emerges from the im Thurn diary. He was, first, not a total stranger to his British collaborator. He was someone with whom im Thurn had evidently worked before. The underlying tone of the first entry in the diary, when X contacts im Thurn and suggests a meeting, is familiar and unsurprised. It is as though the two men expected to hear from each other, especially in connection with anti-Bolshevik activity. X expects im Thurn to be interested in his information and he is not disappointed. Together, they quickly set up a preliminary plan of action: X is to find out as much as he can about Zinoviev's instructions and report back.

That much is immediately clear from the diary. What it indicates about the two men's previous relationship is confirmed in another source, the glossary on the diary which was prepared by Mrs im Thurn for Guy Kindersley, when the latter was writing his own account of the affair. To Kindersley's question about X's identity, she writes in this as follows: 'Mr X was

183

introduced in the course of business by Kadomzev (White Russian aristocrat naval officer) who was in turn introduced by Lady Egerton who was a Rostov'. This reference, additionally, provides the only available indicator of the possible identity of the 'relation' who provided part of X's money: it could have been the White Russian Lady Egerton.

Boris Kadomzev worked with im Thurn as a director of the London Steamship and Trading Corporation, the company which owned the remnants of the fleet of merchant vessels known as the Russian Volunteer Fleet. In the course of business, im Thurn would have been bound to meet a wide selection of anti-Bolsheviks from Eastern Europe. The émigré company was a focus of political and intelligence, as well as business, activities.

Kindersley made no use of Mrs im Thurn's indicator in his own history. And it casts indeed a fairly dim light. But it is a start. Returning to the diary, one may elucidate X somewhat further. He is obviously familiar with the Soviet scene. He refers to 'his old enemy Apfelbaum'. Apfelbaum is another name for Zinoviev, and it might be deduced that X's longstanding enmity with him had begun in Russia during the revolution. This by itself might point to the conclusion that the friend who was passed from Lady Egerton to Kadomzev to im Thurn was a White Russian – one of the many who, travelling round the anti-Bolshevik centres on the continent, might easily have got word of the letter.

However, the use of 'Apfelbaum' suggests more than this. It was a pseudonym attached to Zinoviev particularly by the intelligence services, just as they exploited Jewish-sounding references for Lenin and the other Bolshevik leaders. Therefore it seems likely that X was at least on the fringe of intelligence operations. This, additionally, would strengthen his link with im Thurn, the former British intelligence agent who had never lost touch with the service and never lost his interest in its activities. As a demonstration of his continuing association with intelligence, it is notable that im Thurn seems as familiar with the usage 'Apfelbaum' as does his informant.

The most important question about X is: how central was he to the plot? The diary itself suggests he was badly informed. If it is a true record of X's movements, and if these in turn were faithfully reported by X to im Thurn, X was substantially in the dark. He had merely heard that the letter had arrived. He had to find out, in the course of several days, what exactly was in it, and who had got it. He seems never to have had a copy himself. Certainly he never gave one to im Thurn. As we have seen, im Thurn's main difficulty was that he had to keep on bluffing the authorities into believing he did possess the letter when in fact he did not.

Additionally, several of X's reports can now be seen to be inaccurate. His stories about Maxton having seen the letter, about Rakovsky possessing the original, about MacDonald having cross-examined MacManus when MacManus was in fact out of the country, were all false. Were they purposely false, or were they merely the result of X thinking he knew more than he did?

They could, in theory, have been the over-excited embellishments of a man who wanted to display a more complete knowledge of events than he had. If X was a White Russian on the periphery of anti-Bolshevik affairs, picking up gossip here and there, this is what they could well have been. But in fact it is the least likely possibility. In the end, X *was* able to retail the contents of the letter. His treatment of im Thurn is much more consistent with the theory that he knew how the letter originated, and how its manipulators in Warsaw wanted it to be played. Read with hindsight, the diary, starting with the fact that X knew about the letter two days before it reached the Foreign Office, strongly indicates that X's task was to awaken im Thurn's interest, tantalize him until the moment was ripe, and convince him, by a few well-chosen bits of information, that he himself was an exceedingly well-informed source.

If X wanted to make sure that im Thurn realized the letter was genuine, what better card could he play than the assertion that Rakovsky possessed the original and was concealing it under diplomatic freedom from search? This was the point X kept on reinforcing in im Thurn's mind. After several days' silence, he actually got in touch once again, on 22 October, just as the plot was coming nicely to the boil, to let im Thurn know that he was now 'quite sure' Rakovsky did have it. Likewise, if X wanted to stimulate im Thurn's active indignation at the Government's own intention to conceal the letter, what more effective story to tell than that MacDonald had questioned Mac-Manus about it as early as 25 September?

There remain the references to X in 1928. In his statement to Baldwin, im Thurn spoke of the need to ensure that his informant had time to conclude his affairs in England and get safely away before any hint of his existence appeared in public. At the same time, im Thurn was privately arranging that the Tories should at last pay their debts. These, he insisted then just as he had insisted to Kindersley and Jackson in 1924, were to go entirely to X. Unless im Thurn was deceiving Kindersley, £2,500 was paid over in 1924: this was the money from the 'relation' who had agreed to make up the total of £10,000. In 1928, the rest, from the Tories, was still owing.

Im Thurn's acknowledgement of the 1928 money states what is to happen to X. He is to go to Argentina. There, apart from the lump sum from the Tories, he is to be paid an annuity for ten years from im Thurn's own sources. On the back of his copy of the letter explaining this, im Thurn has written the putative identity which X is to assume: 'Ramon Gomez. Madrid. Seaman.' He is to get his annuity from the hands of 'our agent' in the Argentine, and neither the agent nor anyone else need know who he really is and what he has really done.

But there is something odd here. Im Thurn is aggrieved that the Tories have only paid £5,000, 'leaving', as he notes heavily to Ball, 'the other £5,000 for us to provide'. It is this other £5,000 which is to be paid in instalments of £250 a year, rounded off with a lump £2,500. However, in the 1924 letter clinching the deal with Kindersley, it was made clear that the sum total from all sources which X was to get was £10,000. Yet we know that £2,500 of this was, as im Thurn wrote soon after the election triumph, sent off immediately: 'I am transmitting every penny this afternoon via cable.' Thus, if im Thurn was telling the Tories the truth in 1928, X by then was to get a total of £12,500, even though im Thurn is still speaking as though £10,000 was the sum total. The conclusion must be either that X had succeeded in increasing his sum in the intervening years, or that im Thurn was engaging in some form of subterfuge.

The first possibility is extremely unlikely. It is just the sort of argument which, if it had been true, im Thurn would have

used to reinforce his petulant indignation at having allegedly
been left out of pocket by the Tories. Yet he makes no reference
to it whatever. It seems far more plausible to suggest that he
was simply forgetting, or blithely ignoring, the payment made
in 1924. This in turn suggests that the elaborate description of
the Argentinian trip, of which we know that he made several
rough copies before getting it exactly right, may be unreliable.
For, unless X *had* been able to increase his demand, im Thurn
would not have intended to pay him £5,000 over and above the
Tory money and the £2,500 he had already received.

What is the evidence that the Argentinian trip ever took
place? Certainly, the im Thurn family had property in the
country and having contacts there both from that source and
from his shipping business, Donald im Thurn could easily have
found an agent to pay over the money. On the other hand, this
existing connection with Argentina is a suggestive pointer to
the probability that the entire reference to X's fate was a fabri-
cation, put together in order to impress the Conservatives.

The promised despatch of X would have assured them that
the chance of their machinations' being discovered was now
very remote. The prospect of such discovery must have been a
strong disincentive to their paying anything at all. Once the
chance was removed, they would be much more willing. The
melodramatic journey planned for X would also have impressed them forcibly with the truth of what im Thurn had
told Baldwin: that his informant was in great danger from the
Bolsheviks and their British collaborators, on whom he had
spied and from whom – as Baldwin was given to believe – he
had intrepidly filched the Zinoviev letter. If this was in fact not
at all the way X had got his information, and if im Thurn's role
had been not at all the one which was now on public record
with Baldwin's endorsement – all the more reason to invent a
good story which proclaimed that it was. And what more likely
destination for im Thurn to alight on than Argentina, a far-
away place which he had visited as a boy and where his family
had credible connections?

There is a further, more comprehensive reason for supposing
that the reference to Argentina was a blind. Removed from the
feverish atmosphere of 1928, when the Tories would believe
anything which got them off the hook, it is difficult to see why

187

X, whoever he was, would make such a trip. If he had to get out of Europe, why had he not gone in 1924? What new and special danger existed in 1928 which would compel him to make a rapid getaway under the humble pseudonym of a Spanish sailor, and live out his life in the uncomfortable anonymity which im Thurn prescribed?

It is not impossible, of course. It is conceivable that X, being a professional conspirator, was now in some new trouble, from which his unpaid credit in London would provide a vital means of escape. But if that was the case, why should im Thurn have bothered with anything except getting as much of the Tory money as he could? Im Thurn, who was telling Kindersley by this time that 'my life is horrid and this affair has done me no end of harm', clearly wanted to complete an obligation specifically relating to the letter and then finish with it completely. He certainly was in no mood to be troubled by annuities and agents if he could possibly escape them.

This same letter to Kindersley contains the strongest hint about just where im Thurn's obligation really lay. It was, not surprisingly, in Poland. The letter, written before the Tories had actually come through with the money, said in a rushed postscript: 'Have just had a cable from Warsaw and have communicated with Ball. They *must* settle up with my friend now and finish.'

Thus, the most convincing picture of X is this. He was a representative of Polish intelligence, conceivably Paciorkowski himself (the probable director of the Zinoviev operation), but, if not him, at least an emissary sent by him to use all his resources to ensure maximum impact for the letter. He was a man who knew im Thurn from Kadomzev's introduction and from earlier intelligence work together. He used him, probably among other London contacts. He strung him along, playing on his intense anti-Socialist and anti-Bolshevik feelings. In 1928, after Baldwin's rescue from political embarrassment, he put pressure on im Thurn to recover the unpaid debt. This was transmitted to the Tory leaders. Backed by the realistic threat that all might otherwise be revealed – about their promise to pay and their failure to do so – this worked very effectively, not least on Ball, who was very familiar with the intelligence scene. Whether im Thurn did or did not send the Tory £5,000 to X is not certainly known, although there is no substantial reason for supposing that he did not. What does seem certain is that X never went to Argentina.

But if Polish intelligence told im Thurn, who told the Foreign Office? That is much the more significant question. It was clearly someone very special indeed. It was someone who could convince Crowe, by his mere reputation, that the letter was authentic. We know that Crowe was personally informed of the letter's existence before it started its way up from the bottom of the Foreign Office hierarchy: this was why Strang, as he prepared to append a routine minute, was told to give it special, extended treatment. We also know that Crowe decided very quickly that the letter was authentic, and did not ask for a second opinion from other branches of intelligence.

We would know this anyway from im Thurn's diary. But it is confirmed by the striking fact that the other intelligence agencies, when they eventually had a chance to examine the document, all pronounced it a fake. We have seen the reaction of Childs, at Special Branch: 'There was absolutely no reason to think that this particular effusion was genuine.' His view was endorsed by the Chief Commissioner of Metropolitan Police. Mr Philip Noel-Baker recounted this impressive confirmation in a letter to *The Times* on 22 December 1966. 'The late Sir Walford Selby,' Mr Noel-Baker wrote, 'was Principal Private Secretary to Mr Ramsay MacDonald in the Foreign Office before and during the 1924 election. He remained as Principal Private Secretary until 1932, serving Sir Austen Chamberlain, Mr Arthur Henderson and Sir John Simon. Sir Walford told me many years afterwards – I think it was during the second world war – that in 1925 the Chief Commissioner of the Metropolitan Police had assured him in confidence that, as Chief Commissioner, he had come into possession of absolute proof that the Zinoviev letter was a forgery.'

Nor, it seems, was Scotland Yard alone. MacDonald asserted, in his speech during the 1928 debate, that the heads of other intelligence departments had very confident views: 'The heads of the intelligence departments who received the letter thought it was such nonsense that they described it to me later as 'blank' – hon. members can supply the adjective themselves – tripe.'

Thus, Crowe's opinion that it was far from tripe was a very

exclusive one. How can he have reached it? The best clue is reported by Dalton in his memoirs. Dalton says that Mac-Donald told the Labour parliamentary leaders, when they met to plan their strategy for the 1928 debate, that Crowe was convinced because 'the secret service agent who gave it to the FO had received it from a man who "had never been known to make a mistake".'

Soon after the 1924 election, of course, both Crowe (in his letter to Haldane) and Austen Chamberlain (in his statement to the Commons) claimed that corroboration of this first source had come to light. Chamberlain even alleged that no fewer than four independent and unconnected sources existed for the conclusion that the letter could be traced all the way back to Petrograd. The Conservatives never elaborated on this. But in the light of the new proof of forgery, one of three conclusions seems possible. Either Crowe, and later Chamberlain, was deliberately misled by the intelligence section of the Foreign Office; or intelligence, MI1C, including Sinclair at its head, was deceived by the man who had 'never been known to make a mistake'; or this man made his first mistake.

The first alternative is so unlikely that it can be dismissed. Sinclair may well have had his own reasons for ensuring that the letter – the great coup, as he saw it, of his service, which Labour was threatening to disband – was not concealed by the Government. He might even have sought to redouble the case for its authenticity, at a time when it was still widely suspected, by falsely telling Chamberlain of these other sources. But it is very far-fetched to imagine that Sinclair or anyone else at MI1C in London knowingly circulated a fake. The risk involved would simply not have been worth the possible benefit gained.

This leaves 'the man who never made a mistake'. Dalton's memoirs contain no further clue to his identity, but if the description is to be taken seriously he must have had a startling record as an intelligence operative. If his superiors were to be so uncritical about information presented by this man, he needed a reputation within the secret service verging on the legendary. In short, he must have been someone whose knowledge of Russia was greeted by a complete lack of scepticism in London.

There was, as it happens, a man with these legendary quali-

190

ties working in Europe at the time. He was known as 'the master spy', and his name was Capt. Sidney Reilly. He was widely believed to be the son of an Irish sea captain and a Russian Jewess: in fact, his parents were both Russian, the story of Irish paternity being just one among many of his own fabrications. He had all the qualifications for a life which took him from Russian international trade broker to British secret agent. He was a brilliant linguist in Russian and German, as well as English. He had a highly developed taste for conspiracy and impersonation. One contemporary account pictured him as a man 'of a foolhardy, adventurous nature, a bold, nay, a reckless gambler with fate, whose most ardent desire it was to meet death in the most romantic fashion possible'.

Reilly seems to have begun his career as a secret agent working for the Japanese in Manchuria in 1900. Unfortunately a subordinate whom he had himself hired to work in the firm of timber merchants established to cover espionage activities, was, Reilly discovered, a Russian counter-espionage agent. He left Manchuria rapidly, taking with him only one prize – a lady with whom he had been flirting. After the Russo–Japanese War in 1905 he turned up in St Petersburg and entered Rasputin's entourage. Within the next five years he was recruited by British intelligence. Already an exceptional operator, he lived and spied in Germany in 1917 and 1918. Shortly before the end of the war he returned to Russia, devoting himself to the pursuit, highly fashionable among British intelligence agents, of attempting to overthrow the Bolshevik Government.

Later he actually established himself as an official of the Soviet Government with access to confidential documents from Trotsky's office in the Foreign Ministry, and from the Vyk (the All-Russian Chief Executive Committee). The Russians claim that shortly after he arrived in Russia he took part in a plot to overthrow the Government. And his most ambitious plan – an attempt to kill Lenin – is well authenticated. It was not surprising that when he was tried by a Revolutionary Tribunal in Moscow in 1917, Reilly was absent, and proclaimed an enemy of the workers to be shot on sight. Nevertheless, he was back in Russia the following March taking part in raids organized by a White Russian named Boris Savinkov. On his return to London he became friendly with Winston Churchill, with whom he shared an indiscriminate anti-Bolshevism, and was secure in the devoted admiration of his secret service masters. He was the ideal man to convince Sinclair and the Foreign Office of the letter's authenticity, and he had the contacts – both among the White Russian counter-revolutionaries and the eastern European intelligence services – to make him the ideal, probably the obvious, candidate for the job of transmitting the Zinoviev letter from Europe to Whitehall.

But the evidence is not merely circumstantial. Although no documentary evidence exists to prove that Reilly did bring the letter to London, the number of references, veiled and direct, to Reilly's role – and the absence of any other candidates – make the case exceedingly strong.

The most important oblique reference is in a book compiled by his wife in 1931, *The Adventures of Sidney Reilly, Britain's Master Spy*. Part of the book consists of a description of the plot to supplant Lenin, written by Reilly himself; the rest is Mrs Reilly's account of her husband's activities in the 'twenties, and his eventual disappearance. It contains convincing proof that Reilly was still deeply involved in the émigré department of Russian politics. During August and September of 1924 he was in close contact with White Russians in Paris who were trying to persuade him to return to Russia.

Mrs Reilly's section of the book is often chronologically inexplicit, but it does establish that 'shortly after' the meetings in Paris (i.e. probably in October 1924) Reilly sailed for New York. On the boat, Mrs Reilly writes, her husband was subjected to unusually close surveillance by Bolshevik agents dressed as stewards and pursers. They were particularly interested in Reilly's attaché case, which contained some important papers. Mrs Reilly explains the reason for this as follows: 'During his stay in Europe he had been implicated in a very important political transaction, the details of which I am not at liberty to divulge.' If this is not a certain reference to the Zinoviev letter, it is an irresistibly suggestive description of the affair.

After his death the following year (he did return to Russia, and was captured, interrogated, and shot in November, 1925), the evidence began to mount. In a slightly delayed obituary, the *Sunday Chronicle* stated categorically that Reilly was responsible for the Foreign Office receiving the letter. No source was given for this, but clearly the idea had entered the folklore attaching to the legendary spy. Then, in 1927, Winfried Lüdecke, in one of a series of articles in German and Swiss newspapers which were not translated and published in Britain until 1929, made the assertion equally categorically. 'The transmission by him [Reilly] of the famous Zinoviev letter,' he wrote, 'assumed a world-wide political importance, for its publication in the British press brought about the fall of the MacDonald ministry, frustrated the realization of the proposed Anglo-Russian commercial treaty, and, as a final result, led to the signing of the treaties of Locarno, in virtue of which the other states of Europe presented, under the leadership of Britain, a united front against Soviet Russia.'

Although Lüdecke, too, offers no sources for any of his information, it is, in the context of his section on Reilly, quite convincing. It is one of a series of statements which together justify Lüdecke's assertion that Reilly was a brilliant, if over-romantic, spy. The propaganda content in Lüdecke's articles is non-existent, and there is no reason to suppose that he had any personal or political interest in implicating Reilly in the Zinoviev affair. Nor is it surprising that both the newspaper obituarist and the Swiss journalist assumed that the letter was genuine and Reilly's part in its publication was heroic.

Rather more political bias attaches to the latest and most interesting source pointing to Reilly's involvement in the plot. It was published in Moscow during the post-Stalin thaw in 1966 in a semi-fictionalized account of the OGPU – the Soviet secret police organization – by an elderly Russian novelist named Nikulin. Nikulin had always been a political loyalist. He was, it seems, a devoted member of the Union of authors, and if a book was to be written about the triumphs of the OGPU it is likely that he would have been given access to OGPU's retired officials, and, more important, to its files. It was a period, after all, during which the Russians suddenly became proud of the activities of their own master spies. Richard Sorge, who infiltrated the Japanese Cabinet Office during the second world war, and Rudolph Abel who worked unmolested in the United States for years, were elevated to the ranks of Soviet heroes.

Nikulin's book, called *Mertvaya Zyb* (literally *The Dead*

Swell) contains a lengthy account of Reilly's activities during the 'twenties. It claims that in 1924 in Paris Reilly was contacted by an organization named the 'Trust', which was ostensibly anti-Bolshevik but in fact controlled by the OGPU. It was soon obvious that Reilly wanted to return to Russia 'because of the danger, because he hated the Government, and also to impress his employers, the English Secret Service'.

In September 1925 Reilly went back. He met a member of 'Trust' named Yakushev in Helsinki. But Yakushev, who provided Reilly with forged papers, smuggled him into Russia and took him to a meeting of the 'Trust' outside Moscow, was actually an employee of OGPU. Reilly, unsuspecting, casually informed members of the 'Trust' who were trying to raise funds for their work that they could not rely on help from outside. 'Everyone's house is burning,' he told them. First he suggested that they steal some of Russia's art treasures and sell them in the West. Then he made the claim which is most relevant to this story of the Zinoviev letter.

'Another way of raising money,' Nikulin quotes Reilly as saying, 'is by co-operation with the English Secret Service. You've got to show these gentlemen in intelligence what you're worth. Above all they want information about the Comintern. You say that's difficult? But you can do anything if you have a mind to. If you can't get some real documents from the Comintern you'll have to invent some. A letter from the Comintern's chairman helped the Conservatives win an election. They maintain that it's a fake, but it's the result that counts.'

Nikulin's implication is clear enough: Reilly was not merely involved in the plot, but he knew the letter was forged. 'If you can't get some real documents from the Comintern you'll have to invent some' was the exact motivation of the forgers in Berlin, and of the Polish intelligence agents to whom they probably passed the letter.

But if Reilly knew, it re-opens the speculation about the degree of knowledge available to his employers in London. There is little doubt about Reilly's ability to foist a forgery on the British Government if he was determined to. He was a respected cavalier adventurer with a passionate hatred for the Bolsheviks. In Mrs Reilly's book he writes 'Here in Moscow there is growing to maturity the arch enemy of the human race . . . monsters

194

of crime and perversion. . . . Here the foulest, most monstrous and most obscene passions gibber and swagger in the seats of government.' It was the kind of ideological hatred which offers a convincing motivation for the transmission of a forgery, and the deception of Sinclair, his colleagues in MI1C and the Foreign Office. Their faith in Reilly was allied to ingrained anti-Bolshevism and a desire to be seen to have made an intelligence coup. If they were not party to the plot, they were certainly duped. The probable truth is that they were happy to be duped.

The true intentions of Captain Sidney Reilly will never be conclusively proved. But the powerful suspicion that he knowingly perpetrated the transmission of a forgery adds yet another curiosity to the whole bizarre affair. It points to a probable conclusion which is fitting as well as ironic: the principal culprit for the 1924 landslide against the MacDonald Government was its own master spy.

Appendix A

The complete diary of Donald im Thurn, discovered among Major Guy Kindersley's papers.

October 8th

Met X by appointment at his request. Wanted to tell me that his old enemy Apfelbaum had boasted in Moscow a few days ago that he was entering on a great propaganda war in England and Germany as the cause was apathetic and wanted rousing. He said that he had already sent instructions over here to be used as soon as the Treaty was signed. He rather feared that the present Government would fall soon, if so, it would be up to this end to decide what they were to do. Asked X to find out if this had been received, and if so, by whom.

October 9th

X rang up 6 o'clock to say that so far nothing doing. Wonder what I ought to do. Do nothing, only hearsay so far.

October 10th

X more hopeful, cannot say anything.

October 11th

X has news but thinks it is inadvisable meet me as he is sure he can dot the i's a bit more. He wants me to keep Monday open as far as possible.

October 13th

Informed by X of letter contents and that Maxton had seen it. That it arrived about the 25th. Also he thinks that MacDonald and Henderson knew of its existence some days ago. That Maxton saw Rakovsky some days ago and he thinks R. kept his letter for safety under diplomatic immunity from search. R. apparently advised Maxton say nothing and keep it quiet and cursed Zinoviev for being such a fool to send it at this juncture.

October 14th

Saw A. who did not commit either way but drew deductions but thought he had original or photographic copy. I asked for help and although he was sympathetic he could not help. Saw X. later he asserts about 25th MacDonald asked McManus if he had heard lately from Zinoviev. McManus refused to answer. MacDonald pointed out that if he had done so it would be fatal to let it leak out just then.

October 15th

Rang up Kindersley. Told him come up. 11 o'clock Kindersley and I met Lord Younger. Told him news and wanted guarantee against loss. 3.30 met Younger and Col. Jackson. Gave guarantee and decided on 'Times' publication later. 6 o'clock discovered on deduction A. had no photo of original and could not discover where it was. C. must have only copy as MacDonald knew the 25th and not from Maxton. Dangerous try C. Try and draw Scotland Yard first.

October 16th

Saw Scotland Yard to find out if Departments had seen letter. Answer No. S. would have seen it if circulated, therefore either C. has not circulated or Childs knows and is keeping it dark. Has Childs a copy or a photo. Fear only the former, otherwise circulated most certainly. Must find out. If not, must fix attention on forcing circulation. Met A. who said K. was waiting to hear from C. He thought that it should be more public but would not commit himself. A. offered publish it through me in a perfectly safe manner. K. interested.

October 17th

Much puzzled but certain in conclusion that if MI5 had not got it, C. must. Decide risk everything as time was getting close. Cannot approach C. Better pump Admiralty as to what it knows. If C. is keeping it dark from D.N.I. there will be ructions. If D.N.I. no good will go to D.M.I. Just discovered D.N.I. Hotham. Better not disclose to him if I see him the date of letter. Give wrong date and get it corrected by him in conversation. This will corroborate suspicions and make them certain. Pretend letter dates 5th and stick to it.

October 18th

Saw D.N.I. Got date of letter out of him and deducted that it could not be original. Told him that must pass information on if publication delayed. Saw Scotland Yard. D.N.I. rang up 12 o'clock asking me to ring up MAW. Met MAW lunch. Made discoveries. Promised to do best possible to get it circulated. C. has only copy. No good publishing my news unless I can get the letter circulated departmentally; that will make it authentic. All X's reports seem to be true after all. D.N.I. seems to think I have copy. MAW spoke as if I have. MAW asked me to hold my hand and not to publish. He would talk it over with his chief that afternoon and let me know Monday afternoon. To-day both D.N.I. and MAW asked me if the date of the letter was the 5th and not 15th, so it is proved they have knowledge of 15th letter. Told MAW thought R. had original.

October 20th

Rang up D.N.I. who refused see Jackson and me. A. rang up told me enquiries being made about me re my activities. Told me meet me later. D.N.I. apparently seemed nervous because I had information and meant to publish. K. goes to bed. No news of MAW. Will leave him alone today as his chief trying to trace original. Cannot make out if MAW knows if and when C. told MacDonald. 5.30 saw Alexander who said that now K. was ill he could not see what he could do to help. C. had asked K. to leave letter with him one week but A. thought that as C. knows outside person knows about letter he could cut short the week.

October 21st

C. rang up tell me about circulation. It would take place. At least, he meant me to understand that. Rang up A. Saw Younger. Told him all right (circulation). Met A. 5.45 who corroborated circulation. Cannot rely on getting copy. What the hell! Must play all I can on F.O. fear of publication.

October 22nd

Saw Scotland Yard 10 o'clock. No news. Childs no earthly. Cannot wait any longer. 1.15 saw Robins at the 'Times'. Asked for assistance and explained whole situation and thought now it was safe to move as departmental circulation to C-in-C's taking place immediately. 5.30 saw A. Told me circulation taking place. X quite sure R. has original.

October 23rd

A. rang up. Strongly advised do nothing further as all necessary steps were being taken. Evidently 'Times' getting busy. Saw Browning morning, suggested him moving. Browning thought he knew the very man. Saw Jackson 3.30. Leave it now for 'Times' and Browning's friend. Appointment 5.30 'Times', better break it off today. They will do the needful without interference.

October 24th

'Daily Mail' knows something. Believe 'Times' 'Daily Mail' met late yesterday afternoon and will play the same bluff as mine about the copy. Press forces 3.45 F.O. who gives up letter after 'Mail' asked 'Times' to approach 'Times' F.O. official. Looks alright for us.

October 25th

'Mail' production. Browning rang me up, Sammy rang me up, Kindersley rang me up, etc. etc.

October 26th

Saw Jackson in his private house re X.

October 27th

Browning rang me up. I went round. He told me that on Thursday afternoon he had passed information on to the 'Daily Mail'.

Key to the diary, deduced by the authors:
  R : Christian Rakovsky, Soviet chargé d'affaires
  A : Alexander, an MI5 agent.
  C : Sir Hugh Sinclair, head of MI1C
  S : Miss Bunty Saunders, clerk, Foreign Office.
  K : Sir Vernon Kell, head of MI5.
  MAW : Unknown.
  Sammy : Unknown.
  X : An agent of Polish intelligence.

200

Appendix B

Surviving correspondence from Donald im Thurn to Major Guy Kindersley, M.P. Although the letters are undated, the approximate time they were written has been deduced from their contents.

(Letter 1. Written some time around 16 October 1924)

51, St Mary Axe
London, E.C.3.

Dear Kindersley,

Conditionally on (you know who) putting up not less than £7,500 a relation of mine has promised to add £2,500 making in all £10,000 & will allow me to draw up to a further £2,500 should I deem it necessary later on.

In approaching my relation I did not allow it to be thought that the Conservative Party had anything to do with it, in fact it was not mentioned, nor did I do further than just state a case without giving anything away although my relation is most discreet – you will see by this that if the above is done there will be no necessity to ask ——— for more than the £7,500 & the matter as far as ——— is concerned can be closed permanently.

I think this is very satisfactory at least it will be if I am placed in the position of being able to accept this outside offer.

Don't get sick of it all!

Yours ever
D. C. im Thurn

Use your discretion about above
I don't want to risk hanging [?] anything up as it is all too urgent.

201

(Letter 2. Written on or about 30 October 1924)

51, St Mary Axe,
London, E.C.3.

Dear Kindersley,

Herewith a copy for your 'archives'!

I wonder if you feel a few years younger today. I do! Well! the memory of these last 3 weeks, anxious as they were, will be very sweet to us both as we get older and I shall be grateful to them for the further reason that making but few friends i.e. real friends, I have met the specimen of that almost extinct species – a live and real man.

I hope that this friendship will enable us together to do little bits of good for the old country. My 'relation' was as good as her word – bless her. I am transmitting every penny this afternoon via cable.

She made me promise to ask you to try to get that KBE again last night and as she wouldn't hand over without my promise she has as you see gained her point. It's beastly asking for anything for meself.

Yours ever
C. Donald im Thurn

Sometime if you see Jackson get that paper out of him – if you can.

(Letter 3. Written towards the end of March 1928)

51, St Mary Axe,
London, E.C.3.

Dear ~~Kindersley~~ Guy ?

Thanks for ringing up. Of course I don't know their reasons for delay nor can I guess them except so far as they don't want to honour Marlowe which it would be difficult to avoid doing if they honour us. But that is a small difficulty compared to the other side of the question. Looking on the matter from a detached point of view it seems to be obviously the best policy to recognise publically [sic] at once and finish the business, you being included in Birthday Honours for political services, I could be national services – I think it would be a popular act seeing that I am snowed under from all over Europe and England with congratulations. If they don't do it now doesn't it prove to their enemies that Headquarters know it (the letter and me) to be a fraud or to have emanated from Headquarters as a political stunt.

By not doing the obvious for services rendered over a long period of nearly 4 years I think it would be taken certainly to imply that on further examination Baldwin found that something was wrong with me or the job.

By doing it now in the obvious way it would prove his faith both in me and the job.

Of course *we* mustn't be given it together obviously.

As regards delaying it for so long i.e. until after elections, what do they gain by that as it would resurrect the old faction [?] all over again and would take no one in at all. In fact besides being awfully unfair to us who certainly deserve the above views to outweigh any slight discomfort at Headquarters, I do think they would be making a great mistake politically if they worked it the way they suggest.

Whilst we had our secret baby you and I were content with the service we had done, but once made public & again saving an awkward position I do not think it unnatural to expect recognition now for services 4 years old and again recent ones.

Also how are we to be certain that the Prayer Book may not lead to such a split over disestablishment as to endanger the elections. Or other unforeseen things may arise. Don't forget we have been diddled once by Hdqs and although I trust the crowd there now as I never trusted Jackson still they *may* not be there when the time comes.

At present my life is horrid and this affair has done me no end of harm and many reflections from political enemies are being thrown about and only a public recognition will prove ~~that our affair was not a put up job and that Baldwin~~ to the public that I am worthy of the honour and a principal and not somebodies [sic] tool or agent. All I have said about myself applies to you naturally. Please take this view in any discussions you may have.

Ever Yours,

Donald

Have just had a cable from Warsaw and have communicated with Ball. They *must* settle up with my friend now and finish.

Appendix C

Letters from Donald im Thurn to Conservative Central Office and to Joseph Ball, 2 April 1928.

2nd April, 1928.

The Conservative & Unionist Central Office,
Paris Chambers,
S.W.1.

Dear Sirs,   *Zinovieff Letter.*

I beg to acknowledge the sum of five thousand pounds (£5,000) on behalf of X.

For a period of ten years X will additionally receive two hundred and fifty pounds (£250) a year, paid on the 1st June to him by our Agent in the Argentine. At the end of ten years this payment will cease and he will be paid the sum of two thousand five hundred pounds (£2,500). In case of death this arrangement will cease unless he should have remarried when his widow will be entitled to this arrangement.

He will be given Argentine papers and will therefore be to all intents and purposes Argentine National, which he will never dare to dispute in after life as the punishment in the Argentine for living under false papers is very severe. He will sail as deck hand and on arrival will present himself to out [*sic*] Agent who will only know him under his new name and will know nothing further about him, except that he will pay these yearly sums over to him for the said period of ten years.

Yours faithfully,
C. Donald im Thurn

Copy No.
3 Copies.
(On the back of this copy of this letter, im Thurn has handwritten 'Ramon Gomez. Madrid. Seaman'.)

2nd April, 1928.

J. Ball, Esq.,
Conservative & Unionist Central Office,
Paris Chambers, S.W.1.

Dear Ball,   *Zinovieff Letter*.

I always knew I could trust you and I thank you for having done your very best to fulfil the obligations to X undertaken by the Central Office in 1924.

Of course this action of the Central Office in meeting X's claim for £5,000, leaving the other £5,000, for us to provide, lays the Conservative Party under greater obligation, if that were possible, to Kindersley and me than ever, and as I suppose within a fortnight we may consider the matter closed as regards X for all time there should be no reason for me to write again on the subject, so I would like to point out one or two points.

I know that the P.M. is one of the tiny minority that consider the episode of 1924 as only materially assisting but not vitally affecting the issue of the Elections. The overwhelming opinion throughout Europe is directly opposed to this opinion. Of course I should not be human if I were not with the majority. However allow that point. There is no doubt whatever that the letter smashed the Communists, split the Labour Party, ruined the Liberals, upset any chance of revolution and made the failure of the general strike a foregone conclusion and established the Conservative Party on a basis of solidity which has never existed before and which is likely to exist for many many years to come. I think also that the action of the other day will have a great effect of consolidating the party at the next Elections.

In the P.M.'s speech of the 19th inst. [*sic*] he told the house that as far as he had been able to judge in the 48 hours he had had at his disposal, he had been able to check the proofs as far as possible. Well it seems to me obvious that this is an additional reason why Kindersley and I should be given the recognition previously promised at the earliest convenient moment, say in the Birthday honours, as otherwise it might appear that on further examination the P.M. finds something questionable or wrong either with me personally or with the statement made.

Having had all the newspaper reports from all over England and hundreds of communications also, I do not foresee that there can be any reason to anticipate any flare up of the slightest importance of antagonistic criticism. I consider that Kindersley and I have for a period of four years done a service to the Nation which, from a Political point to say the least, has seldom been beaten.

I do not care about writing all this but at this general clear up I think it only fair to all of us to say what we think, and I know that the distinction would be of enormous assistance to Kindersley and that he thoroughly deserves it.

Yours ever,

C. Donald im Thurn.

Copy No.
Three copies.

Sources and Bibliography

Chapter 1
W. P. Coates: *The 'Zinoviev Letter'* – The case for a full investigation (1928); 'Iconoclast' (M. A. Hamilton): *J. Ramsay MacDonald 1923–25* (1925); L. J. MacFarlane: *The British Communist Party* (1966); W. T. Rodgers & B. Donoughue: *The People into Parliament* (1966); Robert D. Warth: 'The Mystery of the Zinoviev Letter' (*South Atlantic Quarterly*, October 1950); Richard W. Lyman: *The First Labour Government, 1924* (1957); British newspapers, October 1924.

Chapter 2
Ralph Miliband: *Parliamentary Socialism* (1961); Beatrice Webb: *Diaries 1924–32* (ed. M. Cole, 1956); Alan Bullock: *The Life and Times of Ernest Bevin*, Volume I (1960); 'Iconoclast': *op cit.*; Harold Nicholson: *King George V* (1952); Frederick Maurice: *Haldane, 1915–28* (1939); Lyman: *op. cit.*; A. J. P. Taylor: *English History 1914–45* (1965).

Chapter 3
E. H. Carr: *The Bolshevik Revolution*, Volumes I, II & III (1950, 1951, 1953); MacFarlane: *op. cit.*; Louis Fischer: *The Soviets in World Affairs*, Vol II (1930); A. L. P. Dennis: *The Foreign Policies of Soviet Russia* (1924); W. P. and Z. Coates: *A History of Anglo-Soviet Relations* (1943); E. H. Carr: *The Interregnum 1923–24* (1954); British newspapers, 1924.

Chapter 4
Anti-Soviet Forgeries (Workers' Publications, 1927); E. H. Carr: *Socialism in One Country* (1958–60); Carr: *The Bolshevik Revolution*; John Reed: *Ten Days that Shook the World* (1919); Bernard Pares: *History of Russia* (1947); *The Communist Review*, Vol. V, No. 8 (December 1924); Leonard Shapiro: *The Origin of the Communist Autocracy* (1955); Dennis: *op. cit.*; William Appleman Williams: *American-*

Russian Relations 1781–1947 (1952); Isaac Deutscher: *The Prophet Unarmed – Trotsky 1921–29* (1954).

Chapter 5

Interview with Mme Irina Bellegarde; Vladimir Nabokov: *Speak, Memory* (1951); Robert Bruce-Lockhart: *Friends, Foes and Foreigners* (1957); *Maciej Rataj Pamietniki* (Warsaw, 1965); Trial hearing of the forger, Druzhelovsky, Moscow, July 1927; Trial of Johann Schreck, Leipzig, January 1928 (*Vossiche Zeitung*, Berlin Senate Archives); Trial of Vladimir Orlov, Berlin, April–July 1929 (*Vossiche Zeitung*, Berlin Senate Archives); *Anti-Soviet Forgeries* (*op. cit.*)

Chapter 6

The diary of Donald im Thurn, October 1924; Mrs Donald im Thurn's exegesis of the diary; Guy Kindersley: *History of the Zinoviev Letter* (unpublished); Letters from Donald im Thurn to Guy Kindersley, 1924–28; Interviews with Sir Owen O'Malley, Sir Clifford Norton, Mr John im Thurn, Mr W. N. Ewer, Sir Gerald Nabarro; Ramsay MacDonald speeches, 27 October 1924, 19 March 1928; An Inquiry into certain statements made in the course of the case, Iremonger & Co. *v.* Dyne, affecting civil servants (The Fisher Inquiry) (February 1928); John Bulloch: *MI5* (1963); Lord Strang: *Home and Abroad* (1956).

Chapter 7

The diary of Donald im Thurn; Navy List, Army List 1924; Interviews with Mr Philip Cambray, Sir Compton Mackenzie; Wyndham Childs: *Episodes and Reflections* (1931).

Chapter 8

The diary of Donald im Thurn; Newspaper clipping book kept by Donald im Thurn; Letter from Thomas Marlowe to *The Observer*, 4 March 1928; Interviews with Miss Grace Browning, Mr Philip Cambray, Sir Compton Mackenzie, Sir William James, three retired intelligence officers and one retired diplomat who all wish to remain anonymous; William James: *The Eyes of the Navy* – a biographical study of Admiral Sir Reginald Hall (1956); Barbara W. Tuchman: *The Zimmerman*

Telegram (1959); Nourah Waterhouse: *Private and Official* (1942); Army and Navy Lists, 1924, 1925.

Chapter 9

The diary of Donald im Thurn; Marlowe's letter to *The Observer* (*op. cit.*); Interviews with Sir Clifford Norton, Sir Neville Bland, Sir Owen O'Malley, and one retired intelligence officer. Strang: *op. cit.*; Nicholson: *op. cit.*; 'Iconoclast': *op. cit.* Maurice: *op. cit.* J. D. Gregory: *On the Edge of Diplomacy* (1929).

Chapter 10

The British newspapers, October 1924; Charles Higbie: *The British Press in Selected Political Situations, 1924–28* (London University thesis, unpublished).

Chapter 11

Arthur MacManus (ed): *The Zinoviev Letter* (Communist Party of Great Britain, 1925); Philip Snowden: Autobiography (1934); W. P. and Z. Coates: *op. cit.*; Marlowe's letter to *The Observer*. Interview with Mr John Ross Campbell; British newspapers, October–November 1924.

Chapter 12

Interviews with Mr John Ross Campbell, Mr W. N. Ewer, Sir Owen O'Malley; Hansard, December 1924; The Fisher Inquiry (*op. cit.*); British newspapers, November 1924–March 1928.

Chapter 13

Guy Kindersley: *op. cit.*; Hansard, 19 March 1928; Interviews with Viscount Davidson and Viscountess Davidson; Hugh Dalton: *Call Back Yesterday* (1953).

Chapter 14

The diary of Donald im Thurn; Letters from im Thurn to Kindersley; Newspaper clipping book kept by Donald im Thurn; Letters from im Thurn to Joseph Ball and Conservative Central Office; Letter from Joseph Ball to Guy Kindersley; Interviews with Mr Edmund Kindersley, Viscount Davidson;

London *Evening Standard* 20 March 1928; *Sunday Worker* 25 March 1928.

Chapter 15
Letters from im Thurn to Kindersley; Letter from Philip Noel-Baker to *The Times*, 22 December 1966; Dalton: *op. cit.*; Childs: *op. cit.*; Ramsay MacDonald speech, 19 March 1928; Winfried Lüdecke: *Behind the Scenes of Espionage* (1929); Lev Nikulin: *Mertvaya Zyb* (The Dead Swell) (Moscow, 1966); *The Adventures of Sidney Reilly*: a narrative written by himself, edited and compiled by his wife (1931).

Index

211

217

Secret Service, *see* Intelligence Services, British
Seely, Major-General, 126
Selby, Sir Walford, 189
Shaw, Tom, 160–1
Sikorski, Wladyslaw, 61–3, 117
Sinclair, Admiral Sir Hugh:
head of MI1C, 81; im Thurn interview, 90, 106; reasons for involvement, 106–8; probable link with Browning, 107; reliance on 'X', 190
Snowden, Philip:
Labour not 'wild men', 19; and Labour policy, 19; Chancellor of the Exchequer, 20–1; no prior knowledge of Z.L., 82; disappointment at MacDonald, 130–1; criticizes MacDonald in Cabinet, 140–2
Sokolnikov, Commissar for Finance, 28
Sorge, Richard, 193
Sources and bibliography, 207–10
Soviet Union:
rapprochement with reversed, xvii; dual foreign policy, xvii, 35–6, 39; propaganda against Britain, 26–7, 32; diplomatic 'friendly procedure', 28; recognized by Labour Government, 28; failure to export revolution, 37–8; devastation and breakdown, 38; attitudes to Third International, 44–5
Stalin, J. V.:
alleged report to Comintern, 27; as triumvir, 43; 'Socialism in One Country', 44, 45; defeats opposition, 46
Stamfordham, Lord, 20, 142
Strang, William (*later* Lord):
at Foreign Office, 67–9; recollections of Protest Note, 113; MacDonald's instructions unclear, 119
Sunday Chronicle, Reilly obituary, 192

Sunday Express:
attitude to Z.L., 12; publishes Rakovsky's denial, 127; attacks MacDonald, 131, 132; Castlerosse article, 151–2
Sunday Pictorial, Rothermere article, 158
Sunday Times article 'The Red Letter Forgery' (1966), ix, xviii
Sunday Worker investigates im Thurn, 171
Svatogor League, 54

Taboritsky, assassin, 50–1
Terry, Antony, x
Third International, *see* International, Third (Communist)
Thomas, J. H.:
and Labour policy, 19; Colonial Secretary, 20; pride in Empire, 22; no prior knowledge of Z.L., 82; reaction to Z.L., 130–1; on Election defeat, 140; presses for inquiry, 150; taxes Gregory, 152; member of Labour Party inquiry, 152
Thomson, Lord, on Election defeat, 141
Thurn, Conrad Donald im, *see* im Thurn, Conrad Donald
Times, The:
anti-Soviet character, 127–8; welcomes end of Zinoviev affair, 169
Todd, Judith, ix
Trades Union Congress:
analysis of Z.L., 135–9; delegation to Moscow, 147–8
Treaties, Anglo-Soviet (1924), *see* Anglo-Soviet Treaties
Treaty, Anglo-Soviet Commercial (1921), *see* Anglo-Soviet Commercial Treaty
Treaty of Riga, 37
Trevelyan, C. P.:
hostility to Intelligence Services, 108; reaction to Z.L., 131; on Election defeat, 141